"You Want Breakfast Now?"

A Mongol Rally Team Experience

James Druce

1/3 of The Islanders: Scilly Mission

"You Want Breakfast Now?"
A Mongol Rally Team Experience
James Druce

Published by Lulu.com 2011-04-13 (Paperback)
Published by Amazon.co.uk (Kindle version)

Copyright © James Druce 2011

James Druce has asserted his right under the Copyright, Designs and Patents Act, 1988 to be identified as the author of this work

This book is sold subject to the condition that it shall not, by way of trade or otherwise, be lent, resold, hired out or otherwise circulated without the publisher's prior consent in any form of binding or cover other than that in which it is published and without a similar condition including this condition being imposed on the subsequent purchaser.

ISBN 978-1-4476-5963-1

Second Edition

Dedication

To Will, Mackey, Ed & Ems.
Without you, the whole thing would have just been an overly long car journey.

This book is dedicated to everyone who was involved in the Scilly Mission, for without every ounce of support we received, it never would have happened

Contents

Copyright & Publishing Information	2
Dedication	3
Contents	4
What is the Mongol Rally?	6
Preface	8
Day 1 - Mongol Rally 2010 begins!	12
Day 2 - Another day, another field	18
Day 3 - The lone journey begins	24
Day 4 - 4 capitals of 4 countries in 1 day	30
Day 5 - The start of a very long day	36
Day 6 - The second half of a very long day	44
Day 7 - The mysterious Ukraine	55
Day 8 - Itching to set off	62
Day 9 - Hello Russia	69
Day 10 - Getting the hell out of Rostov	78
Day 11 - Mother Russia	84
Day 12 - More good Russia	92
Day 13 - Entering the land of Borat	96
Day 14 - There's a bloody camel	104
Day 15 - Pushing through Kazakhstan	111
Day 16 - Onwards and eastwards	120
Day 17 - Do we look suspicious?	126
Day 18 - You want breakfast now?	135
Day 19 - Entering the atomic wasteland	146
Day 20 - The Geiger Counter would be going crazy	153
Day 21 - Returning to Russia	160
Day 22 - A jolly nice day	168
Day 23 - Hello Altai Mountains	175

Day 24 - Our last border crossings	181
Day 25 - Impounded!	192
Day 26 - Freedom!	202
Day 27 - We should have brought a boat	216
Day 28 - The comforting expanse	229
Day 29 - Loving/Hating the Desert	239
Day 30 - The End Is Near	253
Day 31 - The Final Push	262
Epilogue	274
Afterword	276
Acknowledgements	277
Appendices	
i. Scilly Mission facts & stats	279
ii. Equipment List	281
iii. Route map	283
iv. Hints, tips and suggestions for future teams	284
v. Team Sponsors	285

What is the Mongol Rally?
By The Adventurists

"Imagine you're lost in a massive desert, hundreds of miles from civilisation, driving a car even your granny would be embarrassed by. 50% of your wheels just fell off and a search for tools turns up a dirty sock and two dried apricots.

This is what the Mongol Rally is about. Getting stuck, lost and in trouble, then finding your way out armed with just your wits and the sock and apricots.

It's about setting forth to tackle 1/3 of the surface of the Earth; unprepared, ill-advised and with no idea of what might happen. What you generally find is a whole giant shit heap of adventure.

10,000 miles of pure adventure over mountains, deserts and some of the most remote, challenging terrain on the planet. All in a tiny car designed for doing the weekly shop.

The world has gone soft. Satellite maps and GPS have sucked the juiciness out of exploring and some git has already walked off the edge of all the maps. What if you want things to go wrong. What if you need to escape the hermetically sealed world we live in? Fear not, the solution is here. Take a dump on health & safety – do the Mongol Rally.

10,000 miles of adventuring bliss through deserts, mountains and steppe tackled in a car your Granny would use for shopping. The Mongol Rally is hurling yourself at 1/3 of the Earth's surface in woefully unsuitable vehicles to see what happens.

The Mongol Rally isn't about comfort and it doesn't have a great deal to do with style; what we seek is adventure. The whole point is that it's difficult. So the one litre rule was born. To tackle the worst roads the world can throw at you, you need to turn up to the start line in a Granny mobile with an engine size of under 1 litre (ish).

There is nothing like staring down the bonnet of a Nissan Micra at hundreds of miles of dirt track and foot high rocks. Or driving for 15 hours and only getting 20km then finding out it was in the wrong direction.

The Mongol Rally is supposed to be an adventure not a guided tour. It's about getting out into the world and discovering it for yourself, so we resolutely refuse to give you a route.

Think how much of a second rate adventure it would be if we all followed the same route, like a traffic jam all the way to Mongolia. Rubbish.

The whole reason for undertaking such a challenge? Simple. To raise loads of cash for some incredible charities."

The Rules
(Taken from the Mongol Rally official website)

1) The On Your Own Rule

You are entirely responsible for yourself. If something goes wrong or you get yourself in a right old pickle, you have to get yourself out of it - there is absolutely no support or back-up once you hit the road. When you sign up you will have to sign our team entry agreement where you agree that you're definitely on an adventure, and definitely on your own - so you can't sue our arses when you die!

2) The Charity Money Rule

You and your team need to try your very hardest to raise a minimum of £1000 for the official rally charities by whatever means you see fit. The Mongol Rally is going to raise shed loads of cash for fantastic charities, which is good.

3) The Vehicle Rule

They have to be tiny, and they have to be less than 10 years old unless they're emergency vehicles or a rather undersized scooter of some kind.

Other than these rules you are free to sneak, bribe, cheat, connive and generally out-wit the world to get yourselves to the end. In fact you will probably have to. If you get to the finish line without some good stories to tell, then the Mongol Rally has failed its mission. Which it won't .

Preface

Tresco, Isles of Scilly; a very small island in the most South-Westerly part of the UK, 1.5 square miles of granite amongst the (usually) tempestuous seas. This island is the home to the Scilly Mission boys – James, Will & Nick.

- **James ("The Brains") Druce** – 27 years old. Born and raised in Somerset. Works in HR & Payroll, HM Coastguard Search & Rescue Officer, Ambulance Community Responder

- **Will ("The Beauty") Ash** – 20 years old. Born and raised on Tresco. Works in Land & Game Management, Isles of Scilly Fire fighter

- **Nick ("The Brawn") Mackey** – 28 years old. Born and raised in Somerset. Works as a Heliport Assistant Manager, Heliport Fire Officer, Ambulance Community Responder.

The three of us had been best friends for as long as we'd been on the island, since early 2004. We'd done some "mainland" travelling together, and Will and I once ventured to backpack around Thailand for a month. We knew each other's strengths and weaknesses pretty well!

In late summer of 2009, our usual post-work time was spent equally between our 3 houses and the New Inn, and island life ticked over at the regular pace. We kept our eyes peeled for an opportunity to do something; to get off "the rock" for a considerable amount of time. Island Fever had a tendency to set in after extended periods separated from the rest of the world, and it had been over a year and a half since Will & I had our Thai adventure.

Nothing had seriously been discussed, only ideas thrown around by two of us as Summer gave way to Autumn. One late September morning though, the eureka moment had hit Mackey, for he burst through my office door and shouted "we're going to Mongolia!".

It took a minute for me to realise what he was getting excited about, probably the most excited I'd ever seen him, as he pushed me away from my work computer and typed frantically on the internet. As soon as I saw the website begin to load, I realised what he planned to do; The Mongol Rally.

The Mongol Rally, created and run by The Adventurists, is a charity event; and this gave us reason still to take part. Tresco residents are some of the most avid fundraisers you'll ever see, throwing their support and efforts into raising money for charity – in particular, The Cystic Fibrosis Trust. An island family has an 11 year old daughter that suffers from cystic fibrosis, the UK's most common life-threatening genetic disease. For a decade, the island held an annual marathon (a 26 mile run around a 3 mile lap!) and raised over £500,000. Not bad for an island with 120 permanent residents.

The Mongol Rally, thrown into the spotlight after Jack Osbourne completed it in 2007, involved driving an underpowered car from the UK to Mongolia. We'd watched the program, vividly remembering how epic it would be undertake it. And here Mackey sat, laying the opportunity in front of me.

Well, maybe not as clear-cut as that. Agreeing to go was one thing; we also had to find a place on the rally, get time off work in the peak summer season, buy a car, find sponsors, learn to drive, achieve a basic understand of world geography, plan the trip of a lifetime... the list was dramatic in both length and depth!

First thing was first – Mackey & I equalled two, and we had a space for a third team member. Someone who we knew we'd get along with. Someone who'd appreciate the trip as much as we hoped we would. Someone who'd contribute to the team. Even before we'd reeled off the personal requirements, we knew it was Will we'd be taking. Our assumption was confirmed when he agreed, without question, if he'd like to drive ten thousand miles with us.

Next came the "big steps" – approaching our managers for five or six weeks off during the busiest part of the year; approaching the owner of the island, Mr Dorrien-Smith, and wondering if he'd become our main sponsor (which basically involved his blessing, buying us a car, and countless hours of indirect support); finding willing sponsors who'd see the charity potential behind a 10,000 mile trip and help with the costs; and all this while raising bucket loads of cash for the Cystic Fibrosis Trust.

A rather large hurdle in the way of starting the rally was the small issue of driving licenses. More so in the fact that Will & I didn't possess them. The island of Tresco is beautiful, but rather lacking in motoring opportunities; about 3 miles of road, road that has never seen any sort of roundabout/road marking/traffic lights/traffic. The island doesn't even have a car to practice with – instead making do with Daihatsu vans, golf buggies and tractors.

We were lucky enough to gain a place on the rally, but only Mackey could drive. It would either be some very long driving stints for our sole driving license holder, or Will & I had to learn and take our tests. Failure to pass would be a critical stumbling block – nothing like added pressure!

From the moment we signed up, we had 10 months in which to prepare. This seems like a long time, almost a year – but as Albert Einstein once said:

"Put your hand on a hot stove for a minute, and it seems like an hour. Sit with a pretty girl for an hour, and it seems like a minute. Plan your Mongol Rally trip in 10 months, and it seems like a second. THAT'S relativity."

From the beginning though, we had the greatest resource possible - the island of Tresco. From Mr Dorrien-Smith at the top, to the business managers, islanders, staff and visitors, we found an incredible amount of support and encouragement wherever we looked.

The amount of preparation you have to put in to an undertaking like the Rally is nothing short of unbelievable; whether it's buying the car, mechanically preparing it for the trials ahead, sending out five hundred sponsorship proposal packs, arranging visas for a dozen countries, holding fundraising events to raise charity money, negotiating with potential sponsors, increasing awareness through local media, planning a meticulous route through fifteen countries... Without the support from so many, there is no way we could have started the rally, let alone complete it.

This book is the collection of our blogs; these were written as we progressed through the challenge, and hopefully goes into some detail to help you picture the trials we faced. The aim of publishing as a book is simple – despite living in a remote corner of the country (and not even being able to drive), 11 months after entering we successfully completed the Mongol Rally. I hope this story can show that with a bit of determination, an open mind and willingness to experience everything that is thrown at you – your possibilities are endless.

The full story of our preparations can be found on our website – www.ScillyMission.com

Ten months after the preparations started, we found ourselves at Goodwood Race Track in the UK, our car on the starting grid and about to begin the greatest trip we'd ever experience. What follows is our story, written on the road as it happened...

Day 1 - Mongol Rally 2010 begins!

We arrived at Goodwood at about 7.30pm last night, the night before the launch. We first ended up in a lovely cul-de-sac, having used a slightly wrong postcode, and then mistakenly tried to get access to the track despite our camp site being a mile down the road. Having eventually found the right place, we were graced with an open field of about 30 vehicles, a BBQ stall and a number of white "portacabins". These later proved themselves to be the best portable toilet system you've ever seen. Clean, tidy toilets and urinals; even shower blocks with hot power showers. They were plentiful, they were spotless, and they were fantastic. God knows why I'm describing the toilet facilities in such detail; perhaps as my last camping experience was Glastonbury a few years ago, and I harbour many a dark thought regarding those same facilities.

We set about pitching our tents in the middle of the neatly arranged field, and quickly discovered the ground to be harder than the majority of elements. Each of our three Gelert Solo tents came with 10 pegs; from a total of 30, we had 12 left unscathed and in a relatively straight line. Still, we learnt from other teams who resorted to using a Philips screwdriver in each of the four corners of the tent!

Teams streamed through the field gates throughout the evening and night - every few minutes, some sort of incredible vehicular contraption joined our ranks and set up their living quarters for the night. It was very good to meet some of the teams we'd talked to for the past few months on the internet, all equally excited and panicking, sharing hints and tips where we had them.

The atmosphere of the campsite was a jovial one - teams made an effort and dressed up as weird and wonderful things, such as the four zoo animals and an ice-cream. Lots of Norwegian heavy metal played out from ambulances and Micras, and footballs were carelessly kicked around between posts made up of the camping fire extinguishers. There was even a Rolls Royce, once owned by Sir Jimmy Saville, bought by a team on eBay (and cost £100,000 when new).

Our day, no, our week was a long one - we'd so far travelled many hundreds of miles, and by midnight we felt time had gotten the better of us. We retired to the three coffin-sized tents, nestled in between Pete the Saxo and Team CakeOrDeath's vehicle. Tents just aren't the most soundproof of rooms - every conversation across the entire field was heard, as well as the continually arriving teams. An ice cream van's alluring melody isn't quite the lullaby you might expect, and I think we got to sleep somewhere between 3 and 4am.

I woke at the ungodly hour of 6am, wide awake with anticipation/apprehension/childlike excitement about the day ahead. This was it - the launch of the Mongol Rally 2010. It seemed I was the first up from the entire Mongol Rally contingent, and as a result had the use of those virgin pristine showers. (Last time I mention them, I promise). Will was stirring as I got back to the car, but Mackey enjoyed a lie in, eventually rising after the entire rally. Packing up our tents and campsite was another first for us - we learnt some valuable lessons, and even repacked the car, reducing all unnecessary space and weight.

The culmination of 328 days of planning and excitement finally came to fruition - for us three intrepid explorers (ha!) set off from the pre-rally campsite and made our way to the race circuit...

We headed off about 9am - the earliest that Goodwood race circuit opened its fine doors, but we were quite keen. Having been comically harassed by fake Russian Guards, we were given a bay and told to park up. Once again, we spoke to a few of our rally team mates we were already familiar with, and then began the long wait to the launch later that afternoon. We looked around and saw some teams had visitors; maybe a concerned mother or curious boss wondering what they had given five weeks holiday for.

Us though, we had to be different - we had an incredible entourage: Jo, Steve, Lisa, Jane, Adam, John, Gill, Emily, Sophie, Adam, Jan, Barb, Natasha, Rob, Carolyn, John, Chris, Nigel etc... Family, friends, sponsors etc. Some made the trip from the islands, others travelled from the West Country or London. It was incredibly heart-warming to see those people, who made such an effort, and we thank them - it made a big difference.

Waiting at Goodwood was a long affair, despite the rather genius entertainment provided by the Adventurists, and Buddy the comedian from the rally DVD. Some awards were given out, including to a team that didn't have a car, and instead hired an Enterprise Rent-a-Car (with unlimited mileage). Such a collection of cars, all sharing similar bays to our own, was fantastic - 50 something ambulances graced the paddocks, along with hundreds of bodge jobs and genuinely nice cars, doomed to a fate much worse than they'd ever get in the UK.

We were eventually called up to our starting lines on the race track and watched as the grand stands were full of cheering supporters, generically cheering each and every intrepid team. Of course though, no one cheered louder and more vigorously than our own posse! Will had the honour of driving the lap, and we cruised around in about 5 minutes; somewhat short of Stirling Moss's record of 1 minute 20 seconds.

So, we launched. We started. We set off on what we knew would be an eye opener to each of us, and hopefully the adventure of a life time. Pride and excitement filled the non-existent space in the car as we headed towards Dover, our first stop, to catch the 7.45pm ferry (along with about 30 other teams - we dubbed it "The Party Boat. Upon reaching the port, after a near miss incident where Will wanted to join Pete the Saxo with a brand new Ferrari at 70mph on the motorway, I realised that we had forgotten the ferry tickets. An ominous sign yesteryear perhaps, but computerised number-plate recognition meant we could continue!

We boarded the "Party Boat" - the 7.45 Dover to Calais ferry. Now, this thing was big. Bigger than anything we simple island boys had seen before. It had bars, restaurants, shops etc. We parked up, locked up, admired Pete the Saxo once more, before we explored in the innards of the ship. It wasn't long before we found the bar, and quickly met up with our rally comrades. In fact, 90% of the bar customers were Mongol rallyers. By looking at the lone barman attempting to deal with a queue of thirsty Brits, they didn't know about we were coming.

The hour and a three quarter crossing went nice and smoothly; too fast, in fact. But then the fun began once more as our wheels hit the second country of the day, France, and our first on foreign soil. The

CB radios now came into their own - we absolutely loved it; coming off the ferry, we stayed in contact with a big bunch of convoying teams. A stop at a service station allowed others to catch up, and another fuel stop (in particular, for Maria & Nick of Team Wanderlust in the Perodua Nippa, with it's 20 litre fuel tank), gave us time to chat, meet yet more people and become acquainted with each other and our routes.

Once we'd passed the Dunkirk turn off, teams began to stream off in their own pre-selected directions, and we were left with those teams wanting to push through into the early hours of the morning. We hoped to get good head way into Belgium, aiming to camp outside Brussels somewhere. The few hours drive towards the Belgian capital were the funniest we'd had so far - a convoy of 11 peculiar-looking and unsuitable Mongol Rally cars, all chatting constantly on the CB, including playing some interesting games on the motorway, such as creating a square of 9 Mongol cars (3 x 3) across all the lanes and the passing of snickers bars from car to car. It looked spectacular, but the entire population of the Belgian motorway now hated us all.

The convoy was fantastic; the crème of the crop of the Mongol Rally teams; Team Wanderlust, Team Cake Or Death, Team Catch Us If You Khan, Team Team Mongol Mongol, Team McWhippy, Team Canadian Beavers, Team Domino Pizzas, and others we'd forgotten the name of.

Our plan, once people had began to flag a little bit, was to find a field somewhere and set up a hasty camp for the night. This turned out to be a lot harder than first thought. Despite the fact we'd passed a thousand fields and a thousand forests, each of which would have welcomed 26 weary travellers, we instead ended up in a terrible little village, the name of which I'd forgotten, probably deliberately. While searching for the ideal place to set up, we were threatened with the Police by some angry locals, possibly a little upset that 11 vehicles of rally calibre had woken them up at 3.30am, still chatting and laughing loudly on the CBs outside the streets.

Taking the subtle hint that we should leave, we pushed onwards through the early hours. We came across a few possible sites, but none were overly suitable; the best we had found was next to a busy road, and in front of a busy factory. I'm sure the local police would have loved that! At one point, serious consideration was given to a roundabout. It had impressive plant cover and would be large enough to accommodate us all – but a roundabout it still was.

Eventually though, Mat from Team Team Mongol Mongol found a little dirt track we headed down, which opened up into a mini-field of freshly cut grass, shielded from the road by a row of Belgian trees. By 3.30am, this place looked like a veritable Eden. After a hasty setup of camp, and we bedded down for the first night.....

The night before the start of the Mongol Rally

About to launch from Goodwood Race Track

Day 2 of the Mongol Rally

We awoke to find ourselves in a very peculiar place - a small scraping of common ground next to a field, complete with horse. Despite looking like an enclosed forest clearing at 3am, they were in fact but a single row of trees, patchy at best, the only things separating our temporary home from Brussels - in particular, a busy road and train track.

For the first time, quite possibly ever, Mackey was the first to arise - not just from Scilly Mission, but from the whole convoy. Up, tent packed, and waking me up by 7.30am. I have no idea what happened, how it happened, why it happened, but it did. Mackey was not the last to arise. This brought me hope for the forthcoming challenge; miracles do happen.

As this was the second night we'd camped in our tents, we feel we are getting somewhat confident and skilled in the art of tent erection. Even bringing them down happens with swift and grace, even if we have never managed to fit everything back in the little tent bags (poles and pegs now have their own home within the boot). By 8.30am, we were off - the first team to break away from our small convoy, but we had plans for the next day.

Our idea was as follows - drive down to Bamberg in Germany, where we'd meet with a friend and stay, then head to the Czech Out Party on the Monday - a short four or five hour drive. (For those of you not in the know, or I haven't told a thousand times: the Czech Out Party is the only check point on the rally, held in a 13th Century Castle in very south west of the Czech Republic. It's a lot more of a party than a check point though; thousands of people, live music, free gin (yes, gin) partying with a united struggle ahead of them, before the stragglers retiring to the convincing luxury of their tents).

Packing up camp was a quick affair, but didn't involve us breaking out our Whisperlite Stove, so we needed sustenance. Enter the service station; our giver of life for a few days. We've visited so many in the last few days, the usual topic of conversation upon re-entering Pete the Saxo after a visit usually spawns a five minute conversation identifying the good and bad points about it. This rally is hard-core stuff. Our first stop was before we entered Brussels, where we needed to eat/drink/wash/the rest, and we happily finished off the hand prepared and baked pastries and drank freshly ground coffee. (See what I mean? You can bet Taunton Deane Services don't do that).

I took the first shift of the day after Mackey's guide to driving on the right; and it wasn't too bad at all. No real life threatening moments; instead, I took the boys for a completely deliberate tour around Brussels city centre for about an hour. Also, I learnt that you can't and shouldn't cross a row of dual carriageway traffic whilst turning into a side street. Luckily though, those fuming drivers fell in love with Pete the Saxo, and instead forgave my almost grave mistake.

This Brussels tour lasted about an hour. But, it also gave us a chance to go Wi-Fi stealing. It's our new hobby - basically, to get this blog up on the internet, it involves driving up and down every street we can find at 5mph, constantly refreshing the laptop to see if it pops up with any unsecured wireless. Should we struggle to find one, then it involves us walking along the street with a laptop, trying to home in on the signal. Belgian's are incredibly lax, and a good 50% are free to hijack.

Once we'd escaped the ever tightening grip of the EU capital, we began to make our way down to Germany. European motorway driving is very similar to our own; obviously on the other side, but a few other little differences as well, such as always leaving the other lanes free in case of overtaking (too many middle lane cruisers in the UK). Soon came Liege, followed by Cologne, and Frankfurt approached. I was told off by Mackey for going to fast - apparently 80mph isn't fitting for such a tuned machine such as Pete the Saxo. By this time, I asked my comrades if someone could drive - a five hour sleep proceeded by a five or six hour drive really takes it out of you. Will stepped into the driving seat, Mackey in the navigator booth, and I crashed out within five minutes in the back.

We headed on down past Frankfurt and to Bamberg, with Will experiencing the shock and horror of right hand driving for the first time. As it turns out, he had no near death experiences, and we were very happy with him. Hitting the Autobahns was fun, albeit Pete the Saxo didn't enjoy much of it, keeping to a sensible 70mph.

We have to say a big shout out to our Tresco mechanic Mr Nick Shiles; the man is a genius. Touch wood, the car has performed incredibly; the occasional groan when it's climbing a 10% incline, flat out in 5th gear yet only reaching 45mph, but other than that - superb. Thank you, Mr Shiles, wonder mechanic.

Germany - now that's a country that's surprised us all. Perhaps it's the deep seated hatred still in our minds, burning after all this long time, about the past history we've got together. You know, the 4-1 defeat to them in the World Cup. But we were astonished - the roads were so much better than the rubbish that was Belgium's network (complete with our first pot holes), the scenery was fantastic, and the service stations! Wow. Ok, so 20 cents to use them - but it's all automated. Have a little tinkle, and the urinal lights up. Use the lavatory, and once finished, the thing CLEANS itself - literally scrubs the bowl, cleans the seat, sprays air freshener, and basically wishes you a great day. I need to get me one of them.

We headed to Bamberg, to meet up with Charlotte, a friend who once spent a summer on Tresco. I had her phone numbers in a Facebook message; but accessing Facebook from the road just isn't possible. Enter the three of us doing some more Wi-Fi poaching; trawling the windy streets of a fantastically beautiful town. A fellow rallyer mate warned us about the negativity of Bamberg, but we honestly had no idea what she was talking about. A quaint Bavarian town nestled along either side of the River Maine, everything was just nice. Architecture was appreciable by everyone, it was calm, it was clean, it was tranquil; even the people were crazily fit and constantly jogging or cycling.

Once we'd found a way to get Charlotte's number, we found out she's been taken to hospital the day before - poor Charlotte, and we hope she gets better soon. As a result, we were in Bamberg and were at a bit of a loose end. By this time, it was 7pm, so we thought we'd hit up a traditional German restaurant and have pizzas and beers (I know, pizza isn't the most authentic dish, but pizzerias seem to be everywhere). A walk back to our riverside car followed, admiring the foreign things that were everywhere. I was particularly impressed with their street lighting that hung from one side of the street to the other. No posts littering the streets. Genius! I took photos.

Once well fed, we set off in search of the Czech Republic. Mackey possessed almost telepathic knowledge of the streets of Bamberg, and we quickly found our way back to the motorways. An hour of not so smooth navigation occurred, as we visited Nurnberg, (not deliberately) and danced east to west (and vice versa) a few times, before finally finding our chosen path.

Crossing into the Czech Republic, things did start to change immediately. First thing, rather spookily, it got cold. It might have been because it was 1am, but as soon as we passed the long deserted passport control huts, windows were wound shut and a second layer of clothing added. The roads were quite strange - we travelled uphill for about an hour, constantly straining against the inclines, seemingly on top of the world after all that ascending. Motorways were quite the same, apart from some very dodgy potholes, and long stretches of newly laid tarmac where they thought road markings just weren't needed.

Navigation from here on went a lot smoother - within an hour, we'd found Plzen and our Klatovy turn off, and were confident with our direction. Not long after, we approached Klenovy Castle, unsure with what or whom to expect (considering we were a day early to the party). As it turns out, we were about the 40th team to arrive. Obviously our good thinking, with pushing forward early to enjoy a lazy day, wasn't exclusive to our own team.

A few teams arrived later, about 2am, in a convoy consisting of ambulances and family cars. Whenever two ambulances seem to meet, a battle of sirens and music is guaranteed to follow. This woke up many a team mate camping after a 14 hour driving day, but the ambulances didn't care - they loved the melody battle blaring out of their loudspeakers. Somehow, and we commend this team, a beer pong table was unfolded from their car bonnet, and perhaps the first unofficial sport of the rally was born.

We hit the sack about 3am, after making ourselves some soup to warm us up. Our tents, constantly mocked for their size, still prove to be rather quaint. Who needs head room, or space to get undressed, when they keep you toasty warm?

It was nice to see other teams; we'd travelled for about six hours without seeing another, the last being overtaken somewhere near Siegburg in Germany. It's now time to make a move for the day; we have to get a few bits from Klatovy, hopefully find some fancy dress costume for the party this evening (Jules Verne theme…. I know, we're as lost as you). No doubt carnage will ensue this evening, and then we begin the next stage of the rally; leaving Europe in a few days, and beginning to brave the roads of the outback.

Spirits are high, no real arguments yet; fear not though, they'll eventually get here. We're settling in to a good driving pattern - instead of the planned two hours on, four hours off, we seem to do shifts - I'll do the morning drive, Will does the afternoon, and Mackey concludes the dusk and night driving. I'm sure you can all appreciate how tiring a road trip can be, spending every daylight hour on the road, but our body clocks are slowly adjusting. The most sleep we've had in one stint is about six hours, followed by double that of driving. A power nap in the back between shifts usually tops this up. We are becoming veteran travellers I feel!

The rally is proving to be a little bit expensive, in particular with fuel - we've fed Pete the Saxo a good few Euros worth of fuel. But I'm sure once we get into the 4th world countries of Kyrgyzstan and co, we'll be spending an hours wage for a days driving. We're filming lots - well, as much as there is to film whilst driving in a straight line.

(A footnote - we're currently sat on a garden wall in a strange little back alley behind a block of flats, hiding from locals behind a hedge, picking up a very weak unsecured Wi-Fi connection in order to upload our blog. Now that's effort!!!)

Mackey borrows some Czech Wi-Fi whilst hiding behind a block of flats

Day 3 - The lone journey begins

We got up quite early still; the thin veil of tent provides little protection from a morning Czech sun. As soon as it ascends above the rolling hills around Klenovy Castle, you have little choice but to obey and arise. We needed more sleep, but the rally is already doing strange things to our body clocks - no longer do we follow nature's chosen design, of sleeping at night and working all day. Instead, we go for the bi-daily sleep, the second of which follows our shift driving.

One saving grace though, was the now empty day we had out in front of us after our driving through the night to reach our campsite. On emerging from our coffin shaped/sized tents like ugly butterflies, we noticed that a number of teams had arrived at the Czech Out campsite whilst we slept; a good 50 or 60 teams were now our field mates, and most shared the same sun slavery as us; 9am and every team was up.

The novelty of the tents though, has well and truly worn off. At first, they were practical and something to be proud of. Then, they were cute. Eventually, they were quaint, but now they're just a pain in the ass! They are tiny. So tiny, you have no hope of sitting up inside one, and we have about half a foot of space at each end when lying down (literally). Trying to get dressed before you get up is a near impossibility - the only hope you have is if you undressed in such a way, the clothes were ready to slip back in. We've decided we're going to get into a few countries today and aim to buy some much more generic tents – Will & I have both agreed to sacrifice goods we're carrying to make room.

Camping in general though, isn't too bad. We've done it for four straight nights now (and many more to come); we're all in bad moods in the morning so not much is said, but we go about the morning routines easily enough. However, we think that with this being the 5th day we've not seen a bed, or had a proper shower, we deserve to treat ourselves - tonight, we live like kings. (Well, actually, live like very normal people with such imaginable luxuries as running water and pillows).

The Czech Out party facilities consisted of two portaloos (for 400 odd teams and numerous team mates - think comparable to Glastonbury by the end of the party) and fresh water in two parked water bowsers - both of which found themselves very empty by 9am this morning.

We left the campsite at mid morning, and headed the 15 minutes into Klatovy, a small town similar to Penzance in size. As we approached the town, we pulled into a small retail park which housed a Tesco mega store. By a stroke of good luck, its neighbours were Elektronics World and Takko Fashion. The first provided us with a brand new, working rally phone! I have no idea how much it cost, as the Czech's still haven't fully embraced the Euro (most chagrined shop assistants do take them, but insist on giving you any change in Crowns), and I hadn't looked up the exchange rate. The phone cost me about a thousand crowns. I'm hoping this equates to a tenner, rather than me having to mortgage my little house.

Communicating for basic things on this rally has been relatively straight forward. Lots of being nice and happy, despite most Eastern Europeans looking like they want to kill you (our Eastern European friends aside, of course!). Pointing and describing also works well - but how on earth do you find out whether a particular phone model I was interested in is dual band, and is unlocked for any sim card? You could point and shout until you were red in the face, and I'd doubt you'd be able to get that particular point across.

Luckily though, Will's phone (a £15 bargain) had a very basic internet on it. A quick visit to a text version of Google Translate, and before you knew it, I had in my hands the Czech way of asking "Hello. We can't speak Czech. But can you tell me if this phone is dual band AND unlocked for any sim card? We would also like a car charger. Thanks." Initially a very puzzled look from the retail chap, but once he read, he understood.

Great success.

The other mission for the day was for Will and I to find our fancy dress costumes, the theme of the Czech Out party being 'Jules Verne'. Mackey had already purchased his Captain Nemo costume; and us two had no idea what to do. We were thinking of a generic style gentleman from that era, using modern day clothing. Our luck continued, as we managed to find every piece of it from 3 places.

Have a look at the photos on the website to fully appreciate the effort we went to. Rather disturbingly, the whole outfit (including suit jacket, shirt, cravat, hat and pipe) cost much less than £20 - which did make it easier when we realised that nearly all of it would have to remain in the Czech Republic due to Pete the Saxo being full to bursting point.

A bit of alcohol shopping was also in order; unfortunately I was disturbed to find that even a Tesco Mega store doesn't stock Guinness. But, this meant we had to choose something else, and to choose something local. Our final results were a case of Budvar, a case of Gambrinus (Czech beer), and a bottle of a spirit called Stock. The Budvar was lovely, the Gambrinus remains unopened in the car, and the Stock was quite possibly the worst thing we've ever drunk. I think, after a shot each at our camp, us and our comrades will never drink it again. Even Mackey, whose reputation has most likely preceded him even this far, needed to wash it down with some Budvar.

We've been camping with the Mongol Mongrels - a team comprising of Ed and Emma driving a Peugeot 206. The Islanders love these guys - great company and just generally fantastic people. We all got changed into our costumes by 7pm, and by 7.15pm, it's as if we'd been thrown through the metaphysical barrier and landed firmly within one of Jules's novels.

Will & I were two generic Victorian type gentlemen, standing proud in dark blue budget suit jackets, coloured cravats and fancy frilled shirts (which were in fact Czech maternity blouses).

Mackey filled his role as Captain Nemo well, looking particularly nautical in dark blue trousers, a thick beige polo-neck jumper and flat cap.

Ed looked to put in the most effort with his hand made representation of a squid hat, complete with tentacles fashioned from tights. Emma took the somewhat easier route of choosing a long flowing green dress, and declaring herself to be "some seaweed".

We all wandered up to the impressive Klenovy Castle, a short traipse from our campsite. As we approached the gates, we did notice a few people that had dressed up at the gates, and we were all glad we'd made the effort to join in, and wouldn't be the odd ones out. How wrong we were. Despite it being a Jules Verne theme party, the effort put in by many other rallyers was pathetic! Probably 25% or so made an attempt; the rest dressing as they would on a visit to the local pub. A little disappointed, but then again, we'd dressed up and lots of people liked us for it. But it would have just been fine if the 25% of those good people were dressed in the style that was put before them.

There were the Super Mario brothers, a box of McDonalds fries, Finding Nemos, and a LOT of naked and/or cross-dressing blokes. There is a team in particular that just love to get naked. Any excuse, and they streak around the camp amongst hundreds of cars. It's a bit hot? I'll strip and run! I dropped my drink on myself? I'll strip and run! What's that, the grass is green? I'll strip and run! Another guy wore nothing but the Buff he was given at the launch event (think head band/scarf, stretched around his waist). There are some very interesting pictures of Mackey talking in depth to the previously described chap, completely unaware that his testicles were hung out for all to see. Fear not my friends, myself and Will took the photo before warning Mackey that he had two balls glaring at him.

A BBQ was provided for hundreds and hundreds of attendees, as well as free gin; rather disappointed that I'm not a fan of gin and would have to resort to buying pints at the bar, my mood was elevated somewhat when I discovered they were a single, beautiful Great British pound a pint. Several makeshift bars were temporarily added to the ancient structure we now danced in; they'd added a cinema room showing Jules Verne classics, a shisha room (where we spent quite a while meeting lots of other teams), a Russian disco dancing room (where we spent quite a while making fools of ourselves, but seemed to fit in remarkably well) and live music from a very peculiar line up. All in all, it was an amazing night.

We spent most of the night with Ed & Emma - dancing, drinking and talking the night away. Will and I finished up about 2am. Our bodies still craved sleep, but deep down knew that another night in tents would never satisfy the need properly. Mackey, however, said he was staying behind. I think he fell into his tent at about 4.30am. Despite the party finishing at 4am, many rallyers continued to drink, party and play very loud music until 8am. Much to the annoyance of a few hundred other teams, but you've got to secretly congratulate the effort needed to party till 8am.

I think the Mongol Rally shows camaraderie at it's finest; the atmosphere was incredible, you could literally stop anyone and say hi, and you'd start a long conversation with them - although usually it starts with a pre-scripted list of questions - Your name? Which team? Which car? Which route? Any problems? By the 50th person I'd talk to, I did start to make a couple of things up. "Any problems you ask? Well yes, we did lose a wheel flying down the Autobahn at 130mph, but not to worry - we had a spare."

The three of us are entering the seasoned campers group; we haven't had a shower for five days, but are impressively managing this. The car does not smell like Tresco's dump on a bad day. The use of a small bottle of water, wet wipes, a bit of shower gel and deodorant are keeping us surprisingly well kept. But so far, it's tiring. Very very tiring, to spend five hours concentrating like mad to ensure you don't subconsciously drift over to the left side of the road, and to handle the roundabouts (which is just bizarre to do), and then to spend another eight or nine either navigating or catching up with a 30 minute power nap (or indeed, writing this blog).

This is, of course, just the beginning. These are the first few days, with the nicest roads and conditions we'll find on the entire trip. Within a week, we'll be begging and praying we had more of the days like these. But, it's a challenge after all. For those that claimed it was just a long holiday, or casual road trip to rival a mainland jaunt, I do challenge you to enter the next Mongol Rally…..

The 'coffin' tents

Captain Nemo and two generic Victorian gentlemen

Day 4 - Four capitals of four countries in one day

It was the morning after the Czech Out party; Will was the first up by 8am. Not just the first from the Scilly Mission team - pretty much the entire camp. On a regular day, the hundreds of intrepid travellers would be up, washed, and packed by 8am - but not today. For but a few hours ago, the Czech Out party had finished and many a stumbling participant eventually navigated the maze of wrong tents and guy lines to get home.

There was a great deal of hangover in the air - early risers moved that little bit more slowly than usual, and the water bowsers were taking a hitting. I woke up about 8.30am, luckily without a bad head or any sign of the debauchery of the night before. Will, at this point, had already washed under the fresh water tap and started making a coffee (only for himself, though).

Not long after, the campsite heard a noise.

Heads from countless teams snapped round to their team mates with that inquisitive look - eyes slightly wider, eyebrows raised, mouth slightly ajar but then again pulled in tight.

The noise... there it was again... something between a stirring volcano and a hungry bear. If you've seen Cloverfield, it was that sort of thing. After we'd adjusted for a few seconds, trying to work out where this abominable sound was emanating from, all eyes were drawn down to a tent. A Gelert Solo, in particular. In no time at all, the tent started pushing and stretching, as if nine months pregnant and very ready to deliver the kicking and punching offspring.

The zip was lowered from the inside, and Mackey's head was delivered into the bright, fresh, morning world.

Mackey was awakening. And boy, was he hungover.

Will and I relished in the fact that we were without indications of the previous nights drinking, where as Mackey and his wife beater looked terrible, and acted the most grumpiest since we left Tresco. One eye open, one eye still firmly shut, depth perception lacking as he deflated his mattress.

We were in no real rush to get packed and moving, and spent the next hour or so slowly packing up the Solo tents - Will and I both hoped for the last ever time. We foresee a horrible fire taking place, unfortunately reducing our tents (which would be suitable for a single night's camping) to a pile of polyester ash. We made a coffee on the stove, which we love, and I began the morning shift and headed out of the still packed field.

Our direction was the first capital of the day - Prague. As per usual, we understood the road signs and which turning was ours, but only shortly after passing it. And here begins our first accidental "cultural tour" of the city. I blame it on the fact that they were relaying a good kilometre of the motorway, and we bought a proper map of the area from a service station. This proved to be a great idea, and offered much greater level of detail than our £4 map of Europe (one country per page).

We cruised through Czech relatively fast, and most of it was good driving. Moods weren't overly high though - it had been about a week since we'd all slept in beds. A bit of sleep deprivation was always there, even after waking up, and even after our post-driving sleep. No arguments though, just the lack of singing along to Take That and cheesy pop songs in the car for a few hours, driving within our own worlds, contemplating our own thoughts.

Next on our whirlwind tour of Europe was Austria - again, a very quick dip into the country, scooting past Vienna and onwards. Yet again, a combination of completely illogical junction numbering and unrecognisable place names meant we took a city centre tour of the 2nd capital of the day.

Only spending a few hours in Austria, it was a lovely place as far as we could see - which is the only real bad point in this challenge, there just is no time (at these early stages) for sight seeing and touristy things. The closest we get to a local is paying for fuel at the service stations and asking directions!

Slovakia was next on our list, and we headed towards the 3rd capital, Bratislava. This place strikes you as a stereotypical Soviet stronghold - regular, ugly blocks of flat in those ugly colours; disgruntled beige, depressed lemon, disconsolate grey.

You could tell that we were leaving the relative of the luxury by looking at our fellow motorists; no longer were the large majority of cars shiny and efficient. Instead, their poorer ancestors filled the now questionable roads - Opel Kadets for example held their own against the Audis and BMWs. Driving rules went out the window by this time, which just adds to the level of concentration needed to stay safe yet stay moving - overtaking happens wherever and whenever, usually missing oncoming traffic by seconds.

We saw our first few crashes - in Bratislava city centre, the main street through the grey metropolis was home to lone wheels, crumpled arches, and angry combatants where there were no winners.

East, and onwards, we continued, through the Slovak countryside and entering Hungary. The difference between the neighbouring countries, their borders entwined within each other, is astounding.

Austria & Slovakia, for example, are worlds apart; Austria being well built, clean, a joy to drive through. Slovakia, on the other hand, seems like a 2nd world country, looking more Beirut than Birmingham. These places are a couple of hours apart.

By the time we'd found our 4th capital of the day, Hungary, it was about 10pm-ish and we were all tired - and we'd made the unanimous decision to get ourselves a hotel. As Will said on the way into the city, "Hotel or not, I'd rather sleep in a shop door than another night in those tents". Hotels were all well signposted - the army of street signs on the entering motorway held dozens of 'bed' icons, with arrows pointing in our three directions. We picked one, and followed it.

This turned out to be much harder than we first thought, and went through about six different hotel signs, each desperate to attract your weary wallets, before finally finding one. This one, up little windy side streets of the old city, began us to question what sort of quality we'd be receiving for our money, but the general consensus soon became one of 'just get me a mattress and shower".

As it turns out, the Hotel Budai was a sight for sore eyes - 3 glorious stars of hotel quality, offering clean beds, a power shower, even free Wi-Fi! (Which they pronounce wee-fee. Confused the hell out of us when they started shouting about that). Will was the first to jump in the shower, and Mackey and I set about uploading the first few days worth of photos. As it happens, the laptop, despite being on charge in the car most of the day, had been unplugged and gave us just 15 minutes of power before sleeping until next fed - this was just enough time to upload the last blog.

I jumped in the shower after Mackey, the three of us quite possibly the happiest and most comfortable we'd been in a long time. We send our belated apologies to the night manager of the Hotel Budai - his water bill will be astronomical this month.

Settling down for the night was an equally glorious affair - the only room they had left that night was an apartment style room, with a double and a single room. Due to the fact I'd probably kill one of them whilst catching up on a week's worth of sleep walking, the cousins shared the bigger room and I had the smaller. Within seconds of hitting the beds, we were well and truly asleep. The cost, 50 Euros for all of us, was the best money we'd ever spent.

It seems strange how we've traversed four countries in a single day; 12 hours of driving can take you through a quartet of countries so very different in everything they are. The locals, the history, the culture, the architecture, the past, the present, the future. Our only regret I guess has been scratching the surface, nay lightly brushing the surface, of so much potential - just driving by at a solid 100kmph and almost hoping for a traffic jam, purely to give us time and a chance to take some of the essence in.

A very hungover Mackey wearing a very ghastly shirt

A small section of the Czech Out campsite

Slovakian buildings – architectural repetition for miles

Day 5 - The start of a very long day

Waking up in the luxury of four solid walls and a roof was just as refreshing as falling asleep. We were warm, morning dew had failed to creep into belongings and sleeping bags, and there was no sleeping bag - just a comfy bed, quilt, and a pillow. An actual pillow.

The only downside was the time we got up - alarms were set for 7am. This would give us time to marvel at the wonders of running water and electricity for as long as possible, breakfast, and then be on the road for 8am. The morning view from our bedroom windows was just as amazing as the night time version - a wide panorama stretching across all corners of Budapest, up to and beyond the hills surrounding it.

Breakfast was a strange affair, but only because I had typical tourist desires of a full English. Instead, we went the 'continental' route (but not the continental you'd find in UK hotels etc. - that should instead just be called The French). Hungary, instead, presented to us a platter of meat, cheese and eggs. Being so early, Will and I opted for the only safe option for our English stomachs - cereal and yoghurt. Mackey however, went for the lot. Everything the hotel had to offer, Mackey took advantage of. It was like a cold roast dinner, with egg and cheese, and he loved it.

I craved the full English breakfast.

I did have my first cup of tea though in a very long time, which would have been amazing, if I had put milk into it and not double cream. With nowhere to dispose of the ruined morning drink, and to hide my stupidity, I did the only thing I could do, and drank/chewed on it.

We left the hotel with a rough direction to follow, thanks to a crayon scribbled map of the city from the night manager. Pete the Saxo does quite like city centre driving, and the Hungarians did take notice of the machine, many stopping to turn their heads. That's about it though - no smiles, no waves, no flashing. Perhaps we're not far enough away from home to be a novelty yet, or everyone in the city just shared the early morning feeling.

I started the days driving, as per the nice little shift work we've got ourselves into. Setting off from the nation's capital, it was a pretty uneventful drive.

An indication that we were leaving the comfort of our fair modern world was the road signs. 'National speed limit', 'Give way' and '50kph' were now joined by 'Caution! Horse and Cart'. I kid you not - shortly after our first sign, we spotted our first gypsy wagon. It was if we'd gone back in time, the Saxo being the most advanced piece of technology in a large radius.

Pushing on through the border, we entered the mysterious country of Romania, yet again without any need to stop and show passports. I didn't know much about this country; I'd heard of Romani gypsies, and the fact I can't consider their work application unless they have a work permit from my time in HR.

We started to experience the first of the bad roads - pot holes the size of dinner plates soon appeared, followed by potholes the size of dishwashers. Spoilt by the perfectly smooth M5 motorway we all began to long for, these new roads shocked us. Bemusement and novelty soon wore off as we had to avoid each and every one, especially difficult if there was oncoming traffic. Never the less, I carried on, concentrating as much as I could to stop us falling bumper first to the bottom of the pot hole.

(Did you know, they are called pot holes, because once upon a time, roads were made with clay. Poor beggars used to dig out some, to make a pot or mug or ashtray. Hence pot holes.)

It soon became apparent that more concentration would soon be needed, as the heavens opened and down came the hardest rain we'd seen in years. Visibility was reduced to the number plate of the car 12ft in front, and that was with the lights on. Combine that with the pot hole hell, and we had ourselves an interesting driving combination.

Despite only getting my driving licence a couple of months before the rally, I think many people who've driven for years to have struggled with the conditions. It really was that bad.

But wait! It doesn't stop there. Combine the rain with the pot holes, and add a sprinkling of MAD SUICIDE DRIVERS and there was your recipe for hours of fun. The crazy locals, driving everything from 18 wheeler trucks down to tiny 600cc Ladas, would make a break for the stretch of road in front by pulling out and attempting to overtake, despite the fact the road at the fore would be occupied by oncoming traffic, a bend, a dip or a hill. Many a time, all four, but they still had a go. We saw many a near miss, but they were just that - misses. That must say something about the skill and judgment of these drivers. Either way, Mackey and I both commented about how we were ready to jump into action as ambulance co-responders should anything happen. The first aid kit was in the glove box. We were ready.

The Romanian scenery contrasted greatly to the Hungary we'd just left behind, finding winding mountain roads that seemed to go on for ever; long stretches, sometimes measuring eight kilometres of perfectly uncurling freeway; views that rivalled something out of the Lord of the Rings, that a photograph would never stand a chance of capturing.

I drove for about seven and a half hours, straight. The longest shift I'd done, and I started to feel tired. The efficient machine that we were meant whenever one felt tired, the next jumped into the hot seat, and we rotated our task carousel (I then retired to the lounge, and they moved up to navigator/DJ). Will took over, and began his stint on the roads of Romania. More of the same roads were offered to Will, minus the rain - driving these sorts of roads, despite needing full concentration for hours, was a joy.

Some five hours after Will took the driving seat, dusk had settled and the industrious town of Puspokladany gave us chance to refuel both ourselves and Pete the Saxo. We spotted a Romanian McDonalds. Usually not of importance, but our curiosity of the food on offer got the better of us.

We were surprised (or not?) to find much of the same here as we would find in England, a familiar food that we found surprisingly comforting being far away from home. Stopping for an hour gave us the chance to rid our vehicle of the accumulating rubbish; sandwich wrappers, many empty bottles of water, sweet wrappers that filled the empty cavities of the car with alarming speed.

We headed towards our next target - the Transfaragasan Highway. This is the monster road, rated as the "Best in the World" by

Jeremy Clarkson and the Top Gear team. And do you know what we thought of it?

Not much. It was closed.

That's right, an almighty detour that lasted a good 24 hours of driving, and a big sign on the entrance quite clearly stated it closed at 9pm. I'm guessing because even awesome roads needed sleep.

We pulled off at the side of the junction, and thought it would be quite cool to still get our photo next to it. If it didn't have the opening/closing times on it so very clearly, we quite possibly would have taken someone else's photos and photoshopped ourselves into them.

As we were doing this, precariously slipping down the wet grass embankment and setting up the tripod, an elderly Romanian man came out from his junction-side hotel, and informed us of the close.

We laughed it off, called ourselves idiots, but we'd made the decision to push onwards through the night. Romania is in Europe, probably a £30 flight away. We could spend the extra day somewhere like Kyrgyzstan, a country we'd probably never visit again.

Despite informing him of our plan, the man wasn't having it.

"But I hazh hotel. You come do sleep, then do highway in the morning. When open."

More polite no's were pushed aside by more forceful offerings of a bed to sleep of, and no doubt an incredibly inflated bill by the end of it. By this time, the fact we were in Transylvania, it was now dark, and we were being accosted by a local man, we actually did a little run back to the car. I locked the front passenger door as soon as I got in. Looking back however, this was a little foolish. There were three of us, each standing a foot taller, and he was about 80. Plus I think he only had one arm.

We pushed onwards, and we pushed east, setting ourselves the target of reaching the Ukrainian border before calling it a night. With Mackey at the helm, and darkness surrounding us, it wasn't long before Will fell to sleep in the back.

Just to give you some insight - the back (aka lounge, bedroom, library, billiards room etc.) wasn't all I make it out to be. In reality, our sleeping bags/tents/bags took up the seat behind the driver, stacked floor to roof. Even half of that pathetic seat they claim is in the middle was encroached by the mountain of essentials. All that remained was the left hand seat, and Mackey's orthopaedic V shaped pillow. Sleep involved wedging ones legs where there was space, and being so very tired that the cramp and pain faded into oblivion as you drifted off.

We were annoyed about the Top Gear road - it was one of the main points for doing the rally during initial planning. The fact we'd missed it by an hour was just salt in the wound. Grown men don't cry, but this would probably be an allowed reason.

God, Allah, the Gypsy in the sky; whoever was up there though, obviously heard the quiet patter of our inner tears, and guided Pete the Saxo onto a road like you'd never seen before. In between the cities of Cluj-Napoca and Brasov was a 200km road that took our breaths away for 3 hours. Winding up and down mountains, the view remaining incredible despite the jet black background of the sky, and the roads were utterly deserted. I don't just mean nothing tailgating us, or void of traffic jams - there were literally no other cars on the entire road. In 3 hours, we saw 5.

The point of this? The highway turned into the most amazing race track you've ever seen, and by far the longest. Every corner was taken by Mackey with enthusiasm and glee, drifting onto the other side of the road to get the best race line into the sweeping bends. Despite driving for seven and a half hours, and staying pretty much awake for Will's five, the drive kept me up and responsible for choosing suited music to the experience we were in awe of (although Mackey had a particular fondness for Leona Lewis). We swooped and braked, cornered and accelerated, for 3 hours.

Which, unfortunately, Will slept all of the way through. When he did wake up though, he did question why he kept sliding from one side of his lounge to the other, the mountain of possessions dropping maps and coats on him.

As we approached the end of this road, some real navigation was in order as we found ourselves getting closer and closer to the Ukraine, a country we were all looking forward to – moving out of the EU for the first time. It was about 3.45am; we'd driven for nearly 18 hours without any stops other than fuel (and the traditional Romanian meal). Mackey was determined - he'd set his goal, and boy was he going for it.

The next step involved some little Romanian towns, in order to break through the other side and re-join an A road. The first we entered was Ramnicu-Sarat.

4am. That was the time we found Ramnicu-Sarat, but instead found the town from Silent Hill. It was dark, it was eerie, it was backwards, slightly misty and throughout the streets roamed large packs of wild dogs, barking like deranged beasts at the car. All we needed was a crow bar to start off with, and to be somehow trapped in that town, and it would have been Silent Hill.

It didn't take us long to really wish we had the crow bar. Despite being a very small town, it took us 45 minutes to escape from the eerie maze. The roads were the worst we'd seen, with some pot holes eight inches deep and stretching across an entire lane. Avenues and streets looked identical, all prowled by the rabid packs. As we drove, they'd give chase, even as we circled roundabouts.

We all locked the doors and wound the windows up, and accelerated away. With hindsight, god knows why we did that. I mean, what would the animals have done once they had caught up with Pete the Saxo? Bitten through the armour like a Jaws film? I don't think dogs can even open car doors, especially that one with only three legs.

We had never felt happier to leave a place. We were all about new experiences, but that was just crap.

Dogs continually chased us as we sped around everywhere - even running out and stopping dead, glaring at the car's headlights with teeth exposed. Mackey must have felt his first ever twinge of compassion at these times, because he even stopped before hitting them. (Within the hour though, that compassion had gone and he begged for the chance for a pack of these rabid beasts to challenge him). Will, though, found the whole affair hilarious.

It wasn't going to get any better - as time ticked away and onwards we crept, we made our way through a quartet of smaller hamlets - a collection of wooden housed depression clinging on to the road for a kilometre at a time. I can't remember any of the names of these, and we don't want to. The locals would stop and stare (those doing odd things at 4am, like sacrificing a dog to their gods). Pushing on though, it was about 5am by the time we'd eventually found the wideness of the motorway, heading towards the border town of Galati - the last stop on the weirdest country tour we've ever done.

By this time, Romania had well and truly grated us. The scenery was briefly stunning but then tainted with an enormous storm, the pot holes had exhausted us all, the manic drivers nearly scratched precious Pete, the Top Gear road had closed, the country took 3 times longer to traverse than first planned (despite all other countries being on target) and the creepy towns were just... creepy. Mackey continued to steer into his 11th straight hour, driven purely by hatred of the Eastern European country. The only thing that saved it from Mackey's anger was the abandoned rally road earlier in the night.

Our track record with inner city/town navigation was quite bad. We blamed this though on the map we had (it showed no detail on the inner workings of these large towns and cities) rather than on our natural male abilities to read a map.

Once again doing a "deliberate cultural tour of the city centre", we resorted to pure genius on Mackey's behalf - spotting a big truck with a Russian sticker on the back. Mackey deduced that he'd probably be returning home, and we followed him through some overgrown industrial park along well used train tracks, now nothing more than decorative weed beds.

And, as luck would have it, Russian truck guy did exactly as Mackey hoped - took us straight to the Moldovan border. Some brilliant deduction/pure fluke, but we finally reached the border crossing.

By this time, it was 6am. We had driven, non-stop, for 22 hours, and were exhausted, completely beaten. Romania no doubt has countless gems to behold; the Transylvania Dracula Tour, the fine medieval Palace of Peles, the frescos of the painted monasteries in the north, the rich Romanian vineyards... I'm sure I could go on and on. But our whirlwind tour meant we could not experience what this country had to offer, instead pitting us against angry weather conditions and a maze of substandard road conditions. It was a great shame we didn't have time to really find out about the true Romania.

Proof we visited the Transfăgărășan Highway – although closed, and only possible to make out our silhouettes

An industrial behemoth dominating the horizon

Day 6 - The second half of a very long day

We reached the Moldovan border at about 6am and the place was pretty much deserted. We'd studied our map of Europe a great deal over the past few days, trying in advance to develop a nice efficient route through out target countries. Crossing from Romania to Ukraine looked like a relatively simple affair - they both share a border with Moldova, and from our 1:3,000,000 scale map, it looked as if you could wave to the Moldovan guards at their stations as you simply drive to the Ukrainian front door.

How wrong we were.

It turned out, you need to leave Romania and enter Moldova before even glancing in the direction of the Ukraine. And for some reason, you had to enter Moldova twice. There were actually two stop border controls, one after the other. Both would ask the same questions as the first, which confused me - surely you wouldn't be chatting to the second bunch of power tripping fools if you didn't have a passport in the first place?

Anyway, so we approached the border, for I think the second time we'd had our passports out on this little trip - not bad going really. But then it got interesting; a young guard, baby faced and looking as if he'd just graduated from border college, came over to begin the border procedure. You could tell immediately that he loved his job, proud to wear the pressed trouser and shirt uniform, as he thrust his authority in our faces.

Seemingly power tripping on his own baton and oversized hat, he came over to us and starting talking rubbish (probably Moldovan with hindsight) with aggressive arrogance. He just about conveyed the need for our passports, which he took a great deal of time over.

Stare at the photo......

Stare at us......

Stare at the photo......

Stare at us......

This went on for a good five minutes. OK, so I might have had a little more hair than in my passport photo, and Mackey might have been a little more rotund and haggard, but it was still us. Eventually he was satisfied, and then asked for a green card.

Green card? What on earth is this green card? It's not like we're moving to the US of A and get jobs. We'd never heard of this before, and it dawned on us. This would be our first bribing experience!

The little extortioner started saying "Euros, Euros...", but I'd thought ahead in preparation and hid all of our Euros about myself and Mackey. Never ask where. Our plan, I could then get my wallet out and show him that I only had 5 Euros left in there, and any extortionate demands of his would fail immediately! Ha, I was so proud of myself.

Until that is, he asked for just 15 Euros. Fifteen?! What sort of a terrible extortionist are you? Or perhaps playing it very clever, and keeping the price low to increase successful bribery results? Who knows, but the guy was adamant he was to have 15, or we weren't going through. It was the latter part of that conversation which then made me regret stuffing the notes. For an extra £6 or something, we would have been able to continue our journey and progress to our 9th country. But having already told him we had no more, what were we to do?

That was then he came up with a rather interesting plan, but more of an order than a voluntary idea. A gun wielding colleague of the young border guard, also sporting the oversized peaked hat, got into Pete the Saxo and beckoned Will to get in the drivers seat. Before Mackey and I could ask any concerned questions, Will was ordered to drive through the border into countries anew, leaving us sat next to the deserted border point.

We weren't told much (that we could understand, anyway) and just told to sit down and shut up. We were both concerned about Will. We bumped into another Mongol Rally team on the border, and explained the situation - advising them to hide notes, but keep about 15 Euros around.

About 10 minutes later, Pete the Saxo was seen emerging from the peak of the distant hill that was Ukraine. As it turns out, he'd been taken to a cash point machine to withdraw the money. And furthermore, he wasn't able to get any out. Unbelievably so, the gun wielding master of young William had actually offered to make up the difference from his own money. What?!

It was about now that we bumped into a local who could speak English as they casually made their way towards borders. The guy was beckoned over by the rather OTT group of border warriors, and he quickly explained - the 15 Euros was to buy a "green card" - basically car insurance. The insurance we'd taken out on the mainland only covered us up to the windy roads of Romania - from here on out, we were to buy insurance (aka green cards) at every border.

As good as the local stranger's word, the guard came back armed this time with a smile and a green card. I felt terrible, assuming the worst and expecting him to try and fleece us, whereas it seems he had more patience with us than most would!

My preconceptions of what I thought would happen, my sheer cultural ignorance was astounding. My experience of Moldovan border procedures was very thin on the ground, but the knowledge I seemed to gather from other sources was sadly cynical. Here we were, thousands of miles away from home, and expecting every experience to be suspicious and distrusting. What happened couldn't have been further from this – to have a border guard offer to make our up our financial shortfalls with his own hard earned money?

This was cause for an internal re-evaluation of prejudgements; perhaps we really should be more accepting of what's going on, and be more trusting rather than sheer pessimism.

Card in hand, we were waved towards the gate soldier as we stormed on through and into Moldova. About 150 meters up the road we reached another check point. This time however, it was the Ukraine side.

So that was Moldova. We think we travelled enough through it, all five minutes of it, to claim that they have way too much paperwork, their hats are fantastically oversized, but the people are nice, and I'd quite like to revisit someday. And quite possibly visit a different stretch of the country.

Now we had a little more of an understanding of the customs and passport control procedures, we went to enter the third country that morning. It only took an hour or two for Moldova, and we expected/hoped for the same.

We joined the queue at the border. We got to the front of the queue. We were then told to get back of the queue to fill in paperwork. We filled in paperwork and re-joined the queue. We got to the front of the queue. We told we'd filled it in wrong. Upon asking how we fill it in correctly, we were simply told – Get to the back of the queue.

Very frustrating and wasted a couple of hours, doing nothing but sitting there and slowly inching our way forward towards our goal, before having the small ground yanked away from us.

The guards eventually found time, and we finally had some little green slip of paper in hand, which I think means our passport photos looked liked us and we weren't on any Interpol lists. We only had a single control left to do - Customs. We all knew full well that we had nothing to declare, and nothing to hide. The most questionable thing I'd brought was a hat from the Czech Republic, which was so bad it probably would be classed as contraband. We were dismayed by the idea of emptying the car though, and we knew that had to be done as soon as we were told to pull in to a searching area, and a team of five very bored soldiers came to make our morning a misery.

They went through EVERYTHING - questioned what filter tips were, wanted to open the sealed water containers, went through it all with a fine tooth comb. And they weren't going to be happy until they'd profited from our tribulation, and set about starting to shake us down for money. It seems I, with my limited knowledge of Ukrainian border proceedings, didn't realise you had to declare anything of any remote value on a sheet of paper (despite only having five fields to fill in, our laptop and cameras happily filled these spaces). When questioned about giving him some Euros (for what, I had no idea. New shoes for his children?), I said no - I didn't have a lot on me. His eyes lit up like a child at Christmas.

"You have Euro? You not declare these. Show me now".

I had no choice but to pull my wallet out, and he looked the happiest we'd seen him all day. Out of about 200 Euros, he wanted 100 - else the whole lot was to be officially confiscated, no doubt being pumped back into the Ukrainian economy (ha!). I got the beggar down to 50, and grudgingly paid for my beginners guide to getting fleeced. A vast contrast to our earlier border experience! Perhaps an equal balance of trust and cynicism was warranted.

They also wanted two packs of cigarettes. Not the end of the world when cigarettes cost £5 for 200.

We were out. We made it to the Ukraine, and we sped away from the border by a very eager Pete the Saxo, dying to get back on the open roads and unleash the 1,124cc's of pure might.

This lasted about 20 seconds, followed by the worst road you have ever seen in your life. For you Tresco readers, we'd rather have driven across the North End in every direction imaginable than this road. A very wide road, with a single lane for each opposing direction, but the width was needed to traverse thousands of pot holes. The road, more akin to solid Swiss cheese than the serious transport link it claimed to be, took a lot of patience, a touch of skill, a sprinkling of judgement and a whole dose of 1st gear. It took a very long time to finish the 10km road, and most of which spent driving along the central reservation markings in the middle of the road.

Despite temporarily commanding a broad piece of road, the size of two or three UK lanes, it was never enough - unless you had full use of both directions to navigate these monster holes with their jagged edges, lying in wait to puncture every poor sap that made the mistake of finding the road, you were doomed. Doomed I say!

Spirits were raised however, when Mackey got out of the relative comfort/safety of the car to take a photo, and ended up getting chased 100 metres down the road by a rabid dog. I'd never seen Mackey move so fast. Will was in tears.

Our first Ukrainian target was Odessa - I'm sure many of you have heard of Odessa before, as had we, and were curious to see what it was like. We made our way through A roads, B roads and C roads - all of which were rubbish, full of enormous pot holes that even the locals danced around with practiced ability. By this time, it was about 2pm - and remember, this was the day after we woke up at 7am. By 2pm, we'd been up and driving for 31 hours without stopping; the only sleep being a brief five minutes doze in between piloting our fine craft, or trying work out where we were in a Cyrillic-filled country.

The scenery on the way East was fantastic - we skirted along the Black Sea on a hot summer's day, slowly moving away from countries that saw other glorious Saxos on a daily basis and therefore receiving waves and head turns from many.

Before long, we were just 30 km outside of Odessa, in a large town/small city called Illichivsk. I was driving, and casually headed down a very long straight A road, considerably busier than the previous day's driving but everyone content in moving together at a leisurely 80kph (50mph to you old fashioned British folk).

I cruised along behind a large 18 wheeler, when we heard a loud bang - I'd hit a pot hole, as we had been doing all day - the main roads were so littered with them, you couldn't believe it. But, unlike all of the others that we'd glanced the previous six hours, we could tell straight away this one was more serious - a constant rubbing from the arches could be heard.

This was not a good sign.

We pulled over to the hard shoulder, and Mackey (our most qualified mechanic) began to get to work to try and establish the cause of the problem. First, we changed the wheel, in case it had been bent out of shape during the "incident".

10 minutes later and with the spare wheel firmly and happily on, the rubbing still continued. We worked out that with two people in the car, it was fine. Three however, and we'd be going through a tire every 20 miles or so, and as we were only carrying two spares, this didn't seem like the most efficient use of our resources.

We decided to get off the busy main road, as the pot holes littering the surface could have quite easily caused another "incident" and we were quite vulnerable, barely a meter separating us from the other traffic. Very little in the way of a hard shoulder, just some rough gravel. We pulled into the first side street we could find, the road again strewn with holes and strange tarmac mountains that rose up to a foot above the surface. It was a light industrial area, chain link fences and locked gates were sparsely dotted around us, but gave us plenty of space to investigate the car.

We tried everything we could, with what our limited knowledge and limited resources could afford us. Pete the Saxo was jacked up, the wheel was once again removed, and Mackey set about trying to determine the cause of the rubbing.

About five minutes later, a taxi pulled up, having emerged from deep within the eerie industrious area for no visible apparent reason. The taxi driver opened his window, and enquired in his nicest Ukrainian what was wrong with the car (this part is purely a guess. He most likely was just indiscriminately shouting at us. Although, with hindsight, we know that man to be stoned much of the time, and so he probably assumed we were unicorns or something).

We were grateful for him stopping though, even though he couldn't really help us. Having absolutely no way to communicate with him, to explain our predicament, to beg for assistance, we resigned ourselves to him unable to help us, and solemnly returned to Pete the Saxo's rear arch in a futile attempt to fix it.

That is, of course, until the taxi's passenger got out, and said "Hello, what is the problem?" in the most beautiful English you've ever heard (well, more so because it was the first English we'd heard other than the junk spouted by our own three mouths in a while!). That second, just as the gentleman spoke, was an incredible feeling - here we had our first tangible way of communicating with the locals and really get our quandary explained to them.

The gentleman's name was Rusi, who looked more Brazilian gigolo than Ukrainian taxi passenger. Rusi was tall, tanned as if sunbathing was his full time profession, with slick black hair pulled into a pony tail. He attire suggested he was on his way to an exclusive nightclub reserved purely for the socialites of the city.

Straight away, he dropped whatever he was doing (or just had done) and had a look at the car, dropping to the filthy road to look under the arches despite wearing such smart clothes. Would we really find such assistance in England? By now, it was 10pm - the sky was darkening, and but 10 minutes ago, we were a bit stranded. Now though, we had some hope!

Rusi got on the phone and spoke to a few people, to find a garage that was open at such a late ungodly hour. From what we made out from over hearing the Ukrainian shouting on the phone, not many mechanics liked to stay around at their work place long into the night, but Rusi made it happen. It was about five minutes later when we were escorted through the streets of our first Ukrainian city, until we found a mechanics shop that was opening up - seemingly, just for us (well, Rusi).

A quick look and a few shakes of the head from the mechanics sent our spirits plummeting - had we messed up having just left Europe? We were about 20% through our total mileage target, just a scratch on what the rally was to offer and had to bring. Surely we couldn't be out already? These were the thoughts that clouded our minds as the crew of greasy Ukrainian locals chatted amongst themselves in a very negative tone. Negativity, it seemed, was universally recognisable.

It came to light that a vehicle lift was needed to investigate the underside of Pete the Saxo - a piece of equipment these guys did not own, much to our dismay. Fear not though - Rusi once again got on his phone, looking incredibly out of place in the current situation. I mean, you had us three, looking rough after driving for a week. Half a dozen locals, each wearing only shorts, flip flops and a thin layer of engine oil. And Rusi – still looking dressed to the nines, more suited for a cocktail event at some bar in New York rather than helping 3 stinking blokes and their Citroen Saxo. After a couple of minutes, we were on the road again; this time with Mackey riding with the mysterious Rusi and his strange taxi driver, to lighten the load on poor Pete's arches.

The second garage was slightly out of the city, a mile or two further towards Odessa, and once again looked very much shut when we arrived. The basic workshop was closed, there seemed to be no house attached or behind, so we wondered where the mechanics would emerge from. A knock on the door of the nearby Transit van though, and four of the finest mechanics we'd ever seen stepped out. Very strange, it looked like they were having a party in there.

Rusi provided a translation service, and the mechanics set about the car, but told us to come back the next day - they opened at 9am, but they would start on the car at 6am, and we should be there then. Which presented the next problem - where to stay? How to get there? All of our tents and bags were in the car, and we were hungry, having not eaten properly in several days, and now stranded outside of a city. Once again, enter Rusi. It might seem like we big Rusi up a lot - that's because we do.

With the car in the greasy, but safe hands of the second garage, our own well-being was next to be addressed. We jumped in the taxi that had magically appeared out of nowhere, and were taken to a hotel back in the city. Language barriers were a very hard thing to address - pointing and shouting did help to some extent, but the further we got from home, the more difficult it became.

The beautiful Roman alphabet, those 26 letters, was never something we'd taken for granted before. But what an awakening this trip was already proving to be. Enter a world where Cyrillic ruled, where they used strange letters such as the number 3, a backwards N, and many more that I can't find on a keyboard, and your chance of guessing the translation of a word using Latin origins just becomes impossible. Map reading was an affair that took three times as long - instead of looking for the place name, we now had to spot the combinations of symbols.

This seemed to be a repeating theme, my cultural ignorance. Some of the world's greatest literature was penned in the Cyrillic alphabet – Tolstoy, Dostoyevsky, Gorky – all shaping the world we live in today. Arriving at something so trivial as street signs in this alphabet and finding ourselves unable to cope seems piteous.

We turned up at the hotel, Rusi informing Mackey and Will to grab the bags while he and I went into the hotel. We walked into a very nice establishment, more suited to be nestled amongst the funky boutique hotels of London than the Ukraine, and the receptionist warmly greeted him. I wonder perhaps whether he's on commission, and would get a nice pay cheque if we stayed and spent (this trip is making me so cynical!).

Unfortunately though, there were no rooms, so he just told me we'd find another. On heading back to the car park and my comrades, we went through the wrong door and ended up in the hotel kitchen.

Rather than turn around though, Rusi carried on going through and with me in tow, I watched how everyone would stop working and try and shake Rusi's hand and say hello. Who was this guy?!

It was the same at the second hotel, our godsend for the night - Rusi was a known chap, very recognised, and sorted out the stay - even persuading the hotel kitchen to cook us up some food, despite being 11pm. Before we hit our air conditioned beds and showers though, the thought of which were salivating in our minds, we were told to be up at 5am. Rusi would meet us at 5.30am, and escort us to the garage for an early morning mechanical meet. Who wakes up so early to help strangers? Does he really have no other motive other than to help 3 stranded foreigners?

Food was much needed - we were the only ones in the restaurant, merely accompanied by a single chef and a single waitress. When asked what we wanted, it was more of the language barrier. We resorted to the universal "anything/I don't know", a shrug of the shoulders with hands held high. It must have worked, as 20 minutes later we were graced with plates of don't know, some meat, something red and mashed potato.

We thanked Rusi profusely as he set off, and we marvelled at what lay before us - rooms at 16 degrees centigrade, clean beds, showers etc… I won't go on about how good this was. You people are spoilt in your ways with what you have to hand. Perhaps we'd come back all New Worldly and full of traveller mantras, and appreciate how good we have it at home.

Our first few hours in the Ukraine weren't good - bribes, "the incident", many miles driven. But on the plus side, it was quite cheap, and the Ukrainian women were astonishing. Of course, there are beauties in every country - every European country does hold a collection of stunningly attractive women. Ukraine is different though - driving through the city, 80% of them worthy of turning your head and gasping in awe. We looked into how we'd go about getting a visa to live here.

Our first few moments in the Ukraine

Examining the damage after hitting the pot hole

Day 7 - The mysterious Ukraine

Our second stay in a hotel, the first being in Budapest, was supposed to be a luxury affair. And in a way, it was - very clean, nice, something we'd be happy in anywhere in the world, albeit a bit expensive for the country. The problem was though we didn't really get a chance to appreciate it - after eating our hastily constructed meal of something, some meat, something red and mashed potato, we hit the sack. We were so tired after such a long time driving, that before I knew it the lovely receptionist was calling me with my wake up alarm.

An indication of our exhaustion the night before - I woke up on top of the bed, fully dressed, things still in my pockets.

So, yet another night of minimal sleep, this time six hours (which was our best so far on the rally). We were outside for 5.30am, as agreed with Rusi, along with poorly Pete the Saxo - but no sign of him. We waited and waited, sat in the car outside the hotel, getting slightly worried - without Rusi, we had no hope. As I began to drift off in the back seat, desperate to claw back some of my deserved sleep, Mackey announced the triumphant arrival of our saviour sometime around 6am-ish. Along strolled Rusi, beer in hand, looking as if he'd just stepped out of a nightclub and straight to our aid.

As it turns out, he had just stepped out of a nightclub and straight to our aid.

We all headed to the mechanics, and as good as their word they were up and ready, looking exactly the same as if they'd been up for the previous 12 hours - wearing shorts, oil and a nondescript facial expression. Rusi did the talking, we did the looking worried. Within five minutes, Rusi told us we had to leave them to it for a few hours, and he was to take us on a tour of the city of Illichivsk (or rather straight to the sea front).

The beaches were very nice and clean, and the Black Sea looked constantly inviting. Even at 6.30am, there were large groups of people (locals I believe) going for their morning swim, ready to start the day ahead. We went for a walk, a quick historical tour mainly focusing on the nightclubs, and then were offered a morning coffee.

Always a good way to go, Rusi was then visibly distraught as he looked around trying to find a cafe that was open. He continually apologised as he searched high and low for a vender at the early hour, despite our pleas that we were quite happy to grab a coffee later! What a nice guy.

We ended up at a supermarket, due to Mackey wanting to take advantage of the prices of cigarettes. Marlboro, Marlboro lights, Camels, and many of the other international brand names were being sold for a shocking 75 Griva! (This works out to be about 49 pence a pack).

A very strange thing I noticed, the comparative prices of objects. For example, in the UK - cigarettes are expensive, £6 a pack at the local shop. To put this into perspective, a carrier bag in the UK costs what... 10pence at the most? So you could have sixty carrier bags for the price of 20 cigarettes. In the Ukraine, however, we found shops that sold a carrier bag for 2 Griva. (Cigarettes cost 8 Griva). You could buy 20 cigarettes for the price of 4 carrier bags. Very very strange.

One more example - a packet of every day wet wipes (the travellers essential). Keep in mind that 20 Cigarettes cost about 8 Griva, and a carton of 200 cigarettes cost 75 Griva. The wet wipes? 50 Griva. That's right, either buy the wet wipes, or get 160 cigarettes. The place was mad, and was no wonder why so many people smoked (and chain smoked at that...)

The supermarket, a typically Ukrainian affair, was more just pallet racking stacked floor to ceiling with yet more peculiar pricing on even more peculiar items. We found a cafe at the top floor, not open for another 20 minutes, but we sat and waited - mainly due to the air con, and they seemed to be cooking interesting things for breakfast. This eventually consisted of strange meaty tortellini, along with some deep fried dried cheese. Oh, and cream – the Ukrainians seemed to have single cream with everything (breakfast, lunch and dinner).

As we ate our meaty/creamy breakfast, we received a phone call from Mike and the Mechanics (that wasn't his real name), and he gave us the bad news.

A suspected broken torsion bar.

Not the end of the world in the UK, but Citroen had the distinct lack of foresight never to introduce the Saxo into the Ukraine. It was the first time Mike and co had ever even seen one - Will and I should never be trusted to buy a car again. The only potential solution? To visit a Car Bazaar on the other side of Odessa, a good 60km away, and ask around there. Getting there was tricky, but we had was Rusi - the guy could sort anything out. And as good as his word, he swiftly got in contact with a friend who offered his chauffeur skills. Rusi presented his home for Will & Mackey to stay, as I had the money and accompanied him, and off we went in search for the magic torsion bar replacement.

This turned out to be a nightmare, yet Rusi and friend went completely above and beyond what was asked of them. We cruised through the Ukrainian countryside for the best part of an hour in the sweltering heat, before finally arriving at our destination.

The car bazaar was a strange place, reminiscent of a car boot sale, thousands of cars in orderly lines across a gravel topped filled. We parked up and weaved through the stationary vehicles, an eclectic mishmash of international vehicles. This place was the best place to find car parts from around the world, and the car park demonstrated this.

As we eventually squeezed our way to the front, the actual bazaar revealed itself as a sprawling village made out of old shipping containers. As far as the eye could see left, right and straight ahead, a community built from metal shipping containers. Some of these buildings were three or four containers high, unsympathetically welded together where possible. One nice touch though, was many had double glazing - windows and doors. This place was a hub of the automotive trade in this part of the country, the multicoloured containers each displayed branding and writing offering but a small hint of their international history.

Signs crowded the narrow walk ways amongst the containers, each an obstacle to avoid, but also to take notice, for they pointed in the direction of the shipping container resident that would know about your brand of car. There were only two container shops that had the Citroen sign outside, and both had little in the way of torsion bars for a 2001 Citroen Saxo 1.1 Forte.

They did, however, say they are exactly the same as the one used on the Peugeot 106 - find one of those, and we would be happy. Unfortunately though, this was not the happy ending we know you were looking for. Not only did we traipse the maze of the village and spoke to dozens, Rusi and friend also then drove up and down huge swathes of industrial park around the city in all directions, stopping off at every single breakers yard going.

We were at a loss. No car, stuck in a Ukrainian city, and using alarming amounts of our money staying at hotels. Rusi never gave up. He bought the Ukrainian Auto trader, and set about making phone call after phone call to every advert that mentioned France. Eventually Rusi found that single person in the whole country that had a compatible torsion bar, located in the capital city of Kiev. We placed the order and were promised a next day delivery...

Meanwhile, in the adventures of Mackey and Will.... Rusi had let them stay at his flat, on the 9th floor of a Soviet tower block, just about affording ocean views if you precariously hung over of the balcony. On the lift going up to the top floor, which shrieked and shuddered under the weight of four people, we all noticed a very horrible smell. The three Islanders subtly shot glances to each other. A shockingly horrible smell. It turns out that someone had passed away on one on of the floors, and the decomposing smell filled every corridor and lift shaft that it could, before being discovered and removed.

Rusi showed them in, but apologised for he had nothing to keep them entertained - 100 channels of Ukrainian TV and a view of the city. I don't think this mattered - when I returned after the torsion bar hunt, having spent three or four hours racing around Odessa, Mackey and Will were happily asleep on Rusi's bed.

We had 24 hours to waste, before the new torsion bar would arrive. Rusi liked this; it gave him a chance to show us his favourite part of the city - the night life. Back to our hotel we trundled, begged and received another couple of rooms, and had our second shower in two days. This was luxury. Rusi was to come and collect us at 10.30pm - he'd said earlier that it would be much better if we went in as the four of us, that way we wouldn't have any bother from the security.

A 10.30pm start is very late for us island boys - at this point, we'd usually be on the dance floor at the New Inn, or under the direction of Pete the Marshall and his Jagerbomb orders. We headed down to the hotel bar, and had a few cold beers in the still warm evening (temperatures had reached 37°c that day.)

Beer, another thing that didn't cost a lot. A large beer, bigger than a pint, was about 75 pence.

10.30pm and Rusi came to collect us for the 10 minute taxi drive to the sea front, where the ToGo club awaited. It looked like something from the Flintstones from the outside - windows were just holes in the wall, all made to look very cave-esque. Quite a number of people gathered outside, ready for it to open, as there was some famous guy singing. We have no idea who he was though, despite sounding English, other than we knew he was staying at our hotel. We saw him getting his photograph taken with the receptionist - I just assumed he fancied her, as I did.

We were glad to see the inside of the club looked exactly as it should from the outside - basically a funky cave, but huge. Despite the ticket prices being about £20 each (which was a considerable amount for a club night here), it was packed. As soon as we walked in, we were greeted with shots of Angry Mexicans, prepared by the rather skilful barmen. The place was reputed to be the most expensive in the city, and by the end of the night, we very much agreed - but, we'd done a week of nothing but driving and no socialising; it was time to let our hair down.

Rusi introduced us straight away to three or four Ukrainian women, who along with everyone else in the club, looked incredible. They all loved our English accents, and many wanted to chat. More and more cocktails went down, and Will and I hit the dance floor. Looking back, I think we did well, and did our nation proud. In reality though, through sober hindsight, it could have been very very different.

Many of the locals wanted to know about the rally, as Rusi had mentioned it. We tried explaining using a combination of loud words, and hand signals.

My absolute favourite was Will telling someone

"WE" (collective pointing of the three of us)

"DRIVING" (universally accepted steering wheel motion)

"TO" (two fingers held aloft)

"MONGOLIA" (Pointing far in a very random direction)

I think they all recognised the word Mongolia - but it was the TO bit that got them. As we explained to him after, "two" and "to" aren't phonetically joined anywhere but the UK. Hence why many were wondering why we were driving to Mongolia twice....

We got kicked out of the club at about 4.15am, all in very good spirits as I'm sure you could imagine. We genuinely had an incredible time, made lots of new friends, and got propositioned a lot. I'd write about that bit, but not really suitable for the PG audience we are aiming for! But, the party hadn't finished yet - walking on the beach, a bar was happily collecting the club evictees, and laying on yet more drink. We think we stayed there till about 5.30am - it was certainly light by the time we got back to our hotel (how we got back, none of us know. I woke up with a Do Not Disturb sign on the outside of my room door (which happened to be next to reception), and no idea how it got there. From the beach bar to when we awoke at 10am, we remember nothing.

Cystic Fibrosis Trust graffiti?

Rusi – Our Ukranian saviour

The suspect torsion bar

Day 8 - Itching to set off

So, we awoke in very pleasant surroundings indeed. Our lovely hotel, but yet again only two rooms. As I had a tendency to sleep walk, sleep talk, sleep attempted murder and many other questionable things, the cousins shared again and I had the luxury of my own bed.

Not that any of us appreciated it - we were still very, very drunk when we awoke. No idea why we all were up so early... well, they weren't, but I was. And if I got up, then I needed my wingmen. I drunkenly coasted up the two floors, much to the amusement of the night guard and receptionist, and arrived at their door step. Only the Lord himself would have put them on the top floor, much to the dismay of my balance.

I banged on the door, in my best manager's impression. Surely enough, a very hungover Mackey emerged, wearing nothing but boxer shorts. Why he'd answer the door in just those to the potential manager is beyond me - but he was up!

As with any epic night, the first thing we did was recollect and trade memories where our own failed us. Shortly after my arrival, we got a phone call from reception, reminding us that check out was noon. I bet the other guests didn't get this sort of attentive behaviour!

We sorted our stuff out, which involved repacking rucksacks after every night. It was the same with Pete the Saxo - every single day, whether we roughed it in some foreign field, or stayed in a luxury hotel (Definition of luxury: walls, bed, running water) Pete the Saxo needed repacking - everything got taken out, and then repacked tidily and efficiently. Throughout the day, whether it be a leisurely 12 hour driving day, or a nasty 24 hour driving day, things would most definitely be required from all corners of the car - camera batteries, duct tape to fix something, map etc.

Turned out at 12, we were at a loose end - we were at the hotel on the other side of the city, Rusi wasn't answering his phone, and Pete the Saxo was getting tinkered with at Mike & the Mechanics. We had our backpacks, as well as a smaller one we kept the passports and documents in, and really didn't feel like hiking them around town. We asked the receptionist if we could leave the three big bags somewhere, promising to return within the hour to collect them.

With that lie laid out nicely, we set off in the only direction we knew - the sea (aka location of the previous night's club). From there, we could probably make our way to the bizarre supermarket, and from there to a roadside bar we'd had a drink in, and from there to the tasty kebab place, and from there to Rusi's tower block.

We surprised even ourselves when we managed this - taking no wrong turns at all. The tower block however, was determined to step in the way in our quest for a perfect Rusi visit. The door was card locked - you had to swipe a card to open the main door. We thought we'd act all Jason Bourne, and casually read a newspaper just outside, waiting for an unsuspected resident to leave, while we furtively snuck inside.

I'm not sure what gave it away - we probably read that newspaper upside down (Cyrillic is difficult) or just looked very, very out of place (Mackey was wearing a "wife beater"), but an elderly Ukrainian chap clocked on to us, and made sure that there was no way we'd gain unauthorised entry, blocking our approach with stern Ukrainian words and lots of pointing.

We eventually did get in, buzzed through by Rusi's rather attractive sister, but found he wasn't home. In fact, he hadn't been home since last night. Apparently he'd gone to the beach for a swim and a beer, and would be back later.

The guy hadn't slept for three days. He made us all look pathetic - the man goes wild at a club surrounded by a cluster of willing women, drinking until 8am - but then just goes to the beach for a few hours before starting it all again. We were even more in awe of the man.

Once inside, we found ourselves in the same situation Mackey & Will had the day before - absolutely nothing but Ukrainian television to watch and a 34 degree heat to endure. We did what we were good at when we found the opportunity, and we slept. Rusi returned about 3pm, happy to see us, and still looking and sounding like someone who'd had their regulation eight hours sleep every night. When he returned, he got straight on the case with the torsion bar, making phone call after phone call - to the seller, his manager, the transport company etc.

Long story short, it turned out that the seller had not posted it as promised, despite promising a next day delivery. Rusi was angry - not just at the seller, but at the whole country, and continually apologised for this outrageous behaviour on its behalf. The outcome was either Tuesday delivery to the Ukraine, or send to Volgograd to await our hopeful arrival.

By 6pm-ish, we had a team meeting (not as exciting as it sounds - someone put an idea forward and the other two grunt in agreement), and decided that we should be able to lighten the car enough, or at least redistribute the weight, to stop the rubbing at very low speeds and hopefully get moving again. After 3 days in the same place, all of its amazing attributes aside, we were dying to get moving, even if it did mean driving at 20mph for hundreds of miles.

Rusi took the plan well, considering he was about to lose his 3 new best friends, and made arrangements for a taxi to come and get us, take us to the hotel to collect our bags (the bags that were being left for a few minutes, many hours ago) and then to Mike & the Mechanics just outside of the city. We didn't say a proper goodbye, as we assumed we see him after the car was returned back into our loving hands, and we didn't get the chance to drop in once again, which we were gutted about. But we had his email address and phone number, and would certainly never forget the man who saved us in the Ukraine.

The frenzied yellow taxi, skilfully yet scarily weaving in and out of traffic at 120kph, delivered us safely to our first destination where we ran inside the hotel and kept our heads low. Swiping the bags, we made hasty thanks as we left, and surprisingly got a big chorus of "good lucks" from the security and receptionist, which was nice. Bags in the taxi, we set off on another hair raising rally across the city to Mike's. I think Rusi had phoned and explained, because he seemed to understand what we needed - the car, back in one piece, and to make a move.

Mike then set about refitting the back axle, connecting the brakes and generally re-making Pete the Saxo almost fit for the road. This took about an hour or so - time which we just sat outside on the front half of a victimised Lada in the 35 degree sun. A few locals, the type that would sit in a chair outside and drink the Ukraine's version of Special Brew, did try and chat to us. Not a clue what they were saying, but we think it was more mocking of the fact we were driving 10,000 miles to Mongolia in a French car.

After a seeming age, Pete the Saxo was back in one piece, and work started immediately in rebalancing the load. We removed absolutely everything from the car and started the essential task of creating load equilibrium to take some of the pressure off the wheels. Heavy things, like the spare fuel tanks and tools, were moved forward to the back seats and roof box, while the light but bulky sleeping bags, roll mats and tents were aft wards.

The extra spare wheel we were carrying was a considerable weight in the car, no matter where we put it – it was too much weight in the boot, and too big for the roof box. A eureka moment came to the three of us collectively – the bonnet! Yet more sign language – mimicking a drill action (complete with ridiculous sound effects), and Mike the Mechanic eventually picked up our idea. No guilt or apprehension at all as he wielded his drill and sank the bit down.

A painful minute later, the job was done. Two rough holes in the bonnet, spaced perfectly on which to bolt the spare wheel. It wasn't a pretty job, but instead added an air of adventure to our already venturesome vehicle, even if it did reduce the driver's visibility somewhat.

We were happy with what we'd done - the car seemed efficiently packed for once. We timidly climbed in, and Mackey set about driving down the road. We managed 20 ft down a nice tarmac road, before we heard that ruinous sound - more rubbing from the arches. By this time, we were desperate. It was such a good feeling to be back in the car we hadn't used in days, our home on wheels, a place to be rather than just drift between stranger's flats and strange hotels.

Spirits were low - very low. Mike's mechanics had left for the day, leaving Mike to close up shop. As he shut the big barn doors of the workshop, he'd noticed we'd stopped, and we reversed the car up to him.

Desperation set in - we needed to go, and our desolate faces as we approached Mike said it all. Mackey got out, and started to suggest a quick fix that may help - getting rather physical with the car, with the help of a lump hammer and angle grinder. Trying to explain this to Mike didn't really work - absolutely no English on his part, and most definitely no Ukrainian on ours, even the banging and sawing motions of Mackey's frantic hands yielded no understanding. Mackey then strolled into his work shop, found the butchers tools of choice, and handed them to Mike.

I think he understood then - but wasn't really willing to go all out on Pete the Saxo. What if he misunderstood, and started beating the hell out of our pride and joy? Mackey again took the initiative and started hitting the arches with the hammer. Then, Mike realised he had been given free reign on the car and could cause as much destruction (within reason) as he liked.

Pete the Saxo was jacked up, wheel removed, and Mike started laying into it like a repressed killer - smashing the hell out of the arches, cutting away some of the rear bumper and trim, removing the junk pieces of plastic from inside the curvature of the wheel housings.

It wasn't a pretty sight. Although we needed it done, to see Pete the Saxo go through such anguish was heartbreaking for us all. 10 minutes later, once we'd botched the bad side (and the good side for luck), we set off for a test drive down the abandoned industrial road.

Epic. With the three of us inside, fully laden, we heard no sound from the wheel arches. Was it really a torsion bar, and an extra inch of clearance meant it now worked perfectly? Either way, we were happy. We paid Mike for his time - for looking at the car, dismantling, checking, leaving on ramp for a few days, reassembling, banging and sawing, he charged 500 Griva - about £40. After the success of the banging/sawing/grinding, we tipped him 200 Griva. After all, he just gave us the golden ticket to continue on our voyage of discovery.

Those few minutes picked up our spirits enormously - although unsure if we still had serious problems with the car, we could now move, albeit at a mutually agreed top speed of 40mph (and keeping an extra vigilant look out for pot holes). We left Illichivsk, and headed east, towards the Russian border. We were several days behind on our target itinerary, and so decided to drive all night, sleeping when we weren't driving or navigating our now working vehicle. We set off at 9pm.

We had hundreds of miles to go, and continually swapped driving. By 2am we were all tired, affording little sleep as we had to carousel around our tasks. I felt too tired driving - Mackey & Will were fast asleep, and I noticed myself struggling to concentrate on the empty roads and begun to hallucinate; never a good thing when driving.

We're all sensible, and would never risk anything for something so trivial as gaining a few hours headway, so I pulled into a service station so I could join my comrades in some sleep for an hour or two.

As I pulled up, and tried my best to sleep in the drivers seat (which involves resting your head on the top of the steering wheel, precariously balanced for one move rotated it, sending you downwards and waking up rather sharply). Mackey had a better idea though - despite having the back seat, usually the preferred sleeping area of choice due to having two sides to lean on, he simply got out and lay on the ground outside. We all remained in this awkward, but asleep, positions for a couple of hours before we realised it was time yet again to go.

And onwards towards the Russian border we went.....

Ukrainian mechanic enjoying the spacious boot

Waiting at Rusi's place. Alarming amount of leopard print.

Day 9 - Hello Russia

We drove, and we drove, and we drove. We were desperate to reach Rostov, the border city in Russia that was one of the major crossing points from the Ukraine. We were days behind schedule, and so continued our constant driving, shifting positions when one got tired.

The problems with the car were definitely not all over, but they were better. After we'd gone psycho on the arches with a large hammer, no more rubbing could be heard. This picked us up, and probably gave us the desire and drive to push on as much as we did. There were, however, still some alarming rattles - more a loose exhaust than anything else, and most definitely fixable.

We drove throughout the night, watching the sun set, and after both feeling like a second and a year, watching it rise again. Driving through these dark times wasn't too bad, with the roads being very empty, but was dependent on the road conditions. If you weren't presented with road markings, something we very much take for granted, then the concentration needed to stay on the road and not in a ditch was doubled - making out the hard shoulder, which usually comprised of rough gravel separated by a sharp ending of the road tarmac, needed you to stay continually alert. Which, in turn, simply tired you out even further.

Ukraine does have its stretches of good road - road which you're happy to reach 60mph on, but the large majority was not this good. Constant pot holes, some stretching half the length of the lane resulted in you swerving to miss (oncoming traffic dependant), means it was more of a 40mph country.

Still, onwards we pushed, keeping it sensible by ensuring the driver was fit to do so, rotating when not. We had all previously agreed to not risk anything by trying to gain an extra hour here and there - after all, it was not a race, it was a challenge.

About 6am, I was driving and about to join a large dual carriage way from a smaller road. Both directions were completely empty - not a car to be seen as far as the eyes would let you. I pulled out, and followed the road line as best I could - although it was becoming second nature to us now, driving on the right (aka.

wrong) side of the road, we still liked road markings to follow. These though had faded in the consistently scorching sun, and apparently I might have crossed the corners of two of them. Nothing too bad, we were talking a foot or two and certainly no risk when the only car in the viewable radius was us…

But maybe a risk when there's a police car behind the central reservation.

I heard a blast of a whistle (so old school here) and the white baton they point to where they want you to stop - a baton we would learn to fear. I pulled over, not knowing what I'd done at that point, and waited for PC Ukraine to come over and talk. We'd got to the stage where we all run off a little list of legal checkpoints in our head if we were pulled over… Have we got our passports? Anything in the car that shouldn't be? Were we speeding? Are we all drunk? (I'm joking about the last one Mum, Mum and Mum).

As always with the police procedures, they'd ask for your passports as well as car info - i.e. V5 certificate and green card (insurance). We had everything apart from the green card - although we were given one as we entered the Ukraine, the guard manning the exit gate took it off us as we passed. Very strange, but he seemed to accept the Moldovan one after a quick glance.

Quietly confident we stood well within the law, he asked me to accompany him to his car. Ah, I thought, another bribe attempt. After my expensive tutorial at the border, I would not fall for this one again, and would make my country proud by standing up to these tyrants!

Or not, as the case may be. He showed me where I crossed, and I indeed had nipped the corner of two white lines. Only after standing directly on them, examining the road surface for 30 seconds (such a time frame impossible as you cross them, even at 10mph), you began to make out the faded lines.

But, this was a nice corrupt cop, or as nice as they went. Just 200 Griva (about £14) and he'd let me off. Deal!

We stopped off for the last of our Ukrainian fuel, and pulled into a red service station. Whilst filling up, we noticed the place had Wi-Fi. This was the best thing we'd seen in quite a while - petrol station with a little cafe, and free Wi-Fi (or wee-fee). Fantastic.

Back in the car and we approached the Russian border - something we dreaded after the hearsay and rumours we'd been fed about the extortionate demands from the Ruskis. Renowned for their corruption and high bribes, I began to once again hide our large denomination bills from their greedy fingers, possibly learning from our Moldovan border incident and keeping a small amount out.

Leaving the Ukraine was a simple affair - we purchased our car insurance for Russia, which was more expensive than first thought, as it had to last a month. We approached Ukrainian passport control, crewed by an incensed lone woman, who never once raised a smile or changed the sombre/furious look upon her face, even with us trying to chat her up a bit (for no reason what so ever other than to crack a smile).

Next stop Ukrainian Customs Control, who made sure you don't take anything illegal OUT of the country, which I didn't quite understand, but the guard was quite funny. Probably possessing 20 words of English made the who experience enjoyable - we threw keywords around; driving, Mongolia, shitty Citroen, UK etc., and he got the gist of the story. On opening the boot, and being confronted with a veritable mountain of clothes and junk, he shut it again, laughed and pointed us towards the great Soviet state.

We were in no man's land - the stretch of land between two countries. I don't know the laws of this area, perhaps there are none. Would they object to me claiming an acre, and setting up a sovereign state of my own? Then the thought of those Russian guards, now visible on the horizon carrying guns and looking equally vexed with themselves and everyone, quickly extinguished the idea.

Will inched his way up to the first Russian check point, the passport control. We waited a while, but these were returned to us relatively quick. No bribes needed. Perhaps they were saving the financial raping until the customs point, which has been true of our last country border negotiation.

As suspected, the white baton so dearly loved outside of Europe came out, and pointed to the customs search area. We had heard our friends, Ed & Emma from Team Mongol Mongrels, had a four hour wait here. We had enough water to last, but it was already heating up so early in the morning, and the thought of a similar amount of time at the hands of the guard's patience was a sharp contrast to our early high spirits.

A guard walked over, and did the usual speech… documents, V5, passports, green card etc… He then casually glanced in the back, him too being greeted with a mess like no other. We resigned ourselves to the fate that lay before us - unpacking, explaining, bargaining. He asked Will to follow him to his guard station, alone, where Mackey and I were convinced he'd be sat at a metal table with a lamp shone in his face, cigarette smoke filling the darkened room where two Russians might play good cop/bad cop.

Much to our surprise though, Will came strolling out of there just five minutes later, not looking overly distraught at the thousands we'd have to pay out to continue our journey. Instead, by the time Will had returned to the impounded Saxo, he had a definite smirk on his face. It turned out the guard had agreed to sign the customs declaration sheet, authorising our leave and taking responsibility for us not having any guns, ammunition, knives or drugs, and let us go straight away - all for 20 US Dollars.

£15 to save ourselves four hours in 33 degree heat, drinking bath water temperature liquids, bored and slowly roasting, having to unpack and repack the car? Absolutely.

Could it really be that easy? He told us to hurry up and speed through the gates, for if any other guard stopped us, we'd be liable for more "presents" as they like to call it. Will inched out of the stoppage area, and headed for freedom (or as much as you can hope to find in a Communist country), but we were accosted at the gate by a group of other guards. Damn, we thought in unison - so close.

An older guard approached the window and started saying "money, money" - our £15 escape really was too good to be true. Instead though, his younger apprentice simply explained he wanted some UK money to add to his foreign collection. Mackey scrambled through the door compartments, and handed him the exact sum of £2.37. We waited for his reaction - was he insulted we'd try to fob him off with such a petty amount? No, in fact, he was delighted, and gave us our last wave as we finally said goodbye to the Ukraine, and hello to Russia.

Russia started pretty damn good - the border, at about 30 minutes from start to finish, was by far the quickest and the friendliest. The roads immediately improved - a handful of small potholes every few kilometres, and relatively smooth roads. Things like the expansion plates they put in when building bridges, that let the roads expand and contract in the opposite weather conditions - Ukraine never invented these, and as a result large mountain ranges of tarmac form in the roads, a hazard to all (our sump guard has even visited a few). Russia was smooth.

The scenery was good too, ever changing as we pushed on, from hills and valleys to the flattest land you'd ever seen - stretching to the horizon is every direction imaginable. It did get hotter though - my preconception of Russia was of a Moscow winter, all wearing Richard Barber hats, skating on ice and watching Lada's skid on the snow. But somehow, approaching the city of Rostov, it got hotter. Our thermometer read 38 degrees C. Ok, it might not be the most accurate of instruments (a key ring which doubled as a ruler, compass and thermometer), but this was confirmed by an overheard motorway LED board - 38.5 degrees centigrade. I couldn't remember the last time the UK felt that temperature, if ever.

Buying a car without air-conditioning added to our list of mistakes, as having the windows down did nothing. Russia seemed to be a windy place, and having 38 degree air blown in your face while driving was just incredible. Not the good incredible, just the crazy incredible, like standing in front of a hair dryer for hours on end.

Pete the Saxo happily drove through the heat though, no doubt due to the preparation from our Tresco wonder mechanic Mr Shiles, and we hit the city borders of Rostov sometime in the evening. We thought we'd treat ourselves to a hostel of some sorts - just a bed, larger than the coffin tents we'd else sleep in, as we saved so much potential money from the hands of corruption.

Some hotels to like to advertise as "HOTEL" or "MOTEL", but most stuck to their Cyrillic heritage, and consequently finding one was very hard. The few we did spot seemed to be a step backwards from the comparative advancement of the Ukraine. The language barrier was as big as it would ever be in this city - and Google Translate, which has saved our skin a few times, was on the internet. And these hotels didn't seem to have the internet, let alone Wi-Fi. It took 10 minutes to ascertain whether one accepted Visa, or maybe US dollars (as so many did around the world), and that was with pointing to a Visa card and some dollars. Trying to then enquire whether they had three rooms, two rooms, one room or even a storage shed we could rest our weary heads, was an actual impossibility.

We kept circling the city, and then decided to do a bit of our favourite activity, Wi-Fi stealing. As expected, the number of Wi-Fi networks around a city have been slowly decreasing - nothing too bad up to this point though, Wi-Fi is an established technology, affordable by all. Even the Ukraine had ample networks for us to try and poach. Rostov though did not follow the trend. In a 30 minute drive around the residential areas, we picked up two. To put this in relation to, say, Budapest, we were finding five or six constantly wherever we drove. The possibility of using Google Maps to find a hotel soon disappeared.

Russia seemed to be the first place where a LOT of people were taking notice of the car - everyone now turned and looked, albeit never overly happy to see us. Why, we didn't know, but we weren't getting as many smiles as we thought we might by this far.

Continuing our hunt for lodgings for the night, we persisted with our blind circumnavigation of the city, ending up on a motorway. Cruising along at a very legal speed, we heard that horrible sound - a whistle, and in our side mirrors, a shiny white baton being pointed directly at us. Mackey pulled over, we once again went through the mental checklists - as far as we could see, we were shiny legal. The policeman walked over, requested documents, and also our driving license - a first for us since we started this trip. Mackey obeyed, as you would when confronted with an angry Russian with a sidearm, and waited to find out what bogus law we'd broken this time.

It seemed Mackey had followed my lead, and cut across a white line. Ever so slightly, and just one compared to my criminal two, but Russian cop wanted to see him inside the Police hut they have in the middle of the motorway. It was so very weird to see - a police station, about the size of a tiny bedsit, in the middle of the motorway - those angry police just wandering across all four lanes to talk to a pulled-over driver, expecting the authority-fearing motorists to avoid them.

Which they did. Mackey wandered over, still a bit bemused by strolling across a motorway, and entered the hut. Will and I couldn't work out what he did - as far as we could see, he was in the right. But once again now we'd stopped and had time to examine the rubbish road markings, there was a white line.

Mackey came back looking even crazed than angry Russian cop. His first words as he jogged across the four lanes of oncoming traffic back to the car?

"Do you reckon I could kill all four of them out and get away with it?".

A quick explanation yielded this: Angry Russian Cop had Mackey's driving license and wasn't giving it back unless he paid up $300 - an extortionate price from an extortionate police force. Mackey and his arguing got them down to $150, but they were going no lower. As he handed over his actual driving license, rather than the semi-disposable International Driving Permit, he needed it back. We had no choice to pay, both financially and in team spirit, and Mackey headed off down the motorway. He was fuming - for the first time on the rally, he was literally red in the face. Loudly declaring we were getting the hell out of this city right now, he accelerated down the closest city exit he could find.

Will & I, no all three of us, were tired. We'd been driving for countless hours, and were desperate for sleep. Driving out of the city, especially Mackey having a slight case of the red mist clouding his judgement, wouldn't have worked. We told Mackey this, and his response was to sharply cut across three lanes of a luckily empty roundabout, come skidding to a halt and got out the car.

Will took the helm, and continued the vain hope of finding a hotel. Since our last failed discussion with a receptionist, we'd withdrawn some roubles. How much, we had no idea, but we were willing to pay any amount for a bed. At least with roubles, we could point and do the universal "sleep" sign. We continued this drive for an hour, taking chance turnings and fortuitous junctions, ending up in inner city neighbourhoods that seemed as uneasy as we were, as we continued the hunt.

We tried, and tried, and tried - we couldn't find anything. Taxi drivers didn't want to know if we couldn't speak Russian, and cops certainly didn't help us. Trying to gain the attention of a passerby was a futile venture, the vast majority refusing to even acknowledge us. We had no choice but to find a makeshift campsite for the night and get our heads down.

Will headed out of the city limits for 10 minutes, and took the first gravel topped path he could find away from the main road. Russia is big, and everything about it is big. The fields, for example, are the size of Tresco, stretching to the horizon. We followed a path along a field, and soon came to a small clearing in the light gathering of trees that lay down one side. Car was parked, tents were out, and our trespassing home for the night was done.

Team morale was low - Rostov was the worst introduction to Russia, especially after our easy border crossing. The lack of hotels, the hostility of the locals, the Mackey police incident with huge fine, the now cramped camping in some random field trying to set up camp in the dark, and the fact we had not seen another Mongol Rally team in about five days. You could tell when spirits were down in the car – it was quiet, no chat, nothing but some non-chosen music and the constant buffering of the 38 degree air to listen to. Fingers crossed, the next day we'd be reaching Volgograd and will see the long awaited Mother Russia……..

A Russian military monument in the middle of the countryside

Our home for the night – enormous, empty field

Day 10 - Getting the hell out of Rostov

We awoke in the field to find quite a nice view greeting us - our midnight camp site was on the side of an enormous field, overlooking yet more fields. But it was nice. I had fallen asleep in the car, and apparently requested to stay there once we arrived in my lethargic state. I was so tired on arriving that I slept through the cramp that always accompanied a night in the car. Mackey and Will had set up their tents in the field, without the top sheet and relying on the fly sheet for protection against the army of marauding mosquitoes.

Living rough like this wasn't overly pleasant - ensuring you had bought enough water on the day before was essential, for that water provided you with a wash, a shower, drink, brushing your teeth, making coffee and cooking your breakfast. We were slowly adapting to it though, our bodies grudgingly allowing for a few days before resenting and demanding showers and a proper clean. Toilet facilities were... well, I'm not sure you'd want to read about that bit. Just imagine the sort of hygienic bathroom facilities cavemen for example might have had, and you'd be imagining what we had available.

We got the ability of showering with a bottle of water down to fine art - approximately 0.7 litres of water is the minimum needed to have a wash. This involved walking until you found a handy tree and branches, hanging up your clothes (both dirty and clean), and getting very much naked in the middle of the Russian countryside. So far, no surprise/alarmed farmers tending to their fields finding us, but I had no doubt that would come.

We made coffee on our still wondrous stove, and cracked open some of our breakfast ration packs. Pork sausage, omelette and baked beans in a handy foil packet. Just 10 minutes boiling on our Whisperlite stove, and we tasted the best things ever.

That's one thing we were finding about the rally – we were hardly eating anything. Drinking was another thing – we'd stop three times as much in Russia to buy water than fuel. The temperature reached 45 degrees in the sun - unheard of by us simple island guys. At that temperature, it felt like you were in a fan assisted oven, the hot air rushing through the essentially opened windows slowly cooking us. We were keeping on top of the fluid situation though - a good indicator was our urine. If we weren't drinking lots of water, and I mean lots, to keep it a good pale colour, it began to turn very dark. Certainly not a good thing.

Back to the food - a combination of the heat, and always having to drink, meant we weren't eating half of what we used to. It's not a case of not having food on board - we had a good week's worth of meals in the roof box. It was just not on our minds when we'd crossing countless kilometres in the oven car.

Once we'd showered and eaten, it was another repack of the car, before we set off. The three of us couldn't wait to get the hell out of Rostov, a place that we hated more than ever. The locals, the facilities, the police, everything - a low point on the rally for us, for sure. Our plan was to head east towards the city of Volgograd and do some touristy stuff. Mother Russia was on our original agenda, and we intended to keep to at least some of it.

Russia has more police than imaginable. I had literally seen more police in 24 hours in the first city we'd been to, than six months on the mainland. Ha, I'd seen more police in 10 minutes in Russia than my seven years on the island of Tresco. They like to hang out at junctions, where the unfamiliar motorist might make a little mistake, and with it bring upon themselves a fine that will no doubt double the corrupt policeman's wage for the day. As expected, once we crossed one of these junctions, the baton came out and we pulled over. And once again, we ran through the legal checklists burned into our minds by now - every pull over lead to learning something new, but we were confident this time we were not fineable.

Will didn't have his seat belt on in the back.

Queue the policeman asking to see Mackey in his little hut of extortion. Mackey followed obediently, and the police informed Mackey of the crime. In exchange for letting us go on our way? He wanted a "present". Then, in quite possibly the most brilliant thing Mackey had ever done, said OK. He walked back to the car, got Will, and said

"I present Will Ash".

The policeman obviously got fed up of us English idiots who didn't understand what he really meant, and waved us off. Win!

About 2pm, we considered stopping for some lunch; having breakfast and lunch in one day didn't happen too much. We crossed over a bridge, spanning a small river width, and Will spotted a dirt track that lead down it. A quick U-turn in the road, and we went exploring. The bridge itself was a typical Soviet affair - big, over the top, heavy, solid. Underneath though was a big clearing next to the river, so we stopped for an hour for some sustenance. Out again came the stove, and our lunch of choice was Super Noodles.

Something so simple left us so happy.

Off again we continued, after adding some English graffiti to a Cyrillic covered bridge, with Volgograd in our sights. The drive itself was very uneventful - long roads through thousands of square kilometres of the flattest land imaginable, the horizon swallowing the ends before ever seeing a hill or mountain. We did see an enormous fire from miles back, Will the Tresco fire-fighter getting quite excited to see some fire. It was huge- billowing clouds stretching high into the sky, dwarfing everything around. Just as we were approaching the only hill we'd seen in hours, our Volgograd road turned off to the right, and so we drove away from the action. The fire, looked at with excitement by Will, was forever left behind (we later found out it was very, very big - the Russian army was drafted in to help put it out).

On we went, continually stopping at every other garage for more water, and occasionally fuel. Petrol was 50 pence, which we were happy with, and the water was good quality and plentiful (if rarely cold). Even if we did find a gem of a shop that used it's fridge, the water got hot within five minutes in the car. It was like drinking bath water. 45 degrees was the hottest we'd experienced so far, and we were hoping we get a cold patch soon. Every litre of water you drank, you sweat out the same. A treat for us was to lean forward when driving, chin on the steering wheel - the hot breeze could sweep across our dripping backs and gave us at least 20 seconds of coolness.

This blog is quite horrible, what with the toilets and the washing and the sweat - I do apologise.

The most exciting thing that happened during that drive was one of our tents rolling down the road, having been left on the roof and eventually worked its way free somewhere whilst flying down the motorway. Luckily I spotted it in the rear view mirror, else Mackey and Will would have been getting extremely friendly in the tiny remaining tent.

We approached Volgograd at dusk, and city centre driving in Russia in anything but ideal conditions is a nightmare. Dangerous drivers, pot holes, hot women that you have a tendency to subconsciously follow… in the dark, this just made it all the more dangerous. Finding a hotel this late without pre-planning would be an impossibility, so we were forced to find another makeshift campsite for the night.

Our previous method, of turning down a country lane or path and pitching up out of the way, was proving to be a little more difficult in this area of the gigantic country. Everyone we tried was capped at the end by a village, a factory, or guard dogs. We tried every one on the 5 km running up towards Volgograd, and had to resort to turning around and going even further out.

Four of the lanes proved interesting though - we ended up at a secret Russian army base. I kid you not - absolutely no signs whatsoever, down very small dirt tracks, before coming to a huge enclosed encampment, solid walls surrounding it completely. I think their security is a little lacking though - the four entrance points to this military installation each opened the two rows of security gates as we approached. Very confusing. Probably not as much as the machine gun wielding soldiers, watching as a Citroen Saxo was trying to breech the walls by trying each entrance..

By this time, it was completely dark - which made trying to find a camp site near on impossible. Without looking and looking, we'd probably wake up next to a train track (which almost happened) or somehow inside the army base. Eventually, hours after first attempting, we found a dirt track that led a kilometre off the main road, and a clearing surrounded by high bushes and trees. The ground seemed clear, the grass was tall, but it mattered not - we were tired and needed to sleep.

I couldn't find the poles to my tent, so had the misfortune to sleep in the car again. Will and Mackey camped yet again without top sheets, and all three of us accompanied by some rather hungry mosquitoes. We were tired, we were dirty, we were hungry and hot. After the troubles in Rostov, the long day's driving in the heat, stops and not finding a hotel, spirits were probably at the lowest they'd been the entire trip. Angry swatting of the mosquitoes quickly descended from skilful assassination attempts, through to angry punches, to downright submission. We hit the proverbial sack, hoping for the next day to be a better day and determined to find a long overdue hotel.

Breakfast in the field

Russian fruit juice. Amusing ingredient.

Day 11 - Mother Russia

We all woke early from our makeshift campsite, after quite possibly the worst night's sleep to date. Not able to find my tent poles meant I had the back seat of the car for a consecutive night. With absolutely minimal leg room, the thought of being able to stretch my legs out straight was nothing but a pipe dream. Will and Mackey had their tents set up quite fast the previous night, spurred on by the ever growing army of flying insects attracted to the foreigners in their field.

I woke up to the same five mosquitoes I shared my bedroom with, and the war wounds to prove it. Will and Mackey had an equal amount of fun with their flying friends. With light now upon us, we could survey the land on which we temporarily lived; and it sucked. More of a swamp than a campsite, the slightly marshy ground obviously held home to all manner of nasty bastards, dying to eat us alive.

It was a hot night, both in the car and in the tents, and we got up even more sweaty and dirty than the night before. We had a quick bottled shower, again nothing more than a litre of water and standing in a small clearing, free for the world to see and the mosquitoes to bite. The shower didn't help a great deal - we might have smelt that little bit nicer, but deep down we were hobo like.

We repacked the car, jumped in, and I began the perilous 500 meters out of the wasteland and back on to the main road. We probably did three meters before realising the front right tire was completely flat - our first puncture. Not bad after 3,100 miles or so, but still a bit of a heartbreak and didn't help our already rock-bottom moods.

Mackey and Will set about changing it rather quickly - it was already 32 degrees at 8.30am. Once set, we bolted the ruptured tyre onto the bonnet (part of our weight saving exercise from the Ukraine), and hit the short drive to Volgograd.

Volgograd is a bit city – we thought comparable to Rostov, the hell hole. We were half dreading the city, just in case it shared similar bad attributes to its border brother. Our spirits couldn't take another big fine or police attention. Not that we were arguing amongst ourselves though, the shared hatred of Rostov still keeping the peace within Pete the Saxo, but the drive was a quiet one, interrupted only by the exhaust rattling in a vain attempt to break the awkward silence.

This city holds Mother Russia ("The Motherland Calls") - an absolutely prodigious statue of a sword wielding woman, symbolising the power of Russia in the Battle of Stalingrad. Most definitely on our list of things to see, we entered the city with trepidation - always ensuring we were well within the speed limit, even if it did accord us angry horns from the locals.

We had a rough idea where the big lady stood, so we moved through the main four lane road moving up through the city. Half way up, with all our eyes scanning the landscape to try and see something, Mackey spotted her. A couple of miles away, but she looked ridiculously large, the adjoining buildings reaching her ankles. She stood as tall as the Statue of Liberty. Now we knew where to head, we followed the tip of the sword, and eventually came to the car park.

After paying 50 Roubles to park (and have the car watched, a necessity when it's filled with our precious belongings), we were already in awe of her - standing on the highest hill in the city, looking out over the country, a strange expression on her face and holding her mighty sword up high. We strolled up the pedestrian path, and we think right past the ticket hut. Mainly due to not knowing if it was a ticket hut or not, damn Cyrillic. Either way, we had no angry Russian ticket ladies chasing after us, so on we went.

It was late morning by this time, and it was hot. It reached 40 degrees today, and when you're walking around and only able to carry a very limited amount of water (which always reached bath water temperature after a few minutes), we were in no real rush. Especially as the walk was uphill.

We reached the foot of the Mother, standing on a single story plinth. Looking up gave you that dizzy feeling, forcing you to take a step back. Mackey was the size of one of her toes. We questioned how she was ever built, she looked amazing. Seriously impressed. We walked around, took lots of video and lots of pictures, including the typical tourist poses. A particularly special one of Mackey breaking out the motivating pose, imaginary sword held high and attracting many a disgusted glance from the locals who'd come to pay their respects to the motherland. We apologised.

As well as Mother Russia, there was also a fantastic memorial to World War 2 and it's Russian victims - a mausoleum with a 30 foot stone hand in the centre holding an ever burning flame, a winding ramp around the edges leading you to the bottom of it - huge, open, and it's walls adorned with the names of thousands upon thousands of soldiers who lost their lives. The names, and the walls around, were made from millions of pieces of shiny minerals I dare not try to identify. Flanking the flame were two soldiers, who like our own The Queen's Guards, never moved an inch whilst staring forward at the other in the 35 degree heat. While we were there, we also had the pleasure of watching a changing of the guards ceremony - very cool and very foreign.

There were lots of tacky tourist vendors lining the wishing pool outside - I'd love to have brought home some genuine Russian dolls for my Nan, but Pete the Saxo was already full to bursting point. We had a cold drink in the far too hot sun, admired the 20 foot statues of motivational communist war scenes - a soldier dragging the wounded, another charging into the face of battle, and a soldier throwing a huge snake at the enemy. Yeah, we didn't get the last one either.

Once we'd done our bits, we headed to a supermarket nearby, to grab a few things we needed - a replacement Rally Phone, water and enough materials to bodge job a repair on the rattling exhaust. The phone was a simple enough affair - the lone shop girl loved the English accent, and giggled profusely as she went about fulfilling my needs. My phone needs. We then trawled the aisles of the supermarket, eventually finding the DIY section. We came out with a new tyre iron and some oven gloves. The plan, to wrap the oven gloves around the exhaust as a heat shield, and bungee/cable tie to a bracket above. The team had mixed expectations of the outcome...

On driving through Volgograd, we by chance passed a Citroen dealership with workshop, a shiny oasis of silver and glass amongst the otherwise industrial city limits. Had the last few days of anguish been worth it, and fate had finally dealt us a good hand?? We pulled into the car park, filthy Pete the Saxo standing so very out of place amongst the brand new cars, and headed inside. Seeing the countless Citroen signs surrounding us was a very uplifting feeling!

First thing we noticed, was the abundance of beautiful women working there - literally more inside one car showroom than we'd seen our entire time in Russia up to now. Second thing, it was 16 degrees C. Air conditioned heaven. Third thing, a cafe with cold drinks. Fourth thing, free Wi-Fi in said cafe. And fifth thing, a service manager who understood our need for a torsion bar and shock absorber bolt. Surely this was the yin to the last few days yang?

Thanks to the Wi-Fi and the laptop, Google Translate once again helped us explain the problems. We straight away had the same problem as the Ukraine - they pointed out that this was a Citroen only garage. We pointed out again that it was a Citroen - but he'd never heard of a Saxo. He actually had to look it up before he believed us! Eventually he did though, and got to work. Before long, the service manager had printed out in detail diagrams of the rear axle and we highlighted the parts we needed. By this time, a large queue of impatient locals had formed behind us, but we cared not - we'd finally sort out the car.

That was, of course, until the Russian informed us that the parts we needed were not available in Russia, we couldn't order them, and they wouldn't even look at the car. Heartbroken, we retired to the cold comfort of the Wi-Fi cafe, and re-evaluated our options. We explained to Jo what was going on via Facebook, and she gave our wonder mechanic, who we missed dearly in times like this, a call and acted as the internet to phone translator.

We further explained the problem to Nick back at home - the cause, the effect, the symptoms etc. After a long typing session, he came back with the opinion that it wasn't the torsion bar at all. Rather, I'd just bent the entire car hitting the Ukrainian pot hole. All things considered, this was great news!

Rather jubilant at the news - the car was still injured, but fatal it was not, we enjoyed a few more minutes in the cool surroundings of the Citroen dealership café.

As the laptop battery began to wane, it was time to visit a proper mechanics - we still had the issue of our dangling shock absorber to address. Volgograd, as with any other Russia city, is home to millions of mechanics - all very much required due to a) the rubbish roads throughout Asia b) they all drive Ladas.

We pulled in to the first one we found, this like all the others having ABTOMEKIC or something equally strong and prominent. We got strange looks as a French car they'd never heard of pulled in front of their open double doors, already with a car on the ramp. A few finger points and signals later, we got the point they'd be done in 10 minutes and we'd have their full attention. Before too long in the raging sun, we had the car lift to ourselves, and we said hello to our hopeful saviours - Nikolas Shilez & Alexis Kristofer, as they were therefore known as.

At the Citroen garage beforehand, we'd thought a bit ahead and translated our woes into Russian on the laptop. At the new garage, we opened the laptop and showed them. They looked impressed, because we'd had our problems written in darn Cyrillic despite us being unable to recognise a single character. A few nods, and the car was lifted.

Straight away, the two guys called everyone else in the vicinity over - a few laughs, a few open mouths, and much shaking of heads. They were great though - understanding exactly what we were after, and set about finding the bolt needed. Only when testing the length of some against the now in-place shock absorber, they noticed something else - the bloody Ukrainian garage (aka Mike and the Mechanics) had actually forgotten to put a bolt back in - one of four that holds the rear axle on. So since the Ukraine, since Mike and his incompetence, we'd been driving with the rear left shock absorber hanging loose, and one of the right main chassis mount bolts missing completely.

"Fucking Ukrainians", said Mackey, was the first thing our new garage friends understood.

They didn't have the right sized bolts in stock. Of course they didn't, that would have been far too easy. But surprising us all, Nikolas just jumped in his car and disappeared - to buy the correct one. We were impressed and sanguine, even more so when he returned a couple of minutes later. Once again though, mocking fate ensured that the bolt didn't fit - it was too wide. Once again though, our new best friend just grabbed his angle grinder, and made it the right size. Fantastic.

Shock absorber reattached and the missing main bolt replaced, we were jubilant. Straight away, the car seemed happier - not bouncing all over the place and subconsciously we knew it was now not too likely for the back wheels to fall off. We asked him for the bill - 300 Roubles, or £6. We were so happy we gave him a tenner. Best tenner we've ever spent!

With the car fixed, and our tourist needs done for the day, we then went to find a much needed hotel. We started looking at about 6.30pm, touring the city in daylight and with a better hope of finding one. I'll cut a long story short though - despite checking a few, even having some great German/Russian chaps leaving their dinners and making phone calls for us, it turns out there was a big show of some sort in town. As a result, everywhere would be full.

We were hot, we were hungry, we were thirsty, we were dirty, we were tired. We hadn't had a proper night sleep in a long time - no more than six hours in a night since we started the actual rally. Now to be told that we had little hope of finding a bed, either five stars or a shed, was nearly enough to bring us to tears. It was that bad.

We decided to hit the road, head out of the main city, and attempt to find an out of town hotel. By this time, it was dark and we knew we would struggle - but what other choice did we have. As we drove through the city centre, no banter thrown around by any of us, I was sure I glanced across the words HOTEL on a building. 95% confident of this, we drove around the back of the building to be greeted with a car park, towered over by an enormous Soviet style building - uniform windows and curtains, air conditioners and colours. As if the architects had designed only one strip of the hotel, and copy/pasted it throughout the length.

Surely this had to be a hotel? Then, we spotted something that made us very happy - another Mongol Rally vehicle! If only his place had a room, then our spirits would be soaring.

We walked in, Will and I looking like we were veteran hobos, and enquired. They had rooms. After we'd paid, grabbed our bags, made our way up to the rooms and lay on the bed, we agreed that this was the happiest we'd felt the entire rally up to now. Certainly not the best experience, or the best moment - but to contrast how we'd felt an hour ago, we were now polar opposites away from the gloom and desolation from the past few days.

We had a shower (I won't explain to you how good this was, you'd have no idea how happy it made us. And they were separate showers, just in case my wording suggested otherwise) and headed downstairs to the 24 hour bar for some food.

The menu was all in Cyrillic, of course, and we were just about to play a game of menu roulette (point at a menu item, not able to comprehend a single ingredient, and ask for that) when a lovely receptionist came over. She spoke English, realised we would struggle, and asked us what we'd like. Steak please. With potatoes and a salad. Despite being presented as an upmarket portion size, it wasn't overly good quality, but still tasted incredible. We had a beer, 11.30pm came, and we all retired to our air conditioned beds.

Volgograd, so far, had been incredibly good to us - no police stops at all, the locals seem friendlier, we're getting lots of beeps and waves, we (eventually) found a hotel, Pete the Saxo had been fixed and we'd found other rally teams. Russia had redeemed itself.

Mother Russia and war memorials

Our Russian mechanic saviours - and Mackey

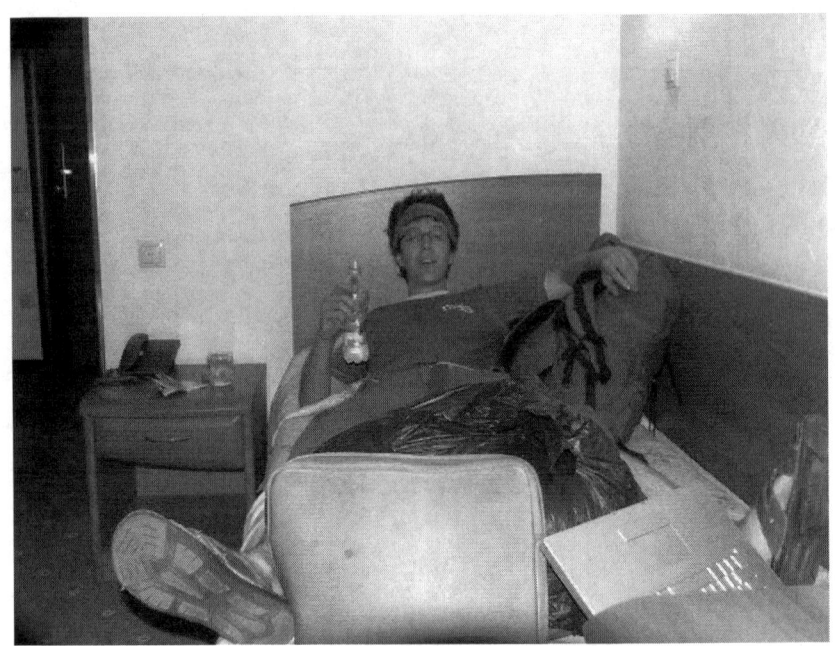
A very good feeling to finally find a hotel and a real bed

Day 12 - More good Russia

We woke up in our favourite environment - in a bed, and an air conditioned room. We got about eight hours sleep, which was our new rally record. After the slog of the past couple of days, we were beginning to enjoy it again. We had a good touristy day yesterday, visiting the might of Mother Russia and war monuments, and had eventually culminated in finding a hotel. Mackey and I shared a room, and Will had the luxury of his own. For some reason, everywhere only has a twin and a single, so we have an unspoken game of "who pays, gets the single". Last night, Will and I had both fought to pay for the hotel, no matter what it had cost. As I'd won the last game, it was only fair to let Will have the single room.

We headed down for breakfast, expecting the same breakfast as we've had throughout most of Europe and Russia, and we were right. Sausage (but not the type we love in the UK, more tinned hot dog style), strange ham, potatoes, vegetables etc... Will and I grabbed some more familiar breakfast comestibles (such as cereal or pancakes), whereas Mackey went all out again, living the Russian dream. I commended him for this.

We packed our stuff, and headed out to the car park, where a few other rally teams had parked their ambulances either side of the Saxo, dwarfing it in comparison. Perhaps if we ever do the Mongol Rally again (I can hear our bosses collectively shaking their head) we'd take an ambulance - so much space inside, teams slept in them, as well as the luxury of standing room. And cupboard space. And... and... I must stop, else I'll get rally envy. We love you, Pete the Saxo.

We chatted with a couple New Zealand/Irish teams, including one who bragged about his fridge in the back of his ambulance. We don't like him anymore. All were going a similar way to us, especially for the first few days - we'd always guessed we'd find more teams as we approached the Russian/Kazakh border, as there are only a couple of roads to use, rather than the millions of route combinations through Europe.

Our target today was Astrakhan - the last city on the way to Borat Land, apparently renowned for its oil wealth and the redevelopment of the city. As we were back onto a semi-tight schedule, Mackey offered to drive to the city. About a six hour drive at Mackey's speeds - Will and I could only legally drive at 43mph in Russia. Due to having our licenses for less than two years, we were limited to a paltry 70kph, even on the open motorways. This felt ridiculous, being overtaken by more Ladas in 10 minutes that you'd see in the UK and Europe your entire life.

We pushed towards Astrakhan. Our map reading skills were improving all the time - whoever was stationed in the front had the responsibility of giving the driver directions, usually in plenty of time but there had been one or two "Four Weddings and a Funeral" moments (mini on the motorway).

On the route, we met up with Team Mongolia Is Our Everest, three lads from Swindon driving a silver Daihatsu Terios. As with the Mongol Rally camaraderie that was beautiful to see, they began to convoy with us and off we headed together.

It was quite an uneventful drive - no police stops, although plenty of police check points. At rather sneaky points along motorways and busy roads, they have watch towers; big circular towers of imposing concrete, something more suited to the bygone days of the Wild West rather than the modern day. We'd spot them in advance, sometimes aided by the flash of headlights from the oncoming traffic - something that doesn't really happen in the UK, motorists warning each other of police, which saved our wallets countless times.

The scenery from the car was much of the same, flat land of enormous proportions as far as the eye could see. Scattered trees, numbering in the dozens rather than the thousands, broke the monotony of the landscape. The road surfaces were relatively very good - Russia obviously has the money to ensure that at least the main roads were somewhat pothole free.

It's a strange place, old Russia. We'd pass countless villages, each looking like they should be in a third world country - shacks and huts, made from scrap wood and looking as if the first storm would wipe any sign of them away. They were the only signs of life between the sprawling larger cities (such as upsetting Rostov and redeeming Volgograd). How they became a superpower though seemed very clear - driving for an hour, we saw dozens of huge army trucks, adapted for different needs - troop carriers, ground to air missile launchers, logistical support etc. We all agreed we'd seen more of a military presence in 1 hour, than our entire lives on UK roads.

As we approached Astrakhan, we were shocked. Stereotypical Soviet industry, heavy in metal rusting after being long abandoned, began to rise from the horizon. Was this the city that had found new money? Were the stories of it being clean that far from the truth? Industrial smoke billowed from the few factories still able to continue their work, and the housing areas looked as distraught as ever. We were a bit worried. Luckily though (well, lucky for us rather than the residents), we drove through and spotted a sign hinting that our target was just that little bit further.

Scilly Mission and Team Mongolia Is Our Everest (TMIOE from here on) took turns in leading the two car convoy, trying to find a hotel. The maps and the Lonely Planet we had both seemed to be out of date. The cheap, no frills hotel we originally searched for seems to have disappeared. We did, however, find a very upmarket establishment, where single rooms were £90. Which, if you've stayed at a good UK hotel (like the Island Hotel, New Inn or Hell Bay for example; Tresco are getting their money's worth from this sponsorship!) wasn't a bad price.

For us, however, hotels were something of a treat every few nights. We simply could not afford them for a month. Their air conditioning and showers might actually save us from killing each other, and all those around us, so we asked the receptionist if she could advise where we could find a slightly more affordable option.

She pointed down river - a huge block of flats style building, albeit right on the edge of the river Volga. It turns out they had rooms - not overly cheap, but how much is a life really worth? We checked in, along with our convoying buddies, and before long were joined by three or four other teams arriving late in the evening. The rooms weren't too bad, though completely overshadowed by the misleading foyer and reception area, stunningly clean and modern, which must have cost as much as the 100 or something rooms put together.

It had air con, it had a shower in a wet room. We were very happy once again.

Ourselves, TMIOE and the Renegade Pencils, a team hailing from New York and driving an ambulance, all got together for some evening beers and food. Once again, menu roulette was about to be played, until I spotted some pictures of pizzas. Six of them, 20 odd Bavarian beers and we all swapped stories of heartbreak and joy, trials and tribulations, all while sat 50 meters away from the perfectly serene river.

Russia has got much better. We like Russia. Although, tomorrow, possibly the next day; Kazakhstan!

The first team seen in a long time - Team Mongolia Is Our Everest

Day 13 - Entering the land of Borat

Astrakhan is a lovely place, but completely filled with police. Russia has an abnormal amount of law enforcement. I know, it's a big country, but it's ridiculous - everywhere we looked there were police with stupid batons, batons that once waved might as well spell out some figure in the local currency, like you might do with a sparkler on bonfire night. Also, strangely enough, there were boy racers everywhere we've been - of course, the quality of the car has certainly dropped from the dizzy heights found at Weston-Super-Mare sea front, but they were still around. Mostly Ladas with a blue neon aerial, doing wheel spins and the like. An international pastime it seemed.

It was always so nice to wake up in a hotel - usually Will (the only one with a phone) setting an alarm to wake us up, so we never completely recharged our batteries, usually deciding to get up at 7.30-8am to begin another long day on the road. But, waking up in a bed, surrounded by walls and the luxury of a ceiling high enough to stand up in, was an amazing feeling.

Another shower for us all, despite being squeaky clean from the night before. We just never knew when the next might be! Breakfast was the usual affair, Mackey going for the breakfast version of a roast dinner, Will and I playing it safe with cereal and fruit, and we were joined by the lads from TMIOE. There we set the rather simple plan for the day - get from Astrakhan to the Russian/Kazakhstan border, a mere 71km away. Fairly difficult to accidentally sway from this simple route, the challenge of getting out the city was the only task to really plan.

We left about 10am-ish - slightly later than usual, but Mackey went about bodging a repair for the rattling exhaust issue we had going on. Nothing bad, but it rattled. A lot. We got so many admiring stares, so many happy and smiley faces waving with enthusiasm, and it was a shame when they all turned to embarrassment and disgust when the exhaust grabbed the attention of half the city.

This repair job involved three key items - some Soviet oven gloves (heat protection with no padding inside, just very thin and raw for strength and efficiency), some bungee cords and cable ties. His plan was simple - wrap the exhaust (quite far from the engine so not incredibly hot) with the oven gloves, cable tie it tight, and then bungee it to the car. Simple!

This was done in front of the hotel, jacked up (the car, not Mackey) and tools spread around. Normally, I think we would have upset a few locals, messing the simple appearance and tidy efficiency they had going on in this particular corner of the city. Luckily though, quite a few other teams had come to seek refuge and filled the parking area with all manners of old ambulances and small cars, all looking as equally good/bad as Pete the Saxo.

With the exhaust fixed, smiles all round when the engine was started and nothing but the little 1.1 litre French engine could be heard (other than Mackey proclaiming he was 'the best' for quite a while), we set off towards the border.

After travelling our first 50km from the hotel, we decided to stop for fuel for the last time this side of the border, being completely unaware of the fuel availability and quality once driving through the Kazakh steppe. We thought it would be best if Pete the Saxo and his jerry cans were full. Here, we met another team - Team Mongolia or Bust, driving a red Suzuki Swift. Two lads from somewhere near Yorkshire-ish, the petrol station then turned into a spontaneous meeting place for teams - eight of us sat around for a while, grabbed some snacks, and chatted away in the scorching mid morning sun exchanging stories of trials and tribulations that had so far presented to us.

The three of us really enjoyed the Mongol Rally fraternity that existed - as soon as you saw another team, that recognisable sticker on the bonnet, everyone would pull in and stop for a chat, exchange hints and tips, and certainly come to any aid should it be required. Most we'd never met before, at the Czech Out party or at Goodwood, but the camaraderie was fantastic.

Temperatures were hot - very hot, touching 40 degrees centigrade, water consistently in demand by the three of us. Cold water was refreshingly beautiful when we could find it, but Russian petrol stations don't push their fridges very hard - most of the water we'd bought, from a trademark Coca Cola fridge, was warmer than our UK tap water in the summer. Thinking about it though, they probably work just as hard as our own, bringing the temperature down 20 degrees or so. If our fridges did that for 80% of the year, we'd just have ice. Also, all fridges in service stations were locked - to get a drink out, the cashier brought out a remote control more suited for a TV, and it magically unlocked. How strange is that?

I'm rambling about fridges far too much.

On the way to the border, we had a river to cross - quite a large one at around half a mile wide and the name of it escaping me, which had the most amazing bridge on. Think of floating pontoons at a marina, but instead spanning a deep river, barely enough room for two cars to pass each other, moving up and down as cars passed over and water passed under it. It cost an extortionate J1.50 to use, but saved us a very long journey upstream to find a bridge. A floating bridge was a first for us, so it made it all the more fun.

We pushed towards the border, getting to our destination just after 1pm, and as luck would have it the queue was remarkably short - five cars, including our own. We were well versed with border procedures by now; before asked by the guard (usually carrying a weapon), we'd have all of our documents in our hands and ready to present. V5, insurance certificate, visas and passports.

Apart from we couldn't find the passports.

Anywhere.

A brief panic, we then thought back to when we last had them - the hotel! The receptionists took them when we checked in, common practice in this part of the world. Had we asked for them back? Ah, then it came back to us.

Mackey checked out first, then Will & I - we asked for our passports, but the receptionist had told us Mackey had them – she'd given them to him. With a satisfied wave, we bid farewell and got in the car, not even thinking to check with Mackey. When told of this story, Mackey denied all knowledge - he certainly didn't have ours, let alone asking for his own (why he didn't, I have no idea).

So, that meant driving the 1.5 hours back to the hotel, in the hottest part of the day. Mackey did the driving; Will & I can only drive at 43mph, which would have turned it into a 2.5 hour journey. A very frustrating few hours round trip lay ahead of us.

Just before getting to the hotel, going via the only route we knew (which happened to involved a short 50 meter one-way street), turning into said street we were greeted by a police car and two baton waving officers, obviously laughing deep inside that an English car had just broken a very obviously law right in front of their eyes.

We played it semi-dumb, which seemed to work. We asked them a few nice questions about Russia, told them where we were going etc. They took Mackey's driving license, this time the International Driving Permit, and made finger gestures that he was to confiscate it. Without arguing, Mackey began to get out the seat and told Will to drive, already resigned in his fate. This had a bizarre response from the cops - they simply gave his license back, and let him carry on down the one-way street!

Once back to the hotel, wallets and licenses intact, I walked in and told them how angry we were - it seemed the receptionist had confused us with some Italians staying in the hotel. Italians?! This was one time the language barrier most definitely worked in their favour. It did however, give us the chance to stand in the 16 degree foyer for ten minutes; comparatively Arctic.

Passports securely in our possession, we again drove (we = Mackey) to the border. As luck wouldn't have it, we were greeted with an enormous queue of vehicles on the Russia side of the border, a sharp contrast to the handful awaiting us on attempt one. We arrived about 3.45pm, and started to queue up, aiming to get through within the hour.

A Mongol Rally team joined the queue, and another, and another, and so on - before long, the majority of the first half of the queue were our comrades, the latter half the Kazakh locals wanting to get home. We met up with teams that we'd spotted and chatted to along the way, including the two Irish/New Zealand ambulances from Volgograd.

Passing through the Russian border went fine - we had to do some photocopying in a very peculiar trailer home, manned by a woman and her daughter working out of their living room, looking like she'd been banished to remain in the trailer forever. Mackey had to have a little shoulder barge with a Kazakh who insisted on pushing in the queue for passport stamps, and lost. Customs took one look at the car boot, crammed full of our life for the past and next two weeks, and simply asked for a souvenir. A miniature bottle of Jim Beam and we were through.

We entered no man's land. Unlike European countries, or even Ukraine/Russia, this no mans land was enormous - a couple of miles long through rolling green hills, bisected by a serene river. We drove for 10 minute or so through this land that presumably belongs to no one, yet maintained better roads that half the countries we've already navigated

As we eventually reached Kazakhstan, and its mighty border control (which strangely was newer and more majestic than any other country so far), a number of rally teams were already queuing to leave no mans land and progress, including Team Stardust (Helen and Victoria, driving a Land Rover ambulance).

Queuing took a couple of hours, but very slowly we inched our way forward. We had thought we might be in luck, as we were at the front of the queue and ready to add our 13th country to our passports. It was never that simple though. We were pulled over to the side of the queue, literally within touching distance of the red and white swing gate that signified the next step. As were a couple of other rally teams. Were we to be searched? But we hadn't even gone through Kazakh passport control.

From what we all could gather, they wanted to let the Kazakhs in first. Fair enough, but we waited hours, all of us continually trying to catch the guards attention and ensure he hadn't forgotten about the Saxo and the Swift, the ambulances and the Pandas, all crazily adorned with stickers and waiting so very patiently at the side of the road. By 8.30pm, the teams came together in true Rally style and road blocked the border.

All four lanes, two for each opposing direction, had an ambulance or two on, aimed directly at the still shut gate, backed up by an armada of tiny cars. Rather than get us all arrested, it seemed to work - we were actually allowed through, much to the annoyance of the guards.

Last step of this tedious crossing was Kazakh customs, and we had no idea what to expect. A few hours previously, I expected the entrance to the gargantuan country as nothing more than a chain fence and a camel herder casually manning it, opening whenever a vehicle approached. But already this had been completely disproved, what with the shiny customs building that dwarfed everything we'd previously seen.

We approached Kazakh customs, and Mackey and I were told to leave the car and walk across to get our passports checked. We entered the shiny building and were seen by a miserable man sweating profusely, in a small room within the expansive building, seemingly the one occupant.

I had to take off my headband to cross - apparently that drastically altered my face and I therefore looked completely different from my passport. It took a few minutes, but we were through - I was the first to walk on the mythical land of Borat. We waited for Will, 100 yards down the road waiting to be searched with the car. Once they finally got to him however, first dealing with another rally team, they simply waved him through. Team reunited, we had entered Kazakhstan.

We drove a couple of minutes down the road, and saw Team Stardust and their ambulance pulled over. We joined them to wait for some other teams, and in true British style they made us all a lovely cup of tea. Ginger, peppermint or white tea was a very welcome evening tipple (about 10pm now), and we chatted and ate Monster Munch as we were joined by other teams, each earning their freedom from no man's land and bureaucracy .

Convoying was great fun - even if the other teams didn't have CB radios, it felt much more relaxed and safe. The lead car set the pace, and the teams behind dutifully followed (or as best we could, the Saxo lacked the ground clearance of a Land Rover ambulance). We'd all agreed to set up camp five minutes away from the border, and drove ever so slightly deeper into the country in the darkness. It was a relatively cool night, certainly cooler than we'd experienced the last few - but still it hovered around the 30 degree mark as we pulled into a small clearing off the road. By clearing, I meant of knee high desert bushes - although it was dark, there was not a tree that could be seen anywhere. Kazakhstan looked big and flat.

All in all, we had eight or nine teams that set up camp together - once tents were set up, excluding those lucky buggers who had the luxury of an ambulance stretcher/bed to sleep on, everyone sat around and retold the stories of their voyage so far; breakdowns, bribes, sights and sounds, foods and drinks. This was what the rally was all about, and we loved it.

Rather strangely, a black 4x4 pulled up next to the road, and out popped two Italians. Very coincidently, they too were travelling to Ulaan Baatar by car, for no other reason than because they wanted to. The Mongol Rally, without being a part of the Mongol Rally. They asked, in very broken English, if anyone knew of a hotel close by. We didn't, but the teams rallied together, and a spare tent and two sleeping bags materialised within minutes.

The majority of the people (us included) retired to tents within an hour, ours once again being laughed at for their similarity to a coffins. It was warm enough for us to not need the top sheet of the tent again, instead sleeping under the netting under-layer, gazing up on the cloudless night to the stars that seemed so different to the ones at home.

Mackey's exhaust repair: Oven gloves, bungee cords, cable ties

The floating bridge across the River Buzan, Russia

Reaching the Russian/Kazakh border for the second time in a day

Day 14 - There's a bloody camel

We awoke at 8am in our rally campsite, a small area packed with ambulances and small cars, tents filling the gaps between. As we slept, it seemed a couple of other teams had spotted our makeshift city and joined us.

Mackey was up first, and delighted in waking us (and everyone else up) at the early hour. It was a good night's sleep, probably the best I'd had camping in the coffins. It was warm enough at night to do without a sleeping bag, but cosy with one. As soon as the morning sun arose over the horizon though, the sleeping bag would fast become a little oven of sweat. Very nice to wake up in the night though, as you'd roll over (as much as the limited space allowed) as per normal, and look straight up; straight up through the mosquito net of the tent and see nothing but expansive sky, with absolutely nothing in the way of artificial illumination to detract from the sheer abundance of stars.

Mackey was now quite well known amongst the camp, as he snored like a bear. A bear with a sinus problem. As we left half the camp still chatting and finishing drinks when we retired the night before, Mackey had fallen asleep quite quickly and started snoring. Much to the amusement of everyone in the immediate area.

We packed up, a somewhat arduous task but we were getting quite good at it, finally able to get the tents back in their ridiculously small tent bags. That must be the sign of a veteran camper, surely.

Half the camp set off for the nearest city of Atrayau, south east of the border. We convoyed with the Danish guys in their ambulance, Team Stardust in theirs, and the red Suzuki swift. Within 10 minutes, we were already beginning to appreciate Kazakhstan. We might have only been a tiny fraction into the great expanse that makes up the 9th largest country in the world, but it was worlds away from Russia. The horizon seemingly stretched to each corner without a hill or mound spoiling the view, impossible to determine how far you were actually seeing.

Will started the day's driving, when we saw something. We saw something splendid. We saw camels. That's right, actual real life camels, just like you'd see in a zoo/on a postcard/imagine in a

Humphrey joke. Eight or nine of the little cheeky devils just hanging out by the side of the road, chewing whatever it is they eat, even admiring Pete the Saxo and watched as we drove past equally engrossed in them.

For me, this strange flat land felt a lot more foreign than anything we'd seen so far. On the inside of Pete the Saxo, high up on the spacious roof, we wrote down each country as we departed it, and were each allowed one word to sum up the just visited state. It was strange to look up and see that my word for the Czech Republic was "foreign". Back then, just a couple of days into the trip, everything seemed so different to our usual UK lives. So much so, the Czech Republic earned the title of being the country that was so different to home. How much we'd already seen compared to that.

The roads in Kazakhstan were as expected for the most - shoddy attempts at a tarmac road, perhaps once a shining example of Kazakh engineering, had become literal mountain ranges of tarmac peaks and troughs. I'm not sure whether it was the sun that damaged these roads so much, or the traffic, but pot holes and raised pinnacles of tarmac poised a constant danger to Pete the Saxo.

We'd learnt from our Ukrainian experience, even if it did turn out to be a small issue. We continually thank our mechanic Nick Shiles for putting on such a fine sump guard - I'd lost count the number of times we'd hit it. It was usually a case of pot holes all around, and the one route you have whilst cruising at 30mph involved one of these tarmac mountains, standing a mighty 10" tall. After inspecting it a few days ago, already bearing a few light scratches from previous roads, I knew we'd rather hit the sump guard and skid over something as opposed to hitting a pot hole and potentially damaging all manner of things on the car.

Small villages littered the roadside, yet again feeling worlds away from the UK or even Russia - half of the domiciles of these steppe inhabitants were nothing more than huts made of wood, mud and straw. We began to get even more waves, or at least a lot more stares, as we cut through their villages on the way to the city. Rather interestingly, next to each settlement no bigger than a hamlet, was their cemetery. Having asked other teams about this, each burial would involve constructing a mausoleum for the recently departed, four elaborate stone walls around the grave. Probably three or four meters along each side, but as far as we could tell, without a roof. Each looked different to its neighbours and a fine way to respect their dead; but worrisome and macabre to see these two laid side by side, the bustling village and the collection of tombs, with the latter usually out-sizing the former.

We convoyed along, losing ground to the high clearance ambulances and having to slow down to properly avoid the constant obstacles, but we'd catch them up every so often as they stopped to change drivers. We found our first Kazakh supermarket, always an exciting thing to marvel at what the locals ate (although usually not risking it too much and going for things we knew and liked!). The prices however have finally changed for the better. Much better. For example - Mackey has found cigarettes for 40 pence a pack. I found a litre of vodka for a pound. A single, UK pound. We bought 25 litres of water, some sweets, vodka, cigarettes, bananas, apples, biscuits, wet wipes, chewing gum, and some other things, and it all came to less than £10. Unbelievable.

With Pete the Saxo now carrying a decent amount of water, which meant we didn't have to stop every hour or so to refuel ourselves, we hit the road once more. Dodging each and every pot hole with care meant we didn't make the best time in the world, but we caught up with our original convoy as we entered Atrayau.

Kazakhstan is the most developed of the 'Stans', and its oil and gas money is being reinvested into the country. Development is everywhere, much more than we thought we'd find in a minor Kazakh city. Shiny new hotels were popping up throughout; the city was clean, filled with nice cars and almost indistinguishable from a European hub. Mackey had found a well recommended hotel in the Lonely Planet guide, that offered air conditioned rooms, showers, free Wi-Fi, and a bar called "Guns & Roses", which played live music every night.

Once we'd discussed this with our motorcade, we all decided to attempt to find it (what with city centre driving in a foreign country not being our specialities. Managing the roads and road systems was fine – it was just finding our way around that was the problem area) and pulled into what we thought might be the car park.

Lots of beeps as we tried to park up, ignored as we assumed just irate locals looking for a parking space themselves or perhaps just showing their support for our great charity rally. As it turned out, we'd parked in the city police headquarters, with many a confused detective looking at us. Quick reverse, and we were out of there.

We blindly drove around, and within a short space of time, found our hotel. It was on one of the main roundabouts, stood 10 storeys tall with the name in neon down one side, but we were still extremely pleased with ourselves. A quick check in before we bundled into the elevator and began our ascent to the 7th floor - a growing tradition it seemed. The rooms were cold, the shower was wet, the bed was comfortable, we were happy.

We cleaned our grubby selves up and changed, still one of the best feelings, and headed down for the free Wi-Fi at the Guns & Roses bar. A half English/half American bar, completely decked out in heavy stained varnished wood but probably the coldest room in Kazakhstan (we think). It was freezing, and we loved sitting there and for the first time since we started the rally, actually considered putting on a second t-shirt. We played some pool, ate some sandwiches, updated some blog and enjoyed our little bit of frigid relaxation.

The Danish team turned up not long after, and decided to stay also at the hotel. They met us in the bar for a few drinks, and we agreed to meet Team Stardust and the Newlyweds at 8pm (The Newlyweds being a young, recently married couple who were doing the Mongol Rally as their honeymoon. How amazing is that?). We had few beers playing pool at the bar, and it quickly got busy with locals coming to see the live music (despite it being on most nights anyway. Perhaps they just heard we were in town).

8pm came, as did our comrades, and we decided to go out and find some local food. The receptionist was adamant that the best Kazakh food would be found in the hotel restaurant, but we wanted to get out of the hotel (and we would be in Kazakhstan long enough to experience lots of Kazakh food). Across the busy roundabout, armed with a policeman and baton whistling at everything he possibly could, was a nice Turkish restaurant. The 10 of us decided there would be as good as anywhere, so Ziggy (from the Danish ambulance) ran and got us a table as we trundled over.

30 seconds later, we were the focus of the policeman's whistle - you couldn't cross the road at anywhere but an official crossing here. We weren't to know, that would be our excuse, but we all ran away before he could even consider telling us otherwise. We got to the restaurant and found it to be quite an upmarket eatery - spacious, air conditioned and with great food. We went through salad, soup and meat although struggled as the last course was unveiled (a platter of kebabs and Turkish meats) - our diminishing diet had meant we fill up rather quickly when offered the luxury of a considerable meal.

Next would be a bar handily located next door, and the 10 of us passed the bouncers and headed up a small flight of stairs. Here, we were presented with two options - to the left seemed a fine upmarket bar, dark and inviting whereas continuing up the stairs, we heard loud music and the potential for some disco dancing (We learnt well from watching Borat. On that note, we had been extremely careful not to drop the "B" bomb and insult anyone within earshot).

Upwards we went, and burst through the double doors into a large hall. A few of the group started disco dancing, while the rest of us realised we'd just barged in on a private party, quite possibly a birthday party, and made for the cool bar downstairs.

The bar was nice. Very nice. We were there quite early, and managed to grab a VIP table in the corner, the 10 of us excited because the menu was in English as well as Cyrillic. We went about choosing, although noticing that the prices equalled those at home.

Then, we saw it. As clear as day, listed on the left hand side about half way down - GUINNESS. I got excited, and the boys joined me in a pint, not knowing what to expect but praying it was nice. The others went for the usual lagers or shorts and a couple of minutes later, the Guinness's arrived.

Unfortunately though, they were quite rubbish. More a can of Guinness Original mixed with a can of budget cola, but it was still the nearest we'd had in a fortnight. Within 15 minutes, after lots of very funny chat (especially with Ziggy and his "what would you rather" questions), we began to notice the place filling up.

Rather than the flip flop wearing, sweaty shirts and shorts rallyers that had been driving for a fortnight and certainly looked it, the place was full of expensive cocktail dresses, suits and shoes that no doubt cost more than many of our vehicles. We, of course, found this funny and then moved back to Guns & Roses for more drinks.

By now, the place was packed - heaving four deep at the bar, and the questionable rock music drowning out us telling our rally stories to each other. I noticed something worrying as well; the number of elderly Western men with young Kazakh women was so similar to my visit to Thailand. Had this become the new Thailand, or was this a regular thing in all foreign cities? We asked at the reception if there was a quiet bar we could all go to, and once again, she said we'd find no better than the hotel's other bar, the Winter Garden. Located about 20 meters from where we asked the question, the receptionist was right - beer around a big table, lots of rallyers, and it went on until who knows what time - I retired at midnight, like a weary Cinderella, and Mackey and Will followed not long after....

Our convoy campsite inside Kazakhstan

The Danish ambulance – Team 'The Mongolian Dream'

Finding Guinness in Kazakhstan!

Day 15 - Pushing through Kazakhstan

It was so nice waking up in a bed. I know, I say that a lot, every time we get a hotel for the night, but it really was a great feeling - although the first few seconds when you woke up, you felt like you were at home, and the first fleeting moments of the day were consumed wondering whether it was a weekday and therefore have work to go to, or a weekend and to lie in just a little. That fall back down to reality, the reality that we were 5,000 miles away from home and had traversed 13 countries, was a bit of a strange one.

Last night was a very good night - a few drinks and dinner with some other teams, lots of stories swapped, generally wonderful. We had a plan where we'd continue with the convoy towards Aral, perhaps look at the dried up sea, and then diagonally negotiate the rest of the enormous country. We discussed set off times over the beers the night before, probably deciding on something entirely unrealistic like 9am (as you do when discussing anything after beer) - we got to breakfast at 9.40am and there was no sign of anyone. We packed up, checked out, this time ensuring passports were very safely with us, and went out to the cars parked right in front of the hotel.

As I mentioned before, the hotel was on a main roundabout in the city, with parking directly out the front for about 10 cars. Pete the Saxo was one of them, along with the Danish ambulance and a handful of other teams. We had asked the receptionist if there was a better place we could park, perhaps the car park we'd spotted behind the hotel. Her answer, in very limited English, was "DANGEROUS."; we left if out the front.

As it transpired though, even directly outside the hotel wasn't overly safe - our passenger door lock had been tampered with and slightly damaged, no doubt trying to get to our bags of dirty washing or the spare air filters in the boot. No entry was gained though. I like to think of this as similar to Knight Rider - but Pete the Saxo taking Kitt's place. The Kazakh intruders were probably trying to jimmy the lock when Pete the Saxo opened his doors, throwing them onto the road. They then tried to throw a brick through Pete the Saxo's window, but it just bounced back and hit them square in the face. Good job, Pete the Saxo.

Strangely enough, one small piece of anti-vandalism had taken place. I'm sure many of you had seen our photos of our friends and family we had on the back of the car - well, someone had ripped Nick Shiles's off the roof box, and stuck it very securely onto the Danish ambulance. We couldn't get it off and back where it belonged without ripping Nick's face. Instead, we took a permanent black marker and wrote on the ambulance, explaining who the man was. Mr Shiles, you might not be with us, but you'll definitely get to Mongolia.

The Danish team didn't show up, and no answer from their door. Looking at the amount these boys drank, they wouldn't be getting up for a long time. In true rally style, Mackey used the permanent marker and wrote a message on their ambulance driver's door, to let them know we'd pushed on and they'd no doubt catch us up.

We headed out of Atyrau, changing up our last remaining Roubles for Tenge, the local currency. On the way out, we saw a shed next to a petrol station and a big stack of tyres outside, reminding us we needed to get ours fixed before we moved further away from civilisation and further into the Kazakh steppe. We pulled in, a few points and gestures later, and the chap knew exactly what we wanted.

I filled up with fuel whilst the boys were waiting for the wheel; 95 octane petrol had now dropped to 45 pence a litre, while the dirtier 90 octane is 35 pence. Not that we'd risk putting it in, but 80 octane fuel was 25 pence a litre. Unreal...

Tyre man successfully fixed our damaged wheel, and I asked for the price. Drawing it in the dust, whether on the floor or on the car windscreen (trust me, there was no point in washing the car, it got filthy after a few minutes in the desert like conditions), was the universally accepted replacement for a pro-forma invoice. He wrote 250 down, which then needed to be converted into our great British pound to ensure no ripping off was underway. It usually took a minute, especially first thing in the morning, as we'd done half a dozen currencies (if not more). The first figure that came to me couldn't have been right, so I checked a bureau de change receipt, and in fact it was - to fix the tyre as good as new cost us £1.

I loved this place. I was actually rich here. I paid him £2, and told him to get a beer with the rest. He was very grateful, overly so, but it didn't seem right. How could we waste £2 on something as trivial as a magazine when that was his morning wages? I know, comparative pricing and everything, but it still felt wrong somehow.

We had a bit of a team meeting. We were over half way through our time, but only just over our mileage target. Usually this would be a good thing, apart from we'd done the luxury of European roads; from here on out was thousands of miles of questionable road (if any) through deserts and steppe. We decided to cut a small portion out of our Kazakh route, the Aral Sea. That's the big sea that dried up when the Russians diverted its source rivers to increase their cotton production, and now the old port and fishing towns lay 50 miles away from the remaining salty water.

We thought it would be cool to go and visit, but we all agreed we'd much rather crack on and definitely do the 28 challenge (or to put it another way, finish on time and keep our jobs – in particular, the guilt I'd feel leaving poor Julie back in the office, alone with my payroll job forever). Even if we did end up to be a few days early as we entered Mongolia, we could spend it in the Altai Mountains. Therefore, from Atrayau, we'd head north east to Oral and west from there.

It was quite a good thing we discussed this in front of Tyre man, as he caught the gist of what we were planning, and grabbed our map. He pointed to the road we had planned to take, a "yellow" road (similar to a British A road) as being very, very bad and would destroy Pete the Saxo. Who were we to argue with a local? We thanked him for the advice, and decided to use a different road moving directly north to get to Oral, a road that would add on 400km to our trip. (With hindsight, the man saved us a lot of trouble. Other teams didn't have the local insight we were graced with, and even a Land Rover had to turn back after 160km – a distance they spent 12 hours covering).

On the way out of the city, which included as always our unintentional tour of the inner workings, we found the road we wanted and sped out of the urban limits. Too fast though it seemed, and I was pulled over by a stationary police car hovering just past our roundabout exit and about 30 feet away from the city end sign.

I came up with a rather good idea the day before - whether it was for speeding, crossing white lines, the fact we drove on the wrong side of the car or whatever rubbish excuse they made up, they'd always end up asking for a large amount of money. Even if you bargained them down, you still had to get the money from your wallet and there was still more we could have haggled it down. So now, whoever was driving, got their wallet emptied - leaving about 2000 Tenge (about £8 or £9).

The lone policeman came up to my window, and straight away asked for our documents. Standard procedure of course, and we learnt from the Mackey incident never to give our real driving license. Instead we gave them the International Driving Permit, an almost disposable but legal alternative. He told me to follow him back to his car - another bribe for another made up rule break no doubt, but I did as instructed and walked the short distance along the hard shoulder to his waiting car (which was a Lada. All police in Russia and Kazakhstan drove Ladas. How on earth are you supposed to keep up with a fleeing villain in a Lada?!).

Once in the car, he had a small TV with a recording of me leaving the roundabout, and accelerating to 76kph. Apparently, according to him writing on his notepad, the limit was 60kph. Ooops. In my defence, there were no signs, and I waited for him to make his next move. Back on the notepad, he wrote the fine; 18,790 Tenge.

Bugger.

I'm thinking this was the official fine though, if we went and did it properly and actually got a receipt for the money, something that certainly never happened before.

I took my pre-prepared wallet from my pocket, and showed him how very little I had, about £7 in his currency. Taking it from the wallet and holding it below the dash level of the car, away from the prying eyes of the motorists whizzing (strictly at 60kph) past, he happily took it and told me I was free to go.

Now, I know I shouldn't have gone fast, but if I'd paid the huge fine, I bet none of it would have gone through the correct channels. But it was quite cool doing under the counter dealings with the local police, I won't deny it. Feel free to laugh at me when I do that with a UK constable (perhaps my good friend PC Kirkham) and get thrown in jail, all without thinking.

From there on, the road was fantastic, the complete opposite of what we'd expected to find. Newly laid tarmac, as straight as an arrow for dozens of kilometres before a slight bend and returning to another long stretch undeviating road. We cruised at 100km an hour (60mph), a speed that would get us where we aimed to be without taking an age, and looking after the car somewhat.

We got to Oral in a half decent time, having stopped for lunch at a roadside canteen used by locals from around the area. As we walked in, the general feeling of the building was of a typical work lunch break; farmers and labourers chatted whilst eating their meals, all keeping a close eye on the time.

Lunch was a delicious combination of noodles and (unidentifiable) meat stew/soup, fried pastry with (unidentifiable) meat inside, and some chai. We met some Italians and Americans, all doing the rally as well, and soon found ourselves alone in the building; it was time to get back to work, and for us to get back on the road.

As we bid farewell to the Italians and Americans, within a few minutes Will got pulled over by the police. Baton out on quite a busy road, we had no idea this time what we had done but already pre-planned and emptied the wallet of those colourful 5000 Tenge bills.

Lights were an issue this time - we had dipped headlights on, following the lead from our fellow road users, but apparently this was wrong - full lights were to be used wherever and whenever we went. Will got escorted to the police hut next to the road, where he was shown video evidence of his fine. The bill? 7000 Tenge.

Preplanning and an emptied wallet meant Will only had 2000.

Great success.

Mackey took the third shift of the day, and I navigated and DJ'ed ("late night love with James Druce" had become a regular feature in the small, cramped car filled with three sweaty men.) Actobe was our next destination, a city further west and closer still to Mongolia. The driving was pretty good, other than the monotony of an unbending road for hours at a time. Even though this was a great road, with minimal pot holes but areas where they just hadn't laid tarmac for 6 ft., driving the monotony made you very tired.

The one thing that kept Mackey driving throughout the evening, and me kept him company, was the first rain drops we'd seen in a week. As soon as the first landed, we could smell it - the rain smell so distinguishable, but a thousand times stronger in the desert road which rarely saw water.

Up ahead, a big lightning storm battled in the clouds, periodically lighting up the night sky and kept us in awe with fork lightning and brief milliseconds when night turned into day. We drove until midnight-ish until we were all tired. We spotted a picnic sign (confused us too, as we were in the middle of no where) and headed into an open car park, handily deserted other than us.

We drove to the far end, found a spot we could lay our coffin tents on the concrete floor without drawing too much attention to ourselves, and we started to unpack the car to begin the dark night.

After a couple of minutes, while the boot was open and things were being removed from the efficient packing (ha!) system, we saw a torch begin to walk towards us. From the hint of moonlight, only just luminescent enough to make out the tree tops, it looked like something from The Hills Have Eyes. Seconds later, we could make out the figure of a man walking towards us - were we not allowed to sleep here? Would we be robbed? Mackey and I already planned to offer Will in exchange for our own lives.

Until the man got within car light, and realised it was a 50 year old Kazakh wearing nothing but underpants. Literally, just a lovely pair of white underpants. He knew a few broken phrases of English, probably a case of repeating them from passing tourists rather than understand the meanings behind them, but was very smiley. We explained what we were doing with gestures and points to the car stickers, and he understood. Possibly. He then said two words which were music to our ears - "Coffee chai?" Absolutely!

We walked/took the car over to the opposite side of the car park, where we noticed a small house of typical Kazakh design - a single story, white boarded and in dire need of Symons Construction. He walked up to the door, and started banging loudly, shouting. This confused us a great deal. Lots of ringing the door bell, shouting and banging. If this wasn't his house, whose was it? And why is he roaming the plains of Kazakhstan with nothing but pants and a torch? Eventually we worked out he was waiting for his wife to answer the door, and invited us in.

It was quite an empty room, apart from a raised area taking up half the space. Almost like a stage in a theatre, on it laid a bright red patterned carpet and a very low round table - a Kazakh chai (tea) table. He got on first and confirmed to us it was a cross your legs at the table affair, and we joined him - still bewildered at the whole situation.

His wife came through some five minutes later with a fresh pot of chai and four bowls (they don't use cups or mugs), and it was delicious. ChaiGuy (I forget his real name) brought out an old school photo album, the photos fading into time, but half way through were some scraps of paper from other Western tourists who'd done the same as us - found a clearing of land off the main road, decided to camp and instead ended up drinking chai with ChaiGuy. We, of course, added our own contact details and a nice message to him and inserted it into the collection of notes I'm sure he'd never been able to understand.

After a couple of cups, he explained this was a cafe for the car park, and I asked how much our drinks were. He asked for 200 Tenge, about 80 pence, for nine cups of much needed chai. Despite looking like it might fall down at any time, and the guilt of the wife who'd been rudely awoken to make us the hot drinks (and actually went back to sleep on the sofa in the room as soon as we started to drink), that was a pretty good deal!

As we got up to leave, and headed back towards the car, ChaiGuy made the sleeping gesture. You know, two hands placed next to your head, eyes briefly closing. We nodded and did the universal tent image, a triangle (despite ours looking like sarcophaguses). He shook his head and led us to a… I don't know what you'd call it. Just outside the front door was a raised floor about 3 ft from the ground. Corrugated board surrounded it up to about 4ft, and then plants grew across a wooden grid surrounding it. With a roof on top. I can't describe it let along name it. Basically a raised platform from the ground, with vines forming the walls. He told us to sleep there - it only had three walls, the fourth completely open to the elements and the bugs. "Mosquitoes" was one word he knew though, and told us there were none.

Ah well, when in Rome - we grabbed our sleeping bags, and lay on the raised platform, the three of us watching the now distant lightning as we fell asleep in the warm Kazakh night. No spooning took place.

Nick Shiles, the Scilly Mission mechanic, somehow ends up on the Danish ambulance

Chai-Guy, the friendly Kazakh, now wearing clothes

Distant hills, a rare sight in the flat expanse

Day 16 - Onwards and eastwards

After our very erratic chancing upon the underpants wearing Kazakh, hospitable to the max, we woke up in our bedroom - the three-sided garden structure, sleeping in our cosy sleeping bags exposed to the open air. Strangely enough, we all agreed it was one of the best nights sleep we'd had, hotels excluded. Most likely due to the space available - one could have stretched out, rolled over, and not hit the confines of the tent. They really were that small, and our aim to buy new ones had yet come up fruitless.

ChaiGuy was up nice and early, I sleepily remembered him coming to check on us outside his cafe very early, chuckling because we were still asleep before walking back inside. We stirred about 8.30am, surprisingly late considering the morning Kazakh sun had beaten down on us for a few hours already. The car was parked a short distance away, just up the garden/wasteland path, and we all got up to change and wash.

Camping hygiene still left a lot to be desired - a bottle of water, wet wipes, shower gel if you were lucky, and as much privacy as the nearby bush afforded you. Even things like brushing your teeth was that little bit harder, and never quite left you with the shiny fresh feeling your bathroom sink always does.

When we returned to our makeshift bedroom to pack up the sleeping bags, the large round chai table had appeared, along with steaming hot tea and bowls. Tea in the morning was an indulgence I'd forgotten about. All of us had, and we appreciated it hugely.

Breakfast consisted of a watermelon we'd bought the day before. A huge watermelon the size of a child, a smaller honeydew melon and a carrier bag full of apples for a couple of pounds from a road stall - fresh and fantastic to start the day. Will operated on the enormous fruit with a 3 inch knife - not the neatest of segments but it all went down very well. ChaiGuy did come over and asked if we wanted some food, but we politely declined.

Before we left, we gave ChaiGuy a small amount of cash (£5) and a packet of cigarettes, for which he was very grateful. Although I think he was more interested in my roll ups. You see, we haven't seen tobacco or rizzlas since the Czech Republic, a few thousand miles back. Every border guard that saw the smoking paraphernalia had to smell it, thinking it was marijuana or another equally forbidden drug. ChaiGuy liked a roll up.

Before setting off, we had a photo with ChaiGuy and he warned us off some road works 25km up the road (all of this done with gestures and writing in the dirt). We set off, and I took the morning shift driving. As foretold, after 15 minutes of fantastic road (albeit straight surrounded by sheer emptiness), the Kazakhs had decided to re-lay the surface and as a result, a temporary road had been built alongside the existing.

I say "built" - more just dug into the dirt, so a semi-flat surface remained, and that left me travelling at a maximum of 30mph, constantly swerving and avoiding the rocks and holes in front of us. Very frustrating driving, and every inch travelled sent tremors through Pete the Saxo, which worried us further.

Many hours later of the same terrible road, Will took the hot seat. We don't know why, or how, but he always managed to start his driving shift as the road magically reappeared, and was given smooth tarmac to slide his way forward. It was an uneventful drive, kilometres of dead straight road surrounded by fields as big as the eye could see.

We stopped off for a spot of lunch, and want to say a big thank you to our anonymous member of the Armed Forces for providing some emergency ration packs. They became a firm favourite in the car from day one, a meal that just needed heating up and had come to our rescue many a time after a 14 hour driving day.

This time, we had chicken chilli & rice, steak and vegetables, beef ravioli and rice in a little layby off the main road. We seemed to be the focus of attention of a Kazakh family also parked, who came to say hello and even asked if we had everything we needed. Kazakh people were proving to be incredibly nice and generous.

Mackey took over, and seemed to have picked up some of Will's good luck - for the next hour or so, the roads were great, not looking out of place in the UK (apart from their abnormally straightness). We had been finding fuel stations every 10 minutes or so, wherever we'd been since we started, but they were certainly thinning out by this point – so much so, forward fuel planning was required. We noticed Pete the Saxo to be rather low on fuel. Maybe it was just us, but Pete the Saxo seemed a little thirsty since Kazakhstan... We weren't sure whether it was the lower quality fuel we'd been using, down to a low of 92, or something else (perhaps a huge rupture in the fuel tank). The little orange fuel warning light came on for the first time. It was nice to see it worked, but meant that we'd have to stop and fill up using our jerry can supply.

We were good boys, and kept 40 litres on board just in case we ran out (in essence, a full tank's worth). We pulled over and did the topping up, our funnel held together with copious amounts of duck tape (it broke before we even got to Goodwood). 10km or so down the road however, within easy reaching distance of running on fumes, we found a petrol station.

We pulled in, filled Pete the Saxo to the top and also replenished our jerry cans. Whilst doing so, Will went to buy more water (despite noticeably cooling the more North we travelled, we were still drinking a lot of water) and a Kazakh man came to admire our fine vehicle. This was a regular event now - rather than just get annoyed because tourists were in the wrong lane, or took up a pump, we were actually an attraction. Cue the scripted explanation of who we were, what we were doing, the receiving party not understanding a single word but loving it anyway.

As Will returned after paying and stocked up on water, the man told us to wait as his son ran up to the fuel station door, and back again - this time with more water and some weird Kazakh cordial. From what we gather, it was a gift from the gentleman to wish us well on our way. Incredibly thankful and more touched than anything - a two minute chat (or incomprehensible words) and he'd bought us a few supplies.

We thanked him profusely, and were about to set off when he told us to wait, and pulled out a bottle of *"Kazakctah"* he'd also bought for us. Apparently it will help us sleep, wherever we were planning to sleep. It looked a bit like brandy, and at 50% proof, should probably be saved for the finish line. Yet more Kazakh hospitality, which was so endearing in this mostly empty country.

We set off, and a couple of hundred meters down the road, the tarmac disappeared for a short stretch. Literally, like the tarmac guys just went for a break at that point and came back to finish the job 50 meters down the road. Driving on uneven rocky ground just made us shudder, Pete the Saxo creaking and groaning at the conditions. But, we thought that was bad. Following this was 100km of the worst road we'd experienced to date. Despite being an "A" road, it was just incredibly bad - pot holes the size of the car, rocks and peaks everywhere, the surface nothing more than dirt.

All the roads in Kazakhstan are quiet - you can drive for 15 minutes even on a motorway and not see another car, and this one was no different, but it was most definitely still a major road. HGVs struggled down it at 10mph, obviously having been shaken and constantly avoiding the countless obstacles for hours for very little headway.

It was dark at this time, which made things all the more interesting. Mackey took the car as if he was Colin McRae himself, and treated the road more like a rally track than a Kazakh highway. Pothole dodging, peak avoiding, basically doing everything we could to stay on the road whilst still ensuring we weren't still there at 5am.

It was a nasty experience - every pot hole we did hit, albeit slowly, sent a huge bang through the chassis. There was nothing we could do though- no pulling off the road, as the Kazakhs liked to raise their roads 6ft or so above the surrounding land. No waiting by the side of it, as the full width was used by opposing traffic, especially as they dodged the same obstructions as us. The only thing to do was push forward, fast enough to do it before we fell asleep but slow enough to try and keep the car in one piece.

The sump guard took an absolute hammering. For those not mechanically minded, the sump guard was a big piece of metal sheet protecting the underside of the car, in particular around the engine. Rather than going over a large rock and smashing the engine to pieces, the sump guard heroically took the pain instead. It really was needed, although nothing worse than hearing a massive bang as an unseen or unavoidable rock scraped underneath.

I was tired, Mackey was tired, and Will was asleep. It was ironic, this country was millions of square kilometres of empty land, space which we'd happily have camped in, but a few feet of height meant we were completely unable to access it.

Eventually, we left the road (if you could call it that) at about 11.30pm. We spotted a tiny dirt path leading down from the main road into a field. Straight onto a ploughed field the size of Tresco, the car bounced up and down the field for a minute until the brakes were applied, engine cut off, and Mackey announced this would be our new home. We are basically a roaming bunch of gypsies.

Will, as did we all, woke up as soon as the engine was turned off, the quietness of the night seemingly more unsettling that the constantly banging and bumping of the rough road. Tents were pitched in record time, again not doing with the top sheet and just using the fly sheet for bug protection, and we quickly fell to sleep between the furrows.

Borat had still not been spotted, and the boys tell me off when I do my impressions a little too loud. "Very nice" as I drive past a bus stop full of Kazakh women was frowned upon, as was saying "I will not move to a small room" in a hotel elevator. We were still hoping though to find Borat's sister.

In all seriousness though, Kazakhstan was shaping up to be an incredible country. Just like my vain attempt at light-hearted comedy above, it was amazing how Western entertainment plants these seeds of anticipation in our minds. Stupid preconceptions and expectations. OK, the roads made you want to cry in places, but the people were friendly, the landscape was incredible, and you just felt happier here. Perhaps it was time to dispel the Borat myth once and for all.

Straight road for miles and miles

A fuel stop and a very full boot

Day 17 - Do we look suspicious?

We set up camp in an enormous field the night before after three hours of shocking road conditions, which pushed us all to breaking point. By car headlamp, it looked like Eden. Tents were set up very fast, we'd got it down to an art; only two tent pegs (well, one tent peg each and a screwdriver each hammered into the hard ground) and the fly sheet to protect us from bugs only.

As it turned out, this sleep deprived decision wasn't the best. At 5am, it started to rain rather heavily. The three of us woke up to find rain beating down on us, slowed briefly by the net a few inches above of our heads. Quite a weird feeling, being toasty warm in our sleeping bags but getting our torpid heads thoroughly soaked.

Within seconds, I'd jumped out of my sleeping bag and coffin tent, and headed straight for the car door. "Screw this, let's go" as I fumbled for the keys. Mackey pointed out it wasn't yet 5am. "Screw that" I apparently said, as I climbed back into my tent. Will made a vain effort to put on his top sheet, before caving in and once again falling to sleep. Luckily the rain stopped shortly after.

We all woke up (again) at about 8am, the sky bright with the morning Kazakh sun and the ground once again hostile and dry. We had indeed camped in between the troughs ploughed into the field, the expanse of land almost hugging us as we slept. Pete the Saxo had bumped over quite a few and the wheels too were nestled in-between the field's trenches.

The usual morning routine began, starting with showers. Separating the main road from our gypsy home was a sparse row of trees, which looked ideal for our private bathroom. Will grabbed his water allowance and travel towel, and went off to wash.

I did the same, giving Will a good 30 meters of clearance by walking further down the tree line and also ensuring I was out of sight of Mackey etc. I mean, we were all friends and shared a tiny space on an epic journey, but that was about all the closeness we wanted to see.

I got very much naked, apart from flip flops (as there are three types of venomous snake in Kazakhstan) and started to shower.

Meagre amounts of water poured over head, shower gel, clean specific areas, another paltry amount to rinse etc.

All was going swimmingly (excuse the pun) until something caught my attention and I saw the flash of two high beam headlights. It seemed that as the roads were so very quiet in Kazakhstan, that I'd separated myself from our car by going completely through the tree line, and instead was quite visible to any passing motorist. Trying to remedy the situation was a disaster; soap suds stung my eyes as I tripped over my shorts. I'm just glad it was this Kazakh highway through nothingness, and not the M5 through Bristol.

We repacked the car, everything coming out and put back in. After our rather drastic "repair" (with the big hammer and angle grinder), we'd trimmed back a lot of the junk plastic trim around the back wheels. One of these "junk plastic trim" pieces filled a gap between the boot and the back wheel. As a result, there was a six inch hole on either side inside the boot, where you could reach through and touch the back wheel. Driving through the steppe, infinitely dustier than even my house, meant everything accumulated a nice amount of red dust.

Onwards we went, and I started the morning shift. The sun was out, despite being a lot cooler that the previous week. Temperatures in the morning were a mere 23 degrees. Practically polar. We headed through Actobe, and stopped off at a big modern supermarket. Shopping here was fun - half the time, we had no idea what we were buying, but could happily afford it all.

Something strange happened here though; we attracted the attention of the security guards, despite looking relatively clean and tidy, showered and wearing fresh clean clothes (they caught us on a good day),. Every business seemed to have an on sight security guard here; supermarkets, banks, shops, even petrol stations.

We grabbed a shopping trolley and started our tour of the aisles, stocking up with both essentials and luxuries. Essentials were things like wet wipes, black bags, copious amounts of water, pot noodles. Luxuries were things like cheese, meat, and finally cool enough weather for a chocolate bar. Pushing the trolley around the first aisle though, despite stocking such low risk items as cleaning cloths and polish, we had SecurityMan quite obviously trying to be subtle and following us.

He even started to talk on his radio, and every time we stopped or turned into the next aisle, SecurityMan was there, keeping his apparent colleagues very much up to date with our location. We didn't take much notice of it to begin with, but then we saw not one but two more shirt wearing employees with radios lurking around; at the next aisle, hiding behind a free standing display of noodles, concealed behind the very transparent glass of the delicatessen.

How dodgy did we really look? Without sounding pompous or arrogant, Pete the Saxo in his frail state was probably worth more than most cars in town. I wanted to get out my wallet and show them I had ample currency to buy our small trolley's worth of goods. It just got weird though when a delicatessen girl followed me around as I browsed separately from the boys. Did they really think this was a tactical decision, to divide our forces and do bad things, finding a chink in their armour? Ah well, it kept me amused for the entire trip as I made the effort to say hi to every covert agent.

We paid for our shopping trolley, pretty much tailed to our car, and started once again on our eastwards journey. Mackey made lunch - bread rolls, weird cheese and weird meat. It was very tasty, and we all ate as I navigated through the city. We were all enjoying city driving at this moment – it was such a contrast to the miles of dead straight road, lots of stopping and starting, darting amongst traffic and lights.

A few minutes later after our en-route lunch, that damned red baton was pointed at us, and we were pulled over by the local police on a busy dual carriageway. The police came over and asked me for my documents, which I duly gave them. My wallet was already emptied of high bills, and I started the distraction tactic - immediately jump into an introduction of who we are, what we were doing, and if they knew the way to the next town. It worked - we were told something about our headlights, yet again, and told to move on.

It wasn't until we'd pulled away when we realised Mackey had been holding a hunting knife the entire time, using it to cut the bread rolls for lunch. Rather a good thing PoliceMan didn't glance in the back!

Forwards we drove, leaving the city and along those straight roads connecting the scattered towns, the conditions of which were an absolute guessing game. Motorways could be 20mph dirt tracks, whereas B roads could be 70mph perfect roads. The further east we were getting seemed to be getting more old school. Huge herds of cattle, sheep and goats roamed free around the empty fields, although gave the impression they preferred grazing on the field boundaries on either side of the road. Quite a few times we'd happily be cruising along at 100kph when we needed to stop, and 100 goats were trotting happily across the road.

I drove for five and a half hours, completely unaware of the time and happy cruising along on the average roads. Will jumped into the hot seat, and as the Will luck would have it, straight away landed on some freshly laid tarmac, not a pot hole in sight. Mackey and I laugh when this happens. If you didn't laugh, you'd cry. Or kill Will.

We stopped for an afternoon snack; Kazakhstan's own Pot Noodle. You might be wondering why we were eating such rubbish, but look at it from our point of view; we wanted something quick, something kind of filling, doable on our stove and with minimal washing up. Pot noodle fulfilled every one of the criteria. We pulled into a picnic area/parking area, and started up the stove, boiling the water needed in about three minutes flat.

Kazakh pot noodles, as it turned out, are rubbish. Don't ever buy one. Oh yeah, and we saw a seagull. It looked exactly like the ones we had at home, but strange as we were a thousand miles or so from the sea. I came to the conclusion that this particular bugger had followed us, from Scilly, like the scavenging flock escorting a weary fishing boat home.

Nice smooth roads continued to present themselves to Will, but a waiting policeman just over the brow of the hill waved the stupid baton and we pulled over. He came over, and did the usual - documents etc. Will's wallet was once again void of anything worth more than £8, but the patrolman wanted Will to accompany him to his car. Standard practice when asking for a bribe - away from the prying ears of the cars occupants and potential recording equipment, but reinforcing the image of power with the blue and white Lada when asking for the "fine".

This time though, Will had actually done something wrong. They replayed his pre-pull over journey on a small screen inside the police car, complete with speedo overlay. It seems Will had been speeding a touch. 81kph in a 60kph zone. Ooops.

This time however, they were almost excited to meet Will. They shook his hand, took an interest in what he was doing (the Mongol Rally rather than the obvious speeding), and let him go with nothing more than a pat on the back. We loved Kazakhstan.

Will pushed on for three hours, smashing through the miles and handing over the reins of the wild stallion that was Pete the Saxo to Mackey. Dusk was falling over the steppe, and Mackey had piggy backed onto Will's luck. For the first hour, roads were great. 120kph was accomplished, unheard of since the German motorways and the odometer struggled to keep up with our headway.

But then again, with Will falling asleep in the back, Mackey's misfortune once more reared its ugly head.

Despite being on a motorway, we saw the first of four signs that we soon learned to dread.

- 90kph
- 70kph
- 50kph
- 30kph

When the sign hit 30kph, you knew something bad was about to arrive. And arrive it did. Despite being on the motorway, or at least a straight well surfaced highway, road works signs directed you off the road, to a hastily made path to the side. We'd had something similar the night before - some semi flat surface dug into the roadside, yet pot holes and large rocks remained everywhere. Driving at anything over 5mph sent shudders down the steering wheel, and every passing car kicked up huge clouds of dust that got inside our vehicle no matter what.

To begin with, we took bets on how long these conditions would last. Road works for 3km, Road works for 8km, Road works for 5km. And before long, the game got tedious and just made us mad when the road works lasted for 25km, shortly followed by another set.

This was due to the Kazakhs with their new found oil/gas wealth, relaying many of the roads and motorways. It was very much needed - but within a couple of years, once the main networks have been finished, the Mongol Rally will be much less of a challenge. Much less indeed, when you can cruise on almost UK standard roads from Calais to Almaty.

Mackey pushed forwards as fast as he could, using both lanes avoiding every hindrance in the way (opposing traffic dependant of course). For a few hours, this was horrible driving - each bang and bump caused Pete the Saxo to bounce around to breaking point. I have to say it was rather skilful driving by Mackey, but I didn't risk telling him that – space was already at a premium without Mackey McRae's ballooning head.

Once we finished a stretch on the temporary road, a large slope and 8ft of height separated us rubbish road dwellers to the freshly laid motorway, and we'd find a dirt ramp that led up to it. Despite not having any road markings, sign posts or anything to indicate we could use it - there was technically nothing to say we couldn't. When safe to do so, we'd shoot up the dirt ramp and onto the virgin tarmac, the smoothness a godsend after rough road hell.

Kazakh drivers would do the same, an unspoken sense of relief filling the flat highway after we all shared the grief of the last trail. We happily cruised along for five or ten minutes, when we noticed something up ahead.

Huge 20ft mounts of dirt in the road, extracted probably from the ditch to either side, and a tarmac machine now blocked our route. This ended our happy motorway experience rather swiftly, and some heavy braking took place as we avoided the abrupt motorway terminus.

Now, we were stuck, six or eight foot above the temporary road still blindly accompanying the motorway to one side. We could see no safe way to re-join the dirt path. The ledge was certainly too much for Pete the Saxo to handle - we'd bottom out long before reaching the bottom. It was nice to see it wasn't just our English stupidity that thought we could get away with using the newly laid motorway and skip the bad road - scores of Kazakh drivers did exactly the same as us, forcing a U turn in the middle of the road and heading away from our target trying to find a way back down.

Dirt ramps did exist every five minutes or so, but a 10 minute motorway drive followed by double backing on ourselves for five minutes, meant we didn't make too much progress. Anything was better than that temporary road though.

This went on, and on, and on. We'd find a stretch of motorway, hit that up for a while, and then those damned signs again. 90kph... 70kph... 50kph... 30kph... and back on to a horrible surface. We'd find a way to sneak on to the motorway again, before ending up at an obstruction and re-finding a way down.

Eventually though, we saw the lights of Astana in the sky, the way every city seeps radiance into the otherwise abandoned night. I think that being able to see this light pollution, and watching it grow every so slightly with every kilometre of hellish road, was the only thing that kept Mackey going.

Astana is the capital of Kazakhstan, after the Prime Minister declared it to be so in 1997 (completely out of the blue, and stripping Almaty of the title). As soon as we approached, a couple of kilometres out, the road surface reappeared and gave Mackey the last bit of vigour to push on and find us a hotel.

Now we knew the Cyrillic for hotel, which looked something *OTeΠb*, we could spot them. It only took five minutes (as opposed to the hours before we learnt their language), and we checked into our £17 a night room for a shower and a sleep.

Mackey finds his new home

Making pot noodles on our fantastic stove

Will being led away by a Kazakh policeman

Kazakh cemetery

Day 18 - You want breakfast now?

We awoke in our hotel, just on the outskirts of the capital city. Some of you might be wondering why we were spending so many nights in hotels recently, and this was supposed to be a challenge. There are a couple of reasons for this; firstly, we'd traversed Kazakhstan. A few thousand miles of ridiculously hot weather, lots of dust and camping in random fields. Just think of the state of Mackey if he wasn't able to shower for a few weeks, and that should be reason enough why a hotel was so needed every now and then.

Secondly, they're rather affordable - £17 a night we could just about to stretch the budget to. Thirdly, a good night's sleep did wonders for team morale. We are three blokes usually very grumpy in the morning, and the first few hours were usually a quiet few hours. Ensuring a good night's sleep did help improve this a lot!

Mackey, yet again, was up bright and early, and hit the included breakfast hard. Will and I thought we'd rather cherish the extra 30 minutes in our beds. Mackey didn't eat alone though, as the hotel had four other rally teams staying. Quite good luck considering there were only 350 teams in the entire world, and dozens of hotels in this city alone.

We packed up, checked out, and headed down to the car park for some comrade banter. The general consensus was that the internet was needed by every team, for updating their respective blogs (although no team seemed to write as much rubbish as me).

Luckily one team knew the location of an internet cafe, a good thing considering our track record of inner city navigation. We headed off in a five car convoy - great fun, be it on the open road or through a busy city centre. As good as their word, the team of Aussies drove us all to a little internet cafe, much to the amusement of city residents completely baffled as the five rally vehicles cruised through town.

The internet cafe was shut. However, a few knocks on the door, and the owner popped his head out from around the building. Seeing ten rallyers, no doubt in his mind seeing walking Tenge (the currency), he was happy to open for us and let us all reconnect to the wider world. The computers were quite interesting though - it took the combined trial and error from all 10 of us to discover the Cyrillic for "Internet Explorer".

It was here we learnt of the tragic death of one of our fellow rally comrades, having been involved in a traffic accident on the east side of Iran. The details of what happened were light, but we understood that two further team members were in hospital. It hit home for us all; not just how dangerous the rally could be, but driving in general. We were making sure we were still being extra safe whilst on the road, but sent our deepest sympathies and thoughts to the families of the team.

As we were finishing up with the internet, another team asked us if we'd registered since being in Kazakhstan. I guess the confused looks on our faces answered their question; apparently all visitors to Kazakhstan had to officially register with immigration by the 5th day of being in the enormous country. Those not doing so faced "being punished to the full extent of Kazakh law". It was then pointed out to us, in black and white (and in English) on the back of our visa slips resting in our passports. A quick count of fingers, and we realised - today was our 5th day.

We weren't the only ignorant team though! Another couple had also skipped over this particular bit of information and were on their 5th day. And so we started our next convoying mission - to get the magic blue stamp on our visa slips which would put us firmly within the boundaries of Kazakh immigration law.

Astana wasn't the biggest city, but it was the capital; all government departments had their freshly built headquarters here, and they lined the main streets - impressive white buildings, each flying the Kazakh flag and unreadable Cyrillic department names. The 10 of us proceeded to the first we found, which even mentioned Immigration (in English) inside the marble floored lobby. The guard dutifully watching the door looked quite perplexed when the 10 of us walked in, obviously the most exciting thing that had happened on his shift.

Unfortunately none of us spoke Kazakh, but that hadn't stopped us so far - lots of pointing at visa slips, inventing a new gesture for "stamp" (as I'm sure you can picture), indicating it was our fifth day etc.; we were told no - this wasn't the right building. They did however point us to the correct building, and off our merry troop went. We left our cars in a central position within the city, within easy walking distance of the buildings, and headed to the second building.

It looked more like a bank than anything else, and we all bunched around a sitting attendant (who looked more like a soldier than anything else) and started our gesturing and questioning. We thought we were doing quite well - within a few minutes, I think he'd ascertained that we were here for something. Very luckily though, behind us in the queue was a lovely Kazakh lady that spoke perfect English, happy to come to our aid. Acting as translator, she picked up what we were after and relayed the information to the semi bewildered assistant/soldier.

He finally understood what we were after, thanks to Kazakh Lady. Huzzah! But not quite - wrong building. Kazakh Lady though was happy to show us where to go. Here was another display of amazing Kazakh hospitality, which had surprised us all but so very likeable. Off we followed, looking more like an arranged tour group now than 10 weary rallyers, around the leafy side streets of Astana.

The place we were after turned out to be the 5th building we visited. Kazakh Lady, if you ever stumble upon this story, we thank you from the bottom of our hearts. A 15 minute walk with you could have easily been a 15 hour mission without you.

It was a travel agent we needed, the 10 of us piling into an office as she considered our request. Yes, they could happily register us and stamp our slips with the magic blue stamp. No problem - just come back the next day and they'd all be done.

A wave of negative "ohhhhh"'s filled the limited space, sufficiently exclaiming this might be a problem in any language. One of the office workers spoke rather good English, and we told her of our plight, and we needed to get going that evening. Eventually she conceded, and said the earliest we could collect our completed visas was 6pm. Good enough for us! It was 1pm by now - giving us five hours to explore the city, take in a bit of culture, and a hint of relaxing; things we hadn't really had a chance to do whilst constantly driving through every daylight hour.

We left Pete the Saxo on a main road, relatively safe and under the shade of the tree lined street, and walked into the city centre.

Astana is a very nice city – an amazing mix of architecture with Soviet, Islamic, Western and futuristic influences. A reputed 8% of the national budget for the entire country is spent on the capital, providing shiny new government buildings and other very ambitious projects. It was clean, the people were friendly, and the weather was perfect for us - a nice 25 degrees, comparatively cool and a welcome change.

We strolled in the general direction of the river that bisected the city, past new tower blocks and developments, and went into the first mall we found. This too was new and clean, air conditioned and filled with shops of surprising calibre - Calvin Klein, Apple, Dunhill, Gucci and other mid to high level brands showed their immaculate window displays off to all who entered. I realise all cities must have their high end shops (Ulaan Baatar in Mongolia has just had Louis Vuitton open a store), but the prices looked even more extortionate when compared to general day-to-day living costs.

We stopped off in the sort of little cafe you find in all shopping centres, once again having pizza - mainly due to being the only thing we could read on the menu, and strangely enough being served in abundance throughout the entire trip - Europe, Russia, Asia, all loving the pizza. The gastronomic currency of beyond.

We browsed around the mall, window shopping more than anything (due to us not needing anything, and certainly not having the space in the car if we did). Maybe it was the way we looked, or the way we dressed, or the way we acted - but once again we had security follow our every move, constantly reporting our whereabouts and actions to his colleagues via radio. We didn't take it personally though - I just made an effort to go and say hello to them all.

Onwards we pushed through the city, casually strolling and attracting quite a few looks from the locals. The city really was spotless - the grass was perfectly cut, there was no litter anywhere (such a contrast from the rest of the country) and the buildings were as shiny as when they were first constructed. We found the river (mainly thanks to Mackey's extraordinary ability as a human compass), and strolled along as if we were tourists to just the one place.

We spotted some pedalos on the river side, dozens of them lined up as if awaiting a mass influx of customers. An influx that would never come though, as we were the only tourists we saw on our city walk. We were tourists after all, so we thought we'd push the boat out (excuse the deliberate pun) and take one of these fine crafts out on the water.

We were the only ones on the entire river, messing around like children but having more fun than we'd had in a week. A 30 minute excursion cost us about £1.60, and we took turns racing along a line of buoys and enjoying the temperate summer weather. Once we'd returned our fine ocean going vessel (that looked ready to sink at any moment) to the amused attendants, we got an ice cream and did some more idling in the sun.

On our gentle amble, we found the "Chelsea English Pub" - a UK pub for UK people. How very boring of us we know, but we couldn't help ourselves. A slice of home? We had to find out what they served that made it so English, and so headed in. We don't want to write too much about this pub, as we accidentally ordered extortionately priced food (the worst Chicken Caesar Salad you'd ever seen for £17).

After the above experience, we noticed it was just fifteen minutes to six, and we were slightly more than that away from the magic visa stamp shop. We headed off, power walking as best we could without looking like tourist knobs, and Mackey broke the group and powered on ahead. He got there just after six, where our passports and now completed visas were eagerly awaiting their return to us.

As we were outside the travel agents, happy and ready to once again push eastwards on our travels, a few other teams drove along the road, and recognised our car immediately - it was our friends Mongolia Is Our Everest, Team Mongolia or Bust, and Team The Two Mongoleers. What were the odds of that?!

They stopped, and we had a rally reunion - a good chat, a swap of the last few days' occurrences and smiles all round. It was great for morale and the chance to convoy onwards with other teams. Unfortunately though, these teams were in the city for the same reason as us - they needed immigration registration. We introduced them to the travel agents, them striking gold on the stamp hunt after our previous misfortune, but were told that they wouldn't be ready until the morning. We had spent the night and day in the city but wanted to push on a bit further (as teams did catch up without noticing), so we bid adieu and off we went.

Our next town was Pavlodar about five hours away, and we decided to take it nice and easy. I'd do half, Will would do half, and Mackey would have a well-earned break.

As it turned out, my shift was the best two and a half hours of driving I'd ever done. The roads were very long and sweeping, crossing over hilly land with golden fields on either side of our empty road. The afternoon sun began to set behind us, showering everything in a red tint light and the hills providing contrasting shadows across sporadic patches of flat land. The road surface was good - not perfect, for there were still a few pot holes and lumps, but that just gave me an excuse to treat it like a deserted rally track; weaving in and out of the obstacles at a sympathetic 60mph, the road ahead visible for miles. Bloc Party was the perfect audio accompaniment to this road, and I drove with a smile on my face for the entire time. A definite high point in the trip for me.

Will's shift started as the last light of the day faded away, and so had to slow down a considerable amount. There was only so far a Citroen could illuminate in front of us, so we took it nice and steady and reached our target of Pavlodar at about 2am. Pavlodar – a repeating industrial town, its skyline dominated by massive rabbit-hole-style apartment blocks. At night it looked very uninspiring, and Mackey drove around the abandoned streets for about 40 minutes, trying to find those magic Cyrillic symbols that spelt "OTeΠbsomething" (hotel).

By the end of the 40 minutes, we were annoyed and tired. Where were these darned hotels?! We resorted to a cheating method; paying a taxi driver to take us to a hotel listed in the Lonely Planet book. A short taxi chase later and £3 lighter, we arrived at the Hotel Sariarka. 12 stories tall, proudly overlooking the River Irtysh (this description came out of the book, as it was pitch black at the time) and with an old-Soviet feel.

Will & I strolled into the hotel and enquired about rooms. Not as simple as it sounds, as we first had to interrupt two security guards (who shall hereby be known as Tweedle Dum and Gollum) from some cheesy soap they were watching on an old CRT television. I say interrupt, as we walked straight up to their counter (adjoining the abandoned reception) and waited. Our flip flops on the faux marble floor made ample sound to attract the attention of anyone in the vicinity, yet still they were glued to their set. A few obvious clearing of throats, and still they watched. Eventually a loud "EXCUSE ME" made them both turn, their facial expressions a mix of annoyance and surprise.

Tweedle Dum stood at least twice the size of Gollum, and moved with an air of unimportance. Every movement he made was at half speed, which could have been due to the late hour we turned up. Gollum, on the other hand, seemed overly excited. He looked very young, as if straight out of school and into the family business, and jumped around with enthusiastic energy. As we described our needs in English, he tilted his head to one side while listening as if to better understand us.

We asked for rooms, to which Gollum then nipped into the back room, returning with a half-asleep receptionist. Her expression was just of anger - how dare anyone awake the night receptionist from the sleep she was enjoying whilst supposed to be working?! We were shown prices, amounts in the thousands that we were just too tired to convert, but the look and feel of the place suggested a ten pound room. Gollum was the only one that spoke any words of English, and so kindly translated (he spoke only 24 words of English though, which we soon found out).

We paid the bill (and £2 to Tweedle Dum to "watch the car for us") and Gollum showed us up to our rooms on the lofty 6th floor. We bundled into the elevator, which scared the hell out of us. If you've ever played Bioshock, it was just like that - a creaking, rocking old steam-punk elevator, complete with a very faulty glowing green floor number display (which counted down 6…5….8….4….3….8….2….8….1…). Unspoken fear gripped us all as the ancient cables struggled to raise the death box to the 6th floor, and spoken relief was exchanged as the door opened and we clambered out.

It was a strange hotel. A very strange hotel. Sort of a bad dream, one where you'd never be able to leave and instead would spend your entire life trying to.

We were shown to our rooms (the "very good" single rooms), and Gollum motioned the eating gesture.

"Breakfast?" we enquired.

"Yes", he replied, "Breakfast", nodding.

We resorted to counting on our fingers to suggest 9am. Lots of confused counting by Gollum - not a case of struggling with English, rather a case of struggling with numbers. After 10 minutes of standing in the corridor, trying to explain we wanted breakfast at 9am, he let us in our three rooms and we presumed he had finally understood.

How very wrong I was.

Five minutes later, after quickly climbing into bed and fast falling into a deep sleep, there was a knock at the door. Straight back up to my room door, I opened it, and there stood Gollum.

"Hello, what's up?" I enquired, hiding my slight frustration as he had tried to be helpful (even if it was just for a few Tenge).

"Breakfast at 6?" he asked.

What?

"No, breakfast at NINE" I said, holding up nine extended fingers.

"Now, I sleep", and showed the universal sleep gesture, two hands against the side of my head. I think he understood. He nodded, said goodbye, and left. Once again, I undressed and got into the rock hard bed, a small feature in the strangest room I'd ever been in; it looked like a Soviet living room from the 50s, complete with two armchairs and the strongest furniture you'd ever seen, everything a horrible shade of green or brown (walls/ceiling/floor included).

Knock knock.

I jumped out of bed, opened the door and kept as nice as possible. Gollum was back, this time with Tweedle Dum. I asked again what I could do for him.

This time, it was to ask whether we liked Pavlodar.

Unbelievable - I almost told them I'd like the city much more if they let me sleep, but I made some excuse about it being too dark and we'd look at it tomorrow. Tonight though, 2.20am, I wanted to

SLEEP. They left me to it, back to the hard bed I went, this time drifting off nicely.

Knock knock.

I couldn't believe it. No guesses to who was at the door yet again - Gollum. I opened the door and looked at him, my mood barely hidden.

"You want breakfast *NOW*?" he enquired.

Unbelievable. How could any one man, be it speaking any language or any age, not understand that we were very simply explaining to him that we wanted breakfast at 9am? Not 6am, not 7am, just 9am. How could any one man then think we wanted breakfast at 2.35am?

I didn't find out until the next morning that Will & Mackey, both asleep in their equally shocking beds, were both wide awake and laughing their heads off, the paper thin walls muting nothing. Gollum eventually left, for the last time that night. I think the look upon my face explained everything; in particular we weren't after breakfast at 2.35am. And so to sleep, we all went.

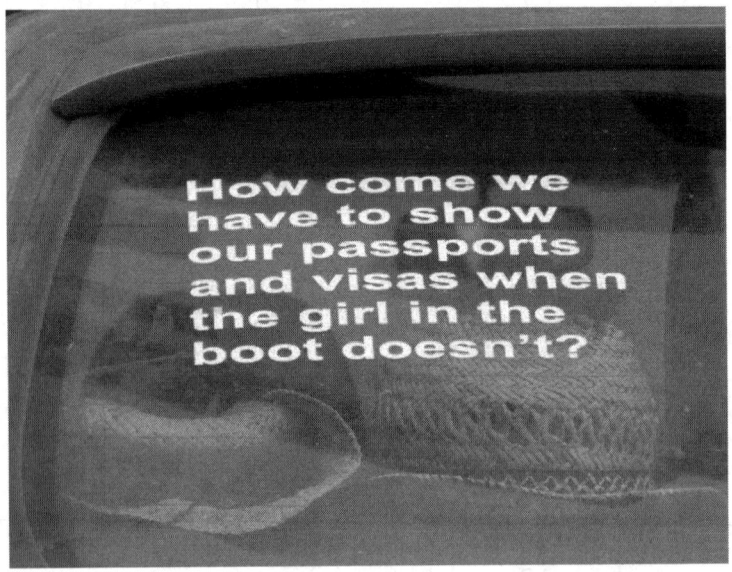

Amusing sign in the back window of a Mongol Rally team car

Astana, the shiny capital of Kazakhstan

Having our first day as tourists, on the Ishmin River

Too familiar not to pay a visit!

Hotel Sariarka – what an experience

Day 19 - Entering the atomic wasteland

We got to sleep after Gollum's 4th visit to my room - the last enquiring whether we wanted breakfast at that ungodly hour. The rooms were just incredible, and not in the good sense of the word. 80% of the room, from the carpets to the ceiling, was the garish shade of Communist green. The other 20% was brown. Just being in the room sucked the joy and happiness from you.

But, it had a bed (albeit a rather firm bed) and was warm and dry; at the end of the day, just what we needed. Having finally got the message through to Gollum that we wanted breakfast at nine, eventually even he counting nine out on his fingers to show he understood, we didn't set any alarms and knew he'd be back with the same ferocity as the night before, and wake us up at 9am.

Knock Knock.

"HALLO. Security. Breakfast now"

It was 8am.

I was tired, but the thought of arguing with him in the futile hope to gain that last hours sleep was too much. I grudgingly got out of bed, answered the door with the best fake smile I could muster, and thanked him for his overly keen wake up.

I told him the boys would come with me, so I banged on Will's door. A few bangs later, and he too was rudely awakened from his sleep. Cruel I know, but Will would want breakfast. And if I was up, then they would be too! A shout through the paper thin walls of the room, and he indicated he was awake. Next stop, just one door down, was Mackey. I tapped on the door with my room key fob, happy with the loud noise it would be making in the room. Tap tap… tap tap…

Gollum was obviously unhappy with my pathetic Western attempts, and pushed me out of the way and hammered the door hard with his fist. Good effort, unneeded but very effective. We heard movement, and a grunt. Mackey was stirring.

I shouted through the door - "Breakfast mate", and a groggy "Yep, I'm up" was heard. And so, I waited in the narrow corridor with Gollum. And waited... and waited... I could hear movement from Will's room, him obviously getting dressed while being blinded by the glaring virescent fixtures and fittings. Mackey's room however, I heard nothing. I banged once more, this time using Gollum's method, and a good 10 seconds later I heard the same "Yep, I'm up", as if it was a subconscious reaction to anything that awoke him.

I waited more, the silence broken by the unheard sound of Gollum just watching me. Just stood there, looking at me, a blank look on his little face. This freaked me out a little bit, so I banged yet again on Mackey's door. "Yep, I'm up" was the reply. I wouldn't be falling for that little trick again - I banged, and banged, until he finally opened the door, about the same time as Will.

We walked, no were actually escorted, to breakfast on the 2nd floor. Being on the 6th would mean another ride in the elevator of doom, the 1950s green floor indicator erratically showing us moving to the 8th floor between the 3rd and 4th. It really was something out of a Stephen King novel - you'd almost expect it to miss the 13th floor all together if we could go that high, for some dark evil lived there.

On the way to breakfast, Gollum said we needed to pay for the food. We were still tired, but Will's suggestion of arguing this sounded absolutely right. I explained we'd paid for a hotel with breakfast, and a minute of arguing using two completely different languages, good old English came out the victor.

We sat in the small restaurant, seating a maximum of 30 people, on a table big enough for us, but small enough that Gollum wouldn't be able to join us. We weren't being nasty, he was just that weird. The previous night, we'd asked how many rooms the hotel had.

2175 was the answer.

I don't think Gollum could count.

The menu was in Cyrillic, but Gollum was there to suggest what we should have. His suggestion was incomprehensible, and our faces probably answered his recommendation. His response was rather simple - walk to another table, where an unknown lone businessman had just been served his breakfast. Gollum scooped up his plate, the meat and eggs piping hot but cooling quick, and walked it over to us.

"?" was his facial expression, hovering the plate under our noses and looking for signs of approval. That looked fine we nodded, but felt terribly guilty that the lone businessman had just had his breakfast stolen from under him to be used as an exhibit for three travelling Westerners. Still, we nodded and ate not long after, sneaking off to our rooms while we were on our own to pack for the day. From the 2nd floor, back up to the 6th, and then back to the lobby, we didn't see our stalky friend again.

Gollum was, in part, exactly what this challenge was all about. OK, he was a colourful character, and gave us a fantastic little story to share with you all. But we were foreigners in his country, clueless about his native Kazakh language, and needed help in finding lodgings for the night. He might have been overly keen and completely unable to count, but to find someone who obviously made an effort with our own language and made the process easier was fantastic. Gollum, we shall never forget you.

Just a quick note regarding the elevator of doom - it was so dodgy, that on arriving at the 2nd floor and the doors opening, Mackey conducted a little scientific test; he jumped up in the air as high as he could, and landed back in the stationary lift. The lift dropped a foot underneath the 2nd floor, resulting in stepping up to disembark. Health and safety would have a field day here.

Despite only having five hours sleep, it was time to move again. Our target today was Semey, a city in the far north western corner of Kazakhstan and near our border gateway back into Russia. Semey was further along the river Irtysh, and probably better known to the world by its Russian name, Semipalatinsk. For this city gained fame when the Soviet military exploded 460 nuclear bombs in the area. Locals say they knew when tests were taking place because the ground would shake - often on a Sunday morning. Radiation was still a serious issue for locals, but we'd read that short term visitors were not in any serious risk.

Either way, the car journey up was still filled with discussions of which super power we'd like to gain. I ended up with teleportation, Will wanted to walk on water (?!) and Mackey wanted his ability to drink beer again.

The road to Semey was pretty good - not too many pot holes, a flat surface on the whole, and so we made quite good time and got to our target by 5pm. Rather than carry on and push forward, we'd finally acquired another phone and had got in touch with the lovely Mongol Mongrels, who were not far behind us. The chance to convoy with our favourite team (along with all the others) at this late stage, probably to the end, was something all three of us wanted and so were happy to wait in town.

We hadn't been using the Lonely Planet guides, as many of the descriptions were rather out of date or inaccurate. An Italian team liked to call it the Lying Planet after many a failed expectation. Semey didn't have a huge piece within the now well used Kazakh edition, but listed three hotels (we weren't sure if this was a random selection, or Semey really did just have three hotels). The descriptions of the three were varying;

"hot water for a few hours a day", "persistence required for a cheap room", "Soviet-style rooms, gloomy with no hot water"; the cream of Semey's hotel crop.

We picked the best, Hotel Binar. We eventually found it, with the use of hiring another taxi driver to take us. Mackey presented the name, the taxi driver nodded, and jumped in the Lada with the driver. This was the first Lada Mackey had ever been in, something that excited him a little too much. His verdict on the car littering the continent? "I like it. Solid".

On arriving at the hotel, we enquired about rooms - three rooms, or at least space for three to sleep. We were given a price, forty something pounds for the three of us with breakfast. It looked like a very nice hotel, and the price was just right. We were showed to the room we would inhabit by a waiting porter, and climbed to the first floor of the two storey hotel. We walked along the main corridor, passing doors regularly on both sides of us, separated by typical single and double room sized gaps. As we approached the end of the corridor though, the dark panelled doors on the right hand side stopped, and a long stretch of door-less beige wall replaced it.

Continuing down the corridor, we noticed half way down the featureless beige wall was a single door - with equal wall on either side. Big room we thought, although let's focus on the room we'd be getting somewhere at the end. As long as it wasn't the gaudy green, we'd be happy.

But of course, this was a happy story - that lone door, separated from its neighbours unlike no other, was most definitely ours. The key was entered for us, opened and we were allowed in. Not into a bedroom though – a foyer. A table and chairs, fridge and mini bar, and huge windows all decked in a delightful relaxing decor. To the left led through to the first bedroom - larger than any room we'd had so far, a huge bed taking centre stage, and this room embellished in passionate reds with long stem roses in a huge vase. A huge window let in light with drapes adorning the walls as if we were in a Hilton. To the right, laid the second bedroom - equal in size to the first, this time a sandy palette suggested a tranquil luxury paradise.

This was our room. No, this was our presidential suite. For £15 each. We were happy. The cousins took the left room, rather worryingly the "passionate" room, and I was left with the "tranquil" room. The bathroom was just as plush, with a full body jet shower. Little did the boys know when claiming their room, was that my room was en-suite. Great success.

We moved Pete the Saxo into the private enclosed car park behind our new home, and Mackey decided to make the most of the remaining daylight hours by attending to the car. After the terrible roads we'd been enduring, the sump guard had taken an absolute battering, and the exhaust loudly rattled every time we accelerated. The exhaust "fix" that was installed (consisting of an oven glove, bungee cord and cable ties) had done us well and survived over 2,000 miles but was very much ready to give up in its task.

Mackey set to work, using a few supplies we picked up en route - the sump guard was removed, and bent back into shape using the car jack. The exhaust was chained back up, and both fixes seemed to work perfectly.

We decided to eat in the empty hotel restaurant, hoping the food was equally nice as our rooms. They'd planned ahead for us ignorant folks, and even presented a menu in English to us - no menu roulette for us today! We each picked a main course, mainly based on the main meaty ingredient rather than understanding what the meal title suggested, as well as soup starters, three extra chips and two extra vegetables. Will was in charge of ordering. We were hungry.

Luckily, the waitress realised the mistake in the over-ordering that Will had made, and our meals came out not long after with sensible amounts of all of the above.

After a very fine meal, we decided to explore the city (or at least close to the hotel) and go out for a few beers. We found somewhere within a street block, sat outside and reflected on the journey so far, anxious to see our friends the following day.

A quick side note that Will wanted to include - on using the toilet facilities at the bar we spent this evening in, Will noticed the long line of urinals separated by a small outcrop of ceramic - as you would see at any pub or restaurant in the UK. These however, were filled with Kazakh men not using them for the traditional use (i.e. a number "1".). Rather, they were utilising them for the full range of bodily functions. I think he felt a bit strange using the centre one of ten to relieve a full bladder surrounding by Kazakh men doing much more.

Hotel Binar – Our luxury oasis in Semey

Cyrillic menu perplexes Will

Day 20 - The Geiger counter would be going crazy

We awoke in luxurious surroundings - our presidential suite and its associated grandeur definitely made up for the shortcomings in comfort the previous few weeks (especially waking up in the swamp). The boys were in the passionate bedroom, the reds and pinks of the walls highlighted nicely against the dark wood floors. Apparently Will was the big spoon that night, Mackey said in the morning.

The boys headed down to breakfast, no doubt an equally impressive spread of morning food. I, however, traded mine for an extra hour in bed - I knew that we'd soon be leaving civilisation, even more so than the transition we'd seen as we'd crossed from Europe to Asia. Hotels, motels, even Holiday Inn's would cease to exist, along with roads. Therefore, my reasoning, was to make the very most of the king sized bed I contently dozed in. I could eat breakfast in the desert!

We all showered (the boys using the suite's bathroom like commoners, myself using my en-suite) and checked out before 11am. Pete the Saxo was in the private car park behind the hotel, protected through the night by the high walls, wrought iron gate and a very bored security guard.

Our plan for today was the Mongol Mongrels - our good friends Ed & Emma, driving their 206 and not seen since the marvellous Czech Out party (they were our adjacent camping buddies). We'd all been dying to meet up, a combination of car troubles and lost rally phones meant our paths had not again crossed, much to the dismay of all five of us.

Ed & Emma were en route from Karkaraly to join us, and sent a text to the recently acquired rally phone number two. Just 250km away - we could be seeing them in a couple hours, else it might take a day, our destiny once again completely dependent on the road conditions. We made the unanimous decision to wait, as long as it took, to reform the most excellent convoy we tasted so briefly in the Czech Republic.

We had the day ahead of us, in the radioactive city of Semey. So far, we'd made quite an effort to avoid all locally grown food, although Mackey swears that the radioactive tomatoes he ate were the tastiest he'd ever sampled. Even when we ordered beers, we endeavoured to buy from as far away as possible. I went for Miller, despite the Americans really not knowing much about good beer.

In the privacy of the private car park, we made the most of our time and decided to give Pete the Saxo some extra special attention. Everything was removed from the car, and the most efficient repacking Kazakhstan had ever seen began. We even tidied; those little bits of rubbish everyone accumulated on a road trip filled an entire black bag. You know the things - Fox's Glacier Mints wrappers, petrol receipts etc...

Once Pete the Saxo looked the tidiest since Goodwood, we thought we'd do something touristy. Semey's entry in the Lonely Planet only spread over a couple of pages, the attractions section merely a long paragraph. One thing they did list however was the nuclear monument, a 50 meter tower representing the Soviet nuclear tests so close to the city. This huge black shrine had a mushroom cloud gap in the middle, with a poignant statue of a mother shielding her baby from the atomic blast.

Walking to the statue, about a kilometre away from the hotel, we crossed over a bridge - a typical strong build with raw steel girders and a lashing of concrete. It stretched about 100 meters, yet swayed horribly when a large truck passed over. This bridge was no doubt built to last generations, but the finishing touches were lacking. Gaps a foot wide provided ridiculous obstacles to jump over as we walked. The country is basically a health and safety lawsuit just waiting to happen!

The river underneath was very pleasant though, although we played a game of "spot some life" in the radiation polluted water, and failed to spot anything bigger than a minnow.

We eventually found the open park area outside the city, but not before coming across wild cannabis growing alongside the road. You could smell it as we sauntered along the hot street - we took a few photos, as it amused us. The passing motorists must have thought we were strange, very strange.

The monument towered over the abandoned park area, and we seemed to be the only tourists that day. It did have a lone security guard patrolling the empty area; we surmised he had the worst job ever, looking so bored as he dawdled around and around the stone memorial.

With that done, our tourist needs satisfied by a very unsatisfying testament, we wandered back into town. This time, the river was home to some naked Kazakh men washing in the fast flowing waters. It looked quite out of place for us, although perhaps that was the norm? The radiation didn't seem to affect them though, as they splashed happily with their three hands.

Will took the lead as we entered the city once more, his stomach guiding the three of us in the aim of finding the nearest restaurant for a spot of lunch. As it turned out, his stomach wasn't too good at navigation. We explored the ghettos and slums of Semey, away from the main roads but assured by Will that this was the "quick way".

An hour later, we re-emerged at the hotel, having bypassed the 20 minute road in our inner city cultural tour. Another 10 minutes, this time sticking to the proven main roads, we found a small restaurant nestled between two buildings, the roof looking more suitable for a garage than a dining establishment. It was a nice place though, the waiter taking special care of us as we were his sole guests.

We had regular text updates from Ed & Emma throughout the day - their going was slow. They had chanced upon some of the worse roads in the country, and as a result the thought of a 60 mph run was nothing more than a fantasy. We waited around in the bar for about three hours, watching women's wrestling on the wall mounted TV whilst eating pizza. Yet more pizza.

Back to the hotel we went after spending the majority of the afternoon at the bar - once again retiring to our hotel car park. I must add though, that we'd checked out of the hotel early that morning, yet our car still remained in the car park. They must have thought we were taking advantage of their facilities - after all, we had used it as a workshop/car wash/valet and now we all sat about in Pete the Saxo watching a movie on the 4 inch screen of the iPod.

Another text came through - Ed & Emma, along with Paul & Laura from the Two Mongoleers, were only 25km away. Even with the shocking roads, our friends were due to be here soon - that was, as long as they had a better ability of inner city navigation and could find the hotel with ease. Unlike us. In every major city we'd been through. Ever.

Whilst waiting in the car park, sectioned off from the rest of Kazakhstan and providing some relaxing time in Pete the Saxo, I caught up with some blogs and Will decided to go on a mission to the nearby shop to get some drinks for us all, to sustain us whilst waiting. Off he set, Tenge in hand and a round trip that should have taken no more than 15 minutes.

Two hours later, Mackey and I began to actually worry about our third team member. Where on earth had he gone to? Did he go to find some fresh water spring to bottle the drinks himself? Did he decide the radioactivity of Semey shouldn't be ingested, and therefore would walk to Astana and get some cold Sprite's there? He had a fairly good sense of direction, managing to re-find the hotel after our nuclear monument visit (albeit the long way round), so not much we could do... other than wait. Eventually though, he popped his little head around the back door of the hotel, and into the car park we were waiting in.

Will had gone for a little stroll and found an internet cafe. A nice use of a couple of hours, but came back completely drink-less for his very thirsty friends. His nickname has now been changed from Willy-One-Bottle (from that time he went to get us drinks, and came back with just his bottle) to Willy-No-Bottles. Apparently he'd spent a nice few hours in the air conditioned room. Even had a few drinks himself!

The hotel receptionist and manager, along with the security guard and gardener, did seem quite perplexed at why we were treating their hotel like... well, a hotel, albeit one we'd checked out of six hours before. But, their frustration would soon be set right; Emma & Laura (Two Mongoleers) arrived at the hotel, and were SO happy to see us. Not only that, as we caught up in reception, the Terios boys from Team This Is Our Everest turned up, as well Team

Desert Beagles. Such a coincidence! But an impressive group was now formed.

Emma was without Ed though; the Peugeot 206 sat two blocks away from the hotel, the exhaust hanging off. Who you gonna call? Why, Nick Mackey of course! Mackey went to investigate the problem, and indeed noticed that the exhaust had fallen off. A very loud drive back to our hotel, and he straight away got to work. The bodge job (the first of several) involved butting the two sheared off ends together with jubilee clips, and lagged them to death with exhaust putty.

We all retired to our rooms, showers still appreciated and welcomed. The plan was to meet at reception, and head out in search of sustenance. At 9pm we wandered from our suite and met up with everyone; Ed, Emma, Tom, Rich, Ian, Jason, Simon, Laura & Paul, and off we went. Despite being in Semey for a few days, our knowledge of fine culinary establishments was limited, and so we all decided to head down the main street en masse.

A short five minutes later, and we found a small bar set underground, that also served food. Perfect we thought, and we tripled their business just by walking through the door. We sat down on two large, back to back tables, the only other customers being a Kazakh family enjoying the local beer. The menu was in Cyrillic, and it came down to Ed to translate using his limited (but incredibly impressive) knowledge. We all picked, but the waitress then pointed out that they only stocked two things on the entire menu; "cheesy cow meat" and "soy sauce beef". Six of each, and we'd share the fruits of our ordering. 'Sharing is caring' was certainly a motto on this trip.

The language was a constant barrier, but we were doing our best to learn all we could. So far, all we'd managed was "yes", "no", "thank you" and "beer". Although the last one, beer - the word is extremely close to "dried fish". Mackey had to walk to the bar and very clearly point at beer when he was brought some dried fish to his table.

The locals spiced things up in the little underground restaurant though, by getting up and dancing to some traditional Kazakh music. Of course, we were British and rebuffed their invitations to dance, although the mood was a jovial one. Before we knew it, it was late and we were all tired - those who had been driving of course, much more than us lay-abouts.

We all sauntered back to the hotel, bid bon-nuit to each other, and retired to our rooms (or suites) for some sleep before the border crossing back into Russia the next day.

The "Stronger Than Death" monument, a memorial to the victims of Semipalatinsk Nuclear Test Site

Questionable Kazakh engineering – this six inch gap spanned the width of the bridge

Good food, good company, good Semey

Day 21 - Returning to Russia

We awoke in the Hotel Binar, Semey, after a very pleasant evening with our comrades. The general mood of the team lifted hugely when we met other teams, something that all the others agreed on. There was only so much lone driving you could do, only so much banter within your car and your team mates you knew so well; to include new people, new topics of discussion, new opinions and company was a fantastic thing. And now we had some of our favourite teams with us, the mood was very good.

We all headed down to breakfast, along with Ed & Emma, and ordered from the Cyrillic & English menus - set breakfast numbers 2 & 7s were on the cards, the usual choice between meat and eggs or fruit and cereal. Mackey, of course, went for the full Kazakh fry up equivalent, whereas I instead went for the healthier option. It came with a pint of yoghurt type liquid though - just in a regular glass, the five of us all unsure what to do with it. Drink it? Spoon it? It was left.

We'd all decided to meet up in the private hotel car park, one we'd grown to know so well, at 8.30am. As with all late night decisions, the chances of us all making our self-made deadline were slim; instead, team members strolled to the collective group of Mongol Rally cars throughout the morning, finally assembling at 9.30am.

We all packed up, each car receiving a reorganisation and repacking despite not getting the tents out, and we set off towards the Kazakh/Russian border. After our previous Russian border incident, we double and triple checked that our passports were firmly in our possession, and not again left with the receptionists.

En masse (by far the best way to travel), we convoyed out of the city and attracted many waves from curious locals. The first bit of rough road, a small pothole that we'd now laugh at after our experience in the Ukraine/Kazakhstan, caused the Mongol Mongrel's exhaust to fall off. Mackey's repair job had lasted 1km.

Percy, the Peugeot 206 driven by Ed & Emma, now sounded like a tank. An actual tank, no doubt throwing up memories of some bygone era for the locals, but we had progress to make and no doubt time at the border to examine the damage. Onwards we pushed, but not too far, before we were pulled over by the Kazakh police.

Unlike their Russian counterparts, the Kazakh police are really rather nice. It seems I hadn't put on my lights (compulsory in these parts), but instead of fining me a rather hefty amount, they just asked me to rectify the situation and sent us on our way. Very refreshing, as the Ruski bastards would no doubt have demanded my right kidney or first born.

We got to the Russian border at 11.15, all making guesses on how long it would take. Six hours was our longest, but we'd become adept to border proceedings after our many - average estimate was three hours. Kazakhstan was done – and what a stunning country it had been. The people were friendly, the police were (generally) respectful, the scenery was difficult to comprehend, the sheer expanse and size of the nation. It'll be interesting to see the developing direction the country is heading in, whether new found oil riches will propel it forward and live up to its size.

I'm not sure what it is; Mackey looking a bit like a terrorist, or perhaps Pete the Saxo looking filthy, but we seem to get searched at every possible opportunity. Ed & Emma had been searched (or a brief look in their car) a couple of times. We however, had Pete the Saxo searched inside and out at nearly every border. Kazakh customs were no different - despite leaving the country, they still made us take everything out and explain half of it to them. What is this? That's a first aid kit. What is that? Imodium. Of course they didn't understand the word, and cue Mackey acting out what Imodium was. A fantastic two minute demonstration, I would have loved to have filmed it all (apart from cameras were banned at border crossings, and I would have been shot).

After the convoy had been searched (well, we had and the rest waved through), we entered the very short No Man's Land and queued at the Russian side. All was going well - passport control, the first of two checks at any side, went smoothly, despite the woman convinced it wasn't me in my passport photo. Will, being the registered owner of the car, was to get processed with Pete the Saxo, so myself and Mackey walked through the border building to get processed individually.

All was well, with a little immigration form to complete before you could proceed. Luckily, Emma & Laura (Two Mongoleers) were very prepared and brought us a plethora of pens to use. Will made a mistake on his, after trying to match up the Cyrillic for "tourist" with the available options on the immigration card. Instead, I think he declared himself as a drug runner or something.

A blank card was quickly obtained and second time lucky, the right combination of strange characters was selected. Somehow, despite not owning it on either iPod, "You don't have to say you love me" popped into my head, and I subconsciously hummed it in the cramped shed/passport control station. Within a couple of minutes, my humming stopped to fully concentrate on the immigration card, and the humming of the song was continued subconsciously by rallyers and locals. It was quite funny.

Onwards we went to the second check - customs.

We were very prepared for the search, already opening the various doors on the car, as the Russian soldiers headed our way. Only a brief search this time however - merely a prodding through the front door compartments and the first aid kits (incredibly, these two areas got searched at every single border. If I ever plan to smuggle drugs across Central Asia, I know where not to keep my stash. With hindsight, anywhere but those two areas were pretty safe.)

A short search - fantastic! Our convoy had also been waved through, and were parked in a car park as soon as you entered the great Soviet country. Onwards we drove, happy with the three hour border crossing and excited to push on.

But it's never that simple, is it? Before we were allowed to proceed, we were asked for our Customs Declaration Sheet. We'd had experience with these before - the Ukraine border guards stinging us for quite a few Euros after not declaring things on them. As a result, we'd promised ourselves we'd list every single item in the car on them, never giving any border guard the chance to again diddle us out of more money. Confident we'd never seen another since then, we told the guard we'd never received one. We didn't know whether we were supposed to have one from our first time in Russia, as we entered Kazakhstan, or as we left Kazakhstan.

Only one guard spoke English, and broken English at that. He made it quite clear that we couldn't proceed without this form and dismissed us. Excellent. We were now stuck in 50 meters of No Man's Land, barred from re-entering Kazakhstan due to our single use visa, and Russia being so close yet so far. Hassling him was the only way we could get anywhere, as he seemed quite content to leave us stewing without hope.

We parked up, in the sinners car park, and tackled him with our paperwork trying to convince him we had never been given a customs declaration form. Lots of talking in Russian with his fellow officers, and he eventually told us we needed one from Kazakhstan. Will, being the owner, was to stroll back into the country we'd just left to get one.

Mackey and I waited, and waited, while Will went to get one. 30 minutes later, he strolled back through the various checkpoints back to the car, empty handed. Apparently the stern Kazakh woman had refused to give him one, and followed the Russian's suit and ignored our pleas.

Our convoy were patiently waiting in relative freedom, parked just behind the chain link fence that separated us. I then told Will we'd get a customs form, even if it meant stealing one, and accompanied him back towards Kazakhstan. By this time, the various guards on the checkpoints were used to us, and simply waved us through as we walked backwards and forwards between the two countries.

Will was right; Kazakh border woman was a pain in the ass. She flatly refused us, muttering "bye bye" - the only English she apparently knew. With our convoy waiting, and this seemingly our only way to continue on the rally, we did what us British do best - we waited. Hanging on her counter would probably be a more apt description, refusing to leave without the hallowed piece of A5 paper.

Eventually though, it worked. She escorted us to a hut, and then another, explaining the problem to the guards who were more than happy to pass the buck to the next. After some time, a guard seemed to understand us and gave us the form to fill out. This took about 20 seconds. Another 10 seconds of stamping it and making it official, we were presented with the declaration and victoriously headed to Russia to attempt to break out.

Will had been to Kazakhstan three times and Russia three times, all in one day.

Whilst the two of us were negotiating/arguing with the Kazakh border, Mackey had wandered over to the chain link fence to give our convoy an update. This was apparently not a good thing to do, as he was shouted at and chased away by an rifle wielding guard, angry that Mackey had broken some international law about conversing with the released. A sniper probably had him in his sights before Mackey made a hasty retreat.

Form in hand, the tired guards eventually let us through, and we reformed the magnificent convoy. Most teams had pushed forward just 10 minutes before we broke free, aiming to find a hotel in the next city of Barnau, leaving only the Mongol Mongrels waiting for us. Ed & Emma, we love you guys.

Towards Barnau we followed, the Russian city so very close to the Altai Mountains. The roads were quite good, avoiding the sparsely laid out pot holes with ease after our previous trials. We entered the city limits late, about 10pm, and found our convoy as we cruised down the main street bisecting the city.

We began the search for the hotel, ever in contact with the other cars thanks to our amazing CB radios (so kindly provided by Sharman Multicom). Laura (Two Mongoleers) voiced her frustration at not being able to spot the Cyrillic for hotel in this ever growing municipality. I pointed out the 30 foot high letters marking 'HOTEL' adorning a skyscraper not too far ahead of us.

We headed towards the shining beacon, and entered the city centre hotel car park. Ed, with his broken exhaust, actually managed to set off a car alarm with his booming car by just pulling in next to it. Absolutely no contact was made - just his faux bad-boy exhaust! We all entered the deserted reception. It was a fairly large hotel; the foyer was open plan, polished floors and even had free Wi-Fi. We checked in, affording ourselves single rooms as a treat (and some privacy for a change), and agreed to meet back in reception in an hour - time for a change into semi-clean clothes and a shower.

I say semi-clean clothes; long gone were the days where we had a freshly laundered t-shirt, or unstained trousers. Washing clothes had become an art, an art which we are slowly picking up. Using a small tube of "Travel Wash", and the hotel room's facilities (be it a bath or a sink), we hand washed to the best of our ability. And for all those that know us, you know the best of our ability was throw it all together, swill it round for 20 seconds and wring the excess water out. Drying clothes though, that's where the magic happened. If the clothes didn't dry out overnight whilst we got some much needed sleep, we took the damp items to our car. Whoever was in the back seat for the morning shift, usually Mackey, then did the drying.

This consisted of one item at a time, holding it out the window. A t-shirt for example, held at the bottom ends and allowing the morning air rushing by the car to fill said t-shirt, and drying it in the process. Our record was the 47 degree air of a Russian heat wave - that managed to dehydrate a t-shirt in less than 30 seconds. Back to the original point - we craved a washing machine.

At the hotel, we discovered a number of other rally teams in habitation; Ultimate Farmer, a French ambulance, a Spanish dude on a motorbike, the two Micras, Skinner & Little in a Swift, and another blue Saxo (this one with a homemade bonnet scoop). By the time we'd all met at reception, it was very late - gone 1am, and all of us in desperate need of food that wasn't crisps or snacks.

Across the city centre road, we found a peculiar permanent marquee erected, filled with empty tables and chairs, as well as a bar. Close to the hotel, and with smiling staff, the group of 24 of us rallyers were more than happy to enter. The poor bar lady, standing no more than 5ft tall and armed with 15 words of English, was overwhelmed by the orders for food and beer coming in, despite us British forming an orderly queue. But, the wait didn't matter - we had rallyers to chat with, and shared stories of highs and lows, both new and old.

The meals eventually came out - one by one. Not a problem when it was just the three of us, but when 24 hungry bodies had all ordered at the same time, it ended up a little bit crazy. The last meal came out over two hours after the first, and even after more unordered dishes materialised. They too were swiftly demolished by the ravished drivers. The last person to eat, a vegetarian who'd ordered 'mushroom carbonara' with the help of someone who spoke the two languages, sat and watched as everyone received and ate. Enquiring with the waitress to the where abouts of her food was answered with blank stares - trying to describe mushroom carbonara with sign language was near on impossible. Mackey ended up coming to the rescue surprisingly, with a very questionable drawing on the back of a napkin of mushroom carbonara. Which actually worked. The dish was served up 15 minutes later.

A few beers later, Emma having finished her delightful dried fish (a variation of "I buy, you wear" – but rather eating) and the majority of the group were feeling the exhaustion after a long day.

It was now 3am, and people began to retire to the luxury of their hotel rooms. Whilst eating however, we heard a reverberating bass line coming from nearby - it seems we'd been eating next door to a Russian nightclub. Never the chance to miss some traditional Russian culture, I voiced my intention to visit. Will was a willing wingman, and eventually Mackey too rose to the challenge. Emma called it a night, but Ed too was to join us. Paul & Laura from the Two Mongoleers also shared our interest for some Russian education, as well as Skinner, Little & Oliver (from a Micra).

We headed in, looking completely out of place from the second we entered. We wore flip flops, shorts or lightweight trousers, and t shirts. The locals however, obviously the wealthy side considering the £10 entry charge, looked somewhat better. Still, onwards we went, ordering a few beers from the packed nightclub whilst attempting to protect our ears from decibels that would have been illegal in the UK.

We grabbed a table, watching the dance floor intently to learn these traditional Russian moves. The fact that they were being performed by stunning local beauties in skimpy sparkly dresses was pure coincidence. This part of Russia, the second half of our two part trip, did seem to hold the more attractive and happy portion of the nation. They were stunning. Not Ukraine stunning, I'll give you that, but enough to keep our posse wide awake until the last orders bell was rang at 4am.

Our Russian was coming along nicely - we could now say: Hello, Thanks, Yes, No, Beer, Chips. The six words that could likely get you through life. I even managed to string five of them together in a sentence which actually worked.

It was a late night - later than we planned, but beers with other rallyers and a chance to witness some Russian dancing was a very welcome break from the thousands of miles we'd done. To our rooms we went, and fell happily to sleep within seconds.

Grabbing a very late dinner in a strange marquee restaurant in Barnau, Russia

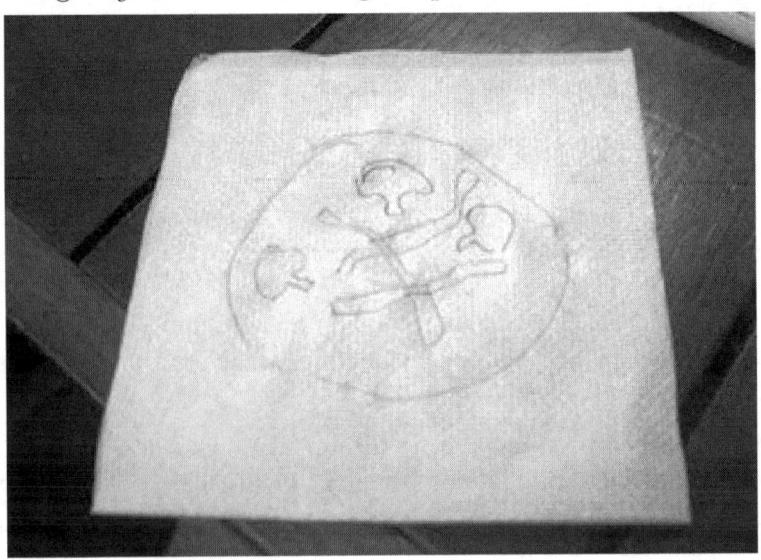

Mackey's successful attempt at ordering Mushroom Carbonara

Day 22 - A jolly nice day

Last night was a good night - a very good night. We didn't get smashed, tipsy was all our feeble exhausted bodies could manage, but we ate well and caught up a lot with other rallyers, both known and previously undiscovered friends. After hitting the sack at 4am, I woke up without any sense of time whatsoever. Not having my phone, a watch, or a clock in the room meant I was completely confused about when in the day I'd decided to awake.

I lay in for a bit, or as best I could with the thought of being the last one up hovering over me like a storm cloud. To keep your team behind was one thing, but to hold up an entire convoy was another. I felt refreshed enough though, showered and sorted my bag out, and headed down to see if they were waiting at reception.

It was 7.30am. Damn. Ah well, I was up and no point in going back to bed, so had a little wander around the area and updated some blogs using the free Wi-Fi, obviously perched on the red leather sofa in front of reception and attracting a few looks accusing me of being too cheap to pay for internet in my room. Which of course couldn't have been further from the truth - nothing would have made me happier than to pay the £2 to get Wi-Fi from the comfort of my own bed, but trying to work out which Cyrillic option on the laptop was to actually pay for it proved to be a fruitless 30 minutes of my time.

Eventually people did stir and began to join my lonely party, the latest getting up at 11am. The plan for today was to push towards the Altai Mountains, the fabled mountain range many have deemed the most beautiful part of the entire rally. Everyone checked out by 11.15am, and a rally party was formed in the car park; more chat, lots of repacking and even a bit of cleaning.

Mackey decided to have another look at Ed's exhaust, his previous attempt at a fix failing after 1km. He needed a few parts - some jubilee clips and other such hardware, so myself, Will and Emma headed into the city to try and find the Russian B&Q. Food was also on the agenda, as we stocked up every few days so we could survive in our camping wilderness (those days where we didn't find ourselves in a cheap hotel of course).

Driving along the main road, we spotted a supermarket - which turned out to be a hardware store. But a supermarket was hidden next door. What fantastic luck. The three of us deemed ourselves Team Supermarket Sweep (little things like that kept us entertained) and we entered and marvelled at yet more foreign products to buy. We ended up filling an entire trolley with essentials such as water and noodles. Lunch was on the menu as well, considering it was now midday and Mackey's repairs usually took a few hours. We bought food including a rotisserie chicken for lunch, and headed back armed with edible and hardware goodies.

Being the first time we'd ever done something like this, it was always a mystery what to take with us from home, and we were learning from the errors of our ways. Some of the things we'd bought from camping websites, convinced they'd be essential, had remained untouched. On the other hand, teams had little bits and bobs that were amazed by. An example - Ed & Emma had the most amazing camping table. Just a little table, that folded into the size of a tent bag. But having a table was the most underrated thing in the world. I think Emma's mum got it for them (Hello Heather!). It provided just a little fraction of civility in the otherwise hobo-like conditions.

Once back at the car park, all the teams were still enjoying their few hours off by re-arranging and cleaning the cars. We set up the table, and Emma & I made lunch for our convoy. Nothing overly complex - bread rolls, freshly roasted chicken and some salad leaves. This turned out to be the tastiest, best lunch we'd had the entire rally. Something about us all coming together, fixing each other's cars whilst others went for supplies, already used to very foreign food by missing the very simple home comforts, and the chicken rolls received rave reviews. Here are some:

Mackey (Scilly Mission): "The best thing I've eaten in my life probably"

Paul (Two Mongoleers): "My only orgasm of the rally"

Will (Scilly Mission): "First proper lunch since we started the rally"

Ed (Mongol Mongrels): "Best lunch since Goodwood"

Laura (Two Mongoleers): "Absolutely magnificent"

Tom (This Is Our Everest): "Damn that's good!!"

Emma & I felt proud and jubilant. They were that good. The car park had transformed itself (or rather we had transformed it) to both a workshop and a cafe, all done in the stunning Russian sun. The hotel were good - they didn't come and tell us all to bugger off once, although I doubt they'd have wanted to what with 24 people enjoying themselves.

Mackey continued to work. Not only did he fix Ed's exhaust (take two) but also got about looking at the Two Mongoleer's sump guard issues. Mackey spent the best part of three hours on the floor, head underneath various engines, and was filthy (more so than usual). Team Supermarket Sweep continued the fantastic rally teamwork by walking along to a nearby clothes shop and picking him out some new threads.

The clothes shop was a strange one; a cross between a Russian Primark and a Russian TK Maxx, and we were there to shop. Of course, we still have the fun game of "I buy, you wear", so I had a little fun picking out some new garments for our resident repair man. My favourite would have to be the bright pink wife-beater, complete with hood. That's right, a pink hooded wife beater. With strange Russian phrases down one side.

Next door to the clothes shop, we found another shop; this time stocking regular budget clothes, and also a wide range of camping equipment. What sheer luck, and this time I bought some plain black t-shirts for Mackey (which of course wouldn't be revealed until he'd first sampled the extra special purchases). Will also spotted some tents - some actual tents that were larger than the average man's coffin. They weren't the cheapest things in the world - in fact, they cost more than their UK counterparts. But a small price to pay for the ability to get dressed/undressed in the relative comfort of your tent. We picked up three, despite toying with the idea of leaving Mackey with a coffin tent (as he loved them so much).

Emma, Will & I got a text as we were leaving the shop and were informed the convoy were waiting for us. We walked the five minutes back to our temporary base, and indeed the majority of cars were preparing to leave. Mackey was black - covered in dirt and oil from spending the lovely day with an engine block but inches from his face.

Mackey didn't know what to say when he received my gifts. He didn't put the pink hooded wife beater straight on – I guessed he wanted to look extra good in it for the finish line. Also in Mackey's bag of presents was the Man Utd kit, complete with BERBATOV along the back (for £5), some hideous lime green tourist t-shirts with RUSSIA on the front, and a new belt. We thought we grabbed the right size, but this was disproved not long after in the hotel car park/cafe/changing room, when two people easily fit into the belt, and the Man Utd kit ended up being for ages 11-12.

We finally left at 3pm - no doubt the hotel over the moon to rid their precious car park of a handful of teams and their faithful drivers. Our convoy of seven now headed south east, towards the mountains.

With a convoy that large, you only went as fast as the slowest team. Luckily, all teams were happy to push on at the speed limit. By this time, we'd conveniently forgotten about the 43mph rule. On our first Russian visit, we paid very strict attention to this rule. Our second though, I'll be honest, we flouted the rule, and quite deliberately.

You see, if a Russian policeman ever asks for your license, they'll accept the International Driving Permit (IDP), which is a legal document and allows the holder to drive in their country. One thing it neglects to mention though is the duration you've held your license.

We convoyed until dusk, leaving the city and the motorways and instead driving along a sweeping A-road, the conditions of which were remarkably good considering the remote corner of Russia we were now in. The road was wide, flanked on both sides by lush thick green forest, one side of which hid from us a river we knew to be there. As light faded away, we decided to look for a group camp site, and the lead car took on the responsibility to find a suitable location.

This little task was completed within fifteen minutes, a further few teams also taking different paths in the aim of finding somewhere appropriate, before one reported finding the perfect site. We all followed, and they stayed true to their word. 50 meters along a dirt track, we came to a clearing just out of sight of the main road. Another dozen or so meters lead through to a sparse collection of mature trees separated by eight or so meters from one another. This wasn't the best bit though; despite finding space for us all, on soft grass, away from the busy road (both audibly and visually), we were on a bank overlooking the Katun River as it swept through the Altai Mountains. It was stunning.

Our bank was three or four meters above the water line, yet overlooked a sweeping meander and the bank opposite. The river was incredibly fast flowing, moving countless millions of litres every minute from the mountains not too far up stream. The soft roar of the ever tumbling eddies and currents provided the perfect backdrop to a pretty much perfect camp site.

We camped with our new best friends Ed & Emma, as well as the rest of our super convoy - The Two Mongoleers, This Is Our Everest and The Desert Beagles. Our new tents even attracted a few comments from the other teams - not because they were anything special (they were very bog standard two man tents), but because of the enormous upgrade from our coffins.

Food was the next thing on the agenda after our gypsy houses had been set up. Emma & I seem to have gained the responsibility for feeding our two teams, and we began to create some culinary magic.

Once again, I feel I should talk about the table – it was just a table, but so very useful when camping. It meant we could prepare, cook and serve without using a bit of flat ground or a rock. And on that table, we did create - Pesto pasta with roast chicken. Cooking on the small stove took a bit of getting used to - only so much could be cooked at once, using the limited water supply, but the end result was the perfect end to a very good (and productive) day.

Good banter was served next, along with an indiscriminate selection of beers we picked up from the Russian supermarket. As we talked, our stomachs full and our patience rested, the stars above us came out in force and bathed the river bank in a gentle luminance - The Plough, Cassiopeia, Orion's Belt; all watching over our band of merry men (and women).

In total, 12 tents were there to share the campsite - a very cool sight next to an incredible river. We retired by midnight, the sound of the ever-surging water providing a relaxing soundtrack that ensured we were all asleep not long after.

Hotel car-park / restaurant

Hotel car-park / workshop

Our long convoy planning our route through Southern Siberia

Mackey had earned his reputation as the convoy mechanic

Day 23 - Hello Altai Mountains

I don't know whether it was waking up in our new tents, or enjoying a relaxing evening by the river, or being in the company of so many good people; but we all enjoyed a fantastic night's sleep, one of the best of our camping days.

Packing away camp was just as efficient these days as setting it up. Ed always seemed to be the first to wake, obviously enjoying rousing the rest of us with gentle calls of "You want breakfast NOW?", and we were all up by 8am. The camp site was just as stunning in the morning as it was at dusk - the ever flowing river providing the perfect backdrop, the tall trees providing ample cover from the sun and the road just far enough to be unnoticed, but close enough to be accessible.

Twenty four torpid rallyers soon emerged from their tents, and began the pack away. We set off about 9am - five cars in our convoy (with the promise of the rest following after) and headed into the ever swelling landscape. This was the beginning of the Altai Mountains, famed for their breath-taking beauty. Even after an hour, we began to appreciate the hold they had on visitors despite the topography only being classed as "hilly". Each sweeping bend along a hillside road offered stunning forest views, and we watched the altimeter creep higher and higher.

After three of driving, we all made the ascent up a particularly large hill and found a roadside cafe. A small wooden shack, built in a traditional circular style with a bbq/fire outside suggested a cafe, anyway. We all parked up, joining a small group of local cars and headed inside. On the menu? Bread and meat, cooked in front of us, for the sum of £1. We sat around outside with a fantastic view of the valleys surrounding us. Dark black clouds swooped in from the west and reduced day to dusk within minutes. Accompanying this dark sky was rain - a lot of rain. We hadn't seen a great deal so far - a storm in Kazakhstan, but not much else.

The rain fell, and it fell. Not the pathetic rain we'd see in the UK - these rain drops were the size of golf balls, smashing the ground where we stood. Quickly retreating to the dry safety of the cafe, we easily filled the small hut. The view was too good to miss though - I went out, sheltering under the one foot overhang of the entrance, and filmed the breath-taking sight, framed by the mountains. The rain wasn't the only thing to come out to perform in front of the camera - hail also joined the party, certainly the first we'd seen on this trip.

Meat and bread went down very well, and we set off towards the Russian/Mongolian border. Every 10 minutes that we progressed, we'd climb for nine of those minutes up ever growing hills, their statuses upgraded from large hills to small mountains. The views were breath-taking, as promised by so many guidebooks and websites. As we skirted across roads carved into the edges of these summits, each valley was as jaw-dropping as the next. Lush, green, commanding views across miles of rivers and forest. Our convoy of five continued, with the aim of finding somewhere to stay so that we could make the border nice and early the next day.

As we entered the collection of peaks, we predictably noticed it was getting a lot colder. The tops of the mountains started to show their snow covered tips, and for the first time all three of us kitted ourselves out in the fantastic team wear provided by BS Embroidery. It had all been sat in the back for a few weeks, the forty-something degree heat deeming them useless. Until now of course, and we looked dapper.

Hours seemed like minutes as we traversed thousands of feet in altitude, stopping several times for photos. Ed in particular was the master photographer, and picked the best spots to stop despite every minute being a potential postcard. Upwards and upwards we went, reaching a peak of 2,235 meters above sea level. Not bad for a day's leisurely driving.

The CB radios were once again proving to be fantastic - this time, we invented "Mongoloke" - a car & CB version of karaoke. Within our convoy there were three teams with radios - Mongol Mongrels, Two Mongoleers and us. This proved to be a great use of our time, each team taking turns in belting out a song whilst cruising through the mountains. The song choices were:

Ed & Emma: Lily Allen (It's not fair) Katy Perry (Hot & Cold) Bryan Adams (Summer of 69)

Laura & Paul: Blur (Park Life)

Us - Tenacious D (Tribute, **** her gently) Verve (Sonnet) Take That (Back for Good)

As we approached the border we passed through a small village - the last settlement before we reached the end of Russia. We made the collective decision to camp near here - far enough away from the border to enjoy our last night in the vast empire, but close enough to make it there when it opened in the morning. As we passed through the village, nestled amongst the towering peaks of the Altai Mountains, we spotted a little motel. A very basic one yet managed to grab a six bed dorm and a two bed room. The girls took the room and the boys took the dorm - six single beds crammed into a room, each with children's duvet covers on. Will got the award for best duvet cover, featuring two cats shouting "Best Friends Forever". It was also luminous green.

Food was on the cards, so team Supermarket Sweep took Pete the Saxo further into the village and eventually found a little shop. What a strange little shop it was as well - it seems to be the standard the further east we get, where everything in the shop was out of reach from the customer. Instead, the shelves behind the long counter were stocked with all manner of goods. The thing you want, you had to ask for. No problem you might think, apart from when you can't speak a word of Russian (other than beer & chips). Lots of pointing, and we managed to get a few bits.

Tonight's menu - pasta, pesto and chorizo type sausage. Russians seem to love frozen pasta, tortellini in particular; supermarket chest freezers are at least 40% full of different types. The shop's freezer was no different, bags and bags of different types. What was in the little parcels of pasta however was a mystery. Fish? Lamb? Chicken? All completely useless in our useless language. Em & I even resorted to making animal noises. The shop woman looked at us with that stare, wondering if we were certifiably insane - that look is universal in any language. Eventually, the lovely and talented Em turned to crude sketches of the various animals on a back of a receipt. Eventually we got our point across - lamb indeed filled the pasta.

With dinner purchased, the three of us headed back to the motel and cooked up a feast in the shared kitchen. We were getting quite adept to the art of culinary camping, as it had fallen to Emma & I to prepare the team meals using nothing but a camping stove. After food, and a couple beers in our big dorm room, night had taken hold of the mountains in which we resided, and we all went to sleep at 11pm; the plan for the next day was to wake up at 5.30am and get to the Russian border for opening time…...

Will washing in the frigid river

Waking up to a river panorama

Group photo at the Altai Mountain café – "Which way to Mongolia?"

Will, Mackey and I in the Altai Mountains

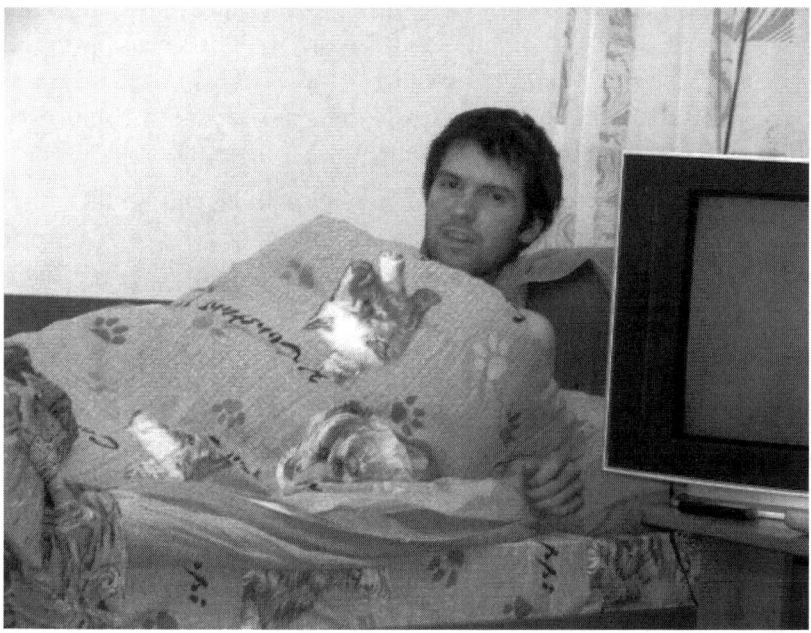

Will in his kitten covered duvet in the 6 bedroom dormitory

Day 24 - Our last border crossings

5.30am. A horrible time in anyone's book, the sort of time you dreaded seeing. That was the time we all got up (as planned), our aim was to reach the Russian border by the time those gates opened and gave us free pass towards Mongolia. It wasn't overly painful this early, as the excitement of our target country so very close got us out of bed.

Us six boys (Will, Mackey, Paul (Two Mongoleers), Ed (Mongol Mongrels) and Matt (The Desert Beagles) and I) woke in our school like dorm, the small window giving us a clue of the rather wet and miserable mountain weather that lay in wait outside for us. It was far too early to make breakfast, instead some Russian breakfast bars (which must be an acquired taste) sustained us. Apart from Mackey, who happily dined on three Marlboro Reds for breakfast.

We loaded up the cars, always nice to do when we hadn't dug the entire boot contents (tents, sleeping bags, food, stove etc.), and headed off. I took the morning shift as per usual, our three cars moving out from the last settlement before the border and into the mountains. There were only three of us now - This Is Our Everest and The Desert Beagles (or at least one team member) decided to camp, and we'd agreed to meet them at the border.

What followed as we left the town were two and a half hours of the most astonishing driving I'd ever done. Probably the wrong turn of phrase, as the Mongol Rally was only the 4th time I'd ever driven with a licence. Perhaps the most incredible drive I'd ever seen? The roads were pretty good, tarmac throughout with only a few potholes to avoid, carved into the sides of mountains and peaks. We snaked around these stunning roads completely astonished at the sights that lay before us - it was still early morning, and dawn clouds hovered all around us. Some above us, on the mountains in which we hugged as we pushed forwards, others glided at our sides as we looked down over the valleys below.

The pot holes, few and far between but still there, simply turned a stunning relaxing drive into a more exciting, stunning relaxing drive. We all happily cruised along at 50mph, slowing as we entered a corner and accelerated out, but constantly dodging obstacles by using both sides of the deserted roads. I'd even go as far as saying that these few hours were the highlight of my driving life, even pipping the surreal Kazakhstan drive a week before.

We reached the Russian border by 9am, just in time for it opening. We weren't the first team there however; a small congregation of rallyers had already formed around the small immigration hut in an unorganised group at the front door. The immigration hut, the first of the border stops we'd be doing today, wasn't quite open. The soldiers manning the border post rocked up forty minutes late, somewhat bemused at the bunch of multicolour vehicles and their intrepid captains waiting for them.

Will & Ed, the registered drivers of the two cars, began to queue up. Within 10 minutes however, Mackey, Emma and I noticed their apparent lack of queuing ability. The bunch of rallyers made a rough queue, slowly inching their way to the front to begin their final push, but Will in particular always ended up at the back. With instructions for him to hold Ed's hand in the line-up, they slowly made progress forward. In the meantime, another Citroen Saxo rally vehicle was queued up behind ours - but this Saxo hadn't been so lucky as Pete the Saxo. Completely knackered, dead to the world, having rolled the last mile to the border down the mountain hills. But Mongolia was so close and the driver certainly wasn't ready to give up without reaching his last country! Mackey and Emma helped him push the car to the border gates. That was the rally spirit.

The border was full of local kids, each with a handful of English (which meant they were infinitely more multilingual than us) and determined to look through our cars for toys or sweets. Mackey got angry, his bear like persona shining through and even growled at the harmless children. This didn't scare them though, as they just giggled at the silly man. Did they have no fear?!

After the immigration checkpoint (step one of five), passport control was next. We sat in the line at the border, a good 50% of cars being fellow Mongol Rally vehicles, every so often inching our way forwards. Bearing in mind that we'd got to the border at 9am, we had travelled maybe 50 meters by the time 3pm came around. That was one thing we'd become very good at - wasting time. Not necessarily doing anything - perhaps reading, or perhaps just sitting there and contemplating life's many issues, but a six hour wait was easy these days.

Waited and waited, we did. As we got closer to the front of the queue, where a lone border soldier was letting cars progress to the next stage, we noticed lots of local vans sweeping alongside the long line and pushing in at the front. Who were these cheeky bastards? Some fine aggressive driving by Mackey kept many at bay, but still they came - on the equivalent of the hard shoulder (in reality a stretch of dirt accompanying the tarmac) and straight to the front.

Will got out to speak to the over-stressed border guard, obviously new at the job else he'd be used to the hordes of Mongol Rally vehicles attempting to cross this time of year. Will discovered the vans intentions; rather than skipping the line to return to Mongolia, they'd drive a kilometre into no man's land, and pick up flour. Yes, regular flour. It seems Mongolian flour sells for a much higher price in Russia, so the vans would meet their waiting accomplices in no man's land, stock up with hundreds of bags, and return to flog their wares at a much higher price. Ingenious, yes - but please, queue like us British!

Ed & Emma, exceptionally British in all the best ways, waited politely near the front of the queue. Obviously indifferent to those pushing in, after all it was their trade, their patience paid off and at 3.30pm they were waved to the front and allowed through. Even though Pete the Saxo still lingered half a dozen cars back, we were happy - the other half of our team were through!

We waited and waited. Yet more flour merchants attempted to push in, angrily rebuffed by Mackey and his hostile revving and acceleration. Some family even got out of their van and stood directly in front of Pete the Saxo so we couldn't move, obviously unfazed by the almost empty threats of the revving engine. Fearless locals, I gave them that. It was soon 5pm, and we started to worry; we already knew the Mongolian side of the border would be shut soon, but we didn't want to get stuck in Russia for another night. After a long while worrying that we'd be camping literally next to our cars in the queue, we were let forward and the long procession of vehicles behind us slowly crept forward the 10ft to fill our gap.

Now past the big metal gates, we were officially being processed at the border. The first step, the immigration hut, was merely a garden shed. This was now passport control. Every country had a different way of doing this; mainly checking your passport was you, your visa was valid and in date, and you weren't on Interpol's most wanted list. Kazakhstan for example was remarkably efficient, but Russia most certainly was not.

The three of us entered the passport control room, a relatively efficient and modern looking structure and filled with such technology as a large bag scanner and computers. This is where the impressiveness of their systems stopped. It was hard to describe without drawing a picture, but the queues for different areas of the building criss-crossed over each other – it was chaos. We queued politely, as we'd learnt to do so well, along one side of the building. But coming the other way, intersecting the queue, was the Mongolians visiting Russia. Intersecting was one thing; to do it at the narrowest point of the whole building, where two people could barely pass each other without some casual touching going on, was just ridiculous.

It got worse, and we guessed there had been a major disaster in Mongolia and no one thought it worthy to inform us - every single Mongolian -> Russian visitor also brought the entire contents of their house/ger - nay, their entire village, over the border with them. Hoards of families were entering the passport control building, carrying dozens of large bags and boxes and expecting to negotiate the small building with them.

The first time we saw this happen, our selves politely queued up yet dozens of huge sacks passed around and in front of us, it was amusing. How could a family carry so much? And even consider moving it by hand through passport control? Each man in the family was lifting everything, from rugs and carpets to food and toys, through the building and into the scanner for approval to enter Russia.

Second time this happened, just a sense of mild annoyance but still tolerable. Bless them and their deciding to move an entire nation's worth of junk to Russia, just as we were trying to cross over.

Third time this happened, it became a mild irritant. After all, the small corridors were filling with sacks and boxes, leaving little room to walk past. Families, feeding their goods forward through the narrow hall, didn't understand the concept of excusing one's self, in case of an accidental nudge or box dropped on foot. Which began to happen with increasing frequency.

Fourth time this happened, we took action. It wasn't the case of us being annoying foreigners, or taking liberties - these Mongolians/Russians/Kazakhs were constantly pushing into our polite queue, destroying any patience we had. Even asking them nicely what they were doing did nothing (rather predictably). Instead, we engaged in a tactic that proved us well on a previous border - the road block. This time, being on foot rather than the cars, the three of us and five other rallyers formed a human wall, blocking all future movements around the building (the majority of movements which were to push in front of us). LOTS of angry locals, furious their dastardly plan to barge through our orderly line had been dashed. Lots of fun, and it worked - we had our brief passport check, and moved to the 3rd checkpoint - Russian Customs.

Customs check points had never been overly fair to us – we had had more searches than any other team we'd spoken to. Russia was no different, despite us leaving the country and therefore assuming the customs search would be a lot more lax than entering a country. We had our car thoroughly sifted, although again they took much more notice in the first aid kits and the front door compartments than anything else.

We were talking soon after this little search (where, of course, they found nothing) - if we ever did want to become drug barons and smuggle narcotics across Europe, we'd simply fill our roof box to the brim. Well, as that was opened just fleetingly once by a border guard, perhaps we'll limit our opiate trafficking to just our rucksacks - they have not been touched at all!

Russian was done. The second time we'd been in the country (well, Mackey's 2nd, my 3rd and Will's 4th after the customs declaration fiasco), and the last of our trip. We waved goodbye to the border guards, and made our way into No Man's Land - that stretch of dirt that separates two mighty countries. As we left Russia, we headed down the tarmac road, flanked on both sides by rolling green hills offering us incredible scenery as we approached our final, target country.

Half way along No Man's Land, we reached a very small Mongolian check point. A lone guard, a shed and a bit of wood claiming to be a barrier. Standing next to a very still Mongolian flag, no wind to unfurl its colourful ensign, the lone guard had a quick look through our passports and raised the bit of wood. I mean barrier.

This was where we first experienced the Mongolian roads. Or to be more precise, the distinct lack of Mongolian roads. Literally, as the Russian half of No Man's Land ended and the Mongolian half began, the tarmac'ers obviously finished their job and returned to their homes. For the tarmac simply gave way to dirt - a pot hole ridden, large rock strewn path cut into the land. Mackey took Pete the Saxo through towards the Mongolian border, reaching a maximum of 20mph as he swerved to avoid every obstacle that could potentially end our little adventure.

We crossed the top of a hill, and below us lay the Mongolian border - looking distinctly quiet, but relatively impressive - structures, offices, not the sort of uncivilised check point I might have envisaged from reading the Lonely Planet.

At the border, we saw Ed & Emma along with the Two Mongoleers queued up amongst a handful of other cars. The border looked very quiet - hardly anyone around, apart from the unofficial Bureau de Change - a rather unscrupulous looking chap flagging down every car that approached the Mongolia, insisting he was the only and best way to convert our Roubles and Tenge (Russia & Kazakhstan) to Togrogs (Mongolia). Without knowing the exchange rate, we were forced to take him up on the offer, which didn't sound too bad. 170 per GPB - the figures alone sound impressive, as that would mean I'd have *thousands* in my wallet. Maybe even ten thousand.

Exchange we did, and headed down to the stopping area we were so used to (passport control followed by customs control). We had only parked up for a minute, behind Ed & Emma who were extremely happy to see us (I think they worried about us, fearing the worst if we left their sight), before we were told to progress directly into a car park. No, car park was the wrong word; holding pen. Impound lot. Concrete cell. A rectangular piece of concrete surrounded by metal fences - this was to be our home for the night, as we'd arrived at closing time. One saving grace was the scenery.

For gazing through the wire fence towards the open land of Mongolia, we were greeted with huge snow topped mountains that could easily have found home on the front of a postcard.

Not to worry though – it's all part of the rally. That had become the official mantra of our teams, the phrase used to put everything into perspective when you were getting financially squeezed by a corrupt guard, you burst a tyre in the middle of the desert, or your exhaust falls off for the 7th time - It's all part of the rally.

We quickly resigned ourselves to the point it might be an uncomfortable, if not interesting, evening. Camping was out of the question, due to an ever growing wind blowing through the new Mongol Rally camp and our tent pegs refusing to get a hold in the concrete flooring. Sleeping in the cars would be the only option…..

Scilly Mission, Mongol Mongrels, Two Mongoleers, This Is Our Everest, The Desert Beagles and a few other teams huddled around a small corner of the pen, the temperature already dropping to the lowest we'd experienced on the entire trip. T shirts, polo's, hoodies and jackets were donned, along with hats and gloves; most definitely the first time they'd seen the light of day since Tresco. Rumour had it was we were free to leave the prison compound and wander into town. And by town, I mean a small collection of homes just 100 meters past the border.

Ed, Emma, Will and I decided to go for supplies - we hadn't banked on getting stuck for a night where we'd struggle to cook. We still had ample supplies in the roof box but the temperature and wind meant cooking would be a struggle, almost promising not to be worth the final effort. The four of us left Mackey and co with the cars, and walked straight through the front door of the compound. No passport check or anything – we just strolled straight into Mongolia.

Which was epic, just this little fact. We had officially reached our final country destination! Well, four of us had anyway.

Onwards we wandered through a very raggedy collection of huts, some baring Cyrillic signs crudely painted on the walls outside. Determining what they meant wasn't the easiest thing in the world, but clues did help - for example, in the lone window of one hut, was 12 or so bottles of different drink (about 10 of which alcoholic). That would be the shop! As we walked further, we smelt food - perhaps a cafe? Easiest way to find out was to enter the shelter...

The temperatures by this point were in very low single figures, and the sky had but an hour of light remaining, but as soon as we walked in the place was incredibly warm and welcoming. It was nothing more than a room claiming to be a cafe, two small tables with a small collection of seats. But the warmth, the warmth! We crowded in, grabbed a small square table and sat down, slowly regaining the feelings in our extremities as the shack pushed heat into us. The menu was a simple one - Buuz. The only thing available, mutton dumplings, handmade and boiled. It didn't take long for us to place an order, and the four almost felt guilty as we relaxed and sat there whilst the rest of our convoy no doubt froze back in the compound.

The food came out from the kitchen a short while later, the kitchen being the other half of the hut separated from the patrons by a brick wall. This brick wall, splitting the room into the two sections, also happened to be part of the oven. As a result, this wall was hot. After being in the bitter wind and very cold temperatures, this wall was an amazing thing. It was just a wall, but thermal opposites from the bitter Mongolian air outside.

Buuz soon became a firm favourite amongst the team - such a simple meal, merely meat dumplings, but oh so tasty and filling. The four of us ate a plate of them, finished a huge flask of chai, and happily sat with our spirits higher now our core temperature resembled normality. We didn't forget out comrades though - ever organised Emma had brought along Tupperware containers with her, and we reordered more buuz to take away.

Leaving the warmth of the cafe/shack and walking outside was a bit of a shock. The 30 minute warm up had pushed the horrible bitterness of the Mongolian summer(?!) from our minds, and walking back into it wasn't overly nice. We headed back to the border compound, once again just strolling through the gates, and re-joined our teams. They were all happy to see us after we waved the still hot dumplings at them, a thousand times more appealing than the thought of attempting to set up a camping stove in the windy conditions.

Mackey and Laura, quite randomly, had heard of a hotel in town. I say hotel, but it was actually someone's bedroom. The small huts were generally split into two - a large bedroom area, and a sitting room/kitchen. The locals were obviously trying to capitalize on the rallyer situation, by offering their sleeping quarters for a small price. Mackey and Laura had heard this, and decided to share someone's bedroom with a collection of other assorted visitors. For the equivalent of £2 a night, they'd have walls and a roof over their head, and even a fire in the room to keep them warm.

The hard-core rest of us however, decided to man up and sleep with the cars. We couldn't leave Pete the Saxo or Percy the 206 alone, who could?! The sun was setting over the mountains, the temperature plummeting as the last rays were blocked by the towering snow tipped peaks.

Rather than just retire to our own beds/cars, we decided to utilise our body heats for a little longer, and all piled into Pete the Saxo. Four of us (Will, Ed, Emma & I) managed to just about squeeze into the car, by far the fullest it had ever been but we quickly warmed it up. It was getting late, so instead we put on some quiet music and all had a little sing song. We all sat there, looking out into the blackness of the Mongolian sky, avidly aware of the coldness behind the windscreen whilst quietly muttering away to the lyrics of everything from AC/DC to Glee until we all started to drift off….

The stunning Altai Mountains

The Russian/Mongolian border crossing, mainly comprised of rally teams

No Mans Land, a stunning stretch of lonely terrain

Buuz – Mongolian lamb dumplings

Day 25 - Impounded!

We woke up literally a few meters away from Mongolia - our target country for the aptly named Mongol Rally. Sleeping in Pete the Saxo, despite its greatness, was never a comfortable thing what with it being about four foot wide. Mackey, the night before, had decided to desert his team mates and rock up to a hotel for the evening (or a small house where the locals would give up their beds for £2) and so Will and I awoke in the cramped conditions at 7am.

I had the back seat, Will had the front seats. Both were as bad as each other; Will had the awkwardness of the gear stick and hand break to contend with, whereas I slept nestled into fuel cans and seatbelt clips. Neither gave us a chance to stretch our legs throughout the entire night, which was a killer. Not overly cold, what with our super 4 season sleeping bags, but having your knees constantly at a 90 degree angle gave you a very broken night's sleep, stirring every 30 minutes to change position.

The look in both of our eyes showed we shared the same tiredness and pain, and unzipping our sleeping bags and opening the car doors, we were shocked to see white everywhere. A lot of white. Not only had the night brought minus-four degree temperatures, it seems it had also deposited a lovely layer of snow on everything - cars, the metal fence we were beginning to call our home, and coating the hills and mountains around us.

As soon as the doors were opened, the frigid air quickly replaced the warmth in the car, and the light came flooding in. Luckily we were already dressed, what with the previous night's temperature and the rather limited interior space of the car suggesting it would be a good idea just to sleep in our clothes! Ed & Emma were already up, having politely waited to 7.30am before starting their car to generate some much needed heat. Paul from the Two Mongoleers also began to rise, as the makeshift curtains in his car (i.e. t-shirts in the windows) began to fall and the sight of the snow flooded the Polo.

The morale of the Mongol Rally campsite (aka. impound lot) was surprisingly good; the snow and ice, ultimate contrasts from the 45 degree heat we'd all experienced a week or two previous, kept us amused and bewildered rather than depressing us all in our cold state like it maybe should have. Hats and gloves were unveiled from people's rucksacks for the first time... well, those people who had the foresight to pack them. I had plenty of hats, but only fingerless gloves that made me look somewhat homeless. Layers of clothes turned out to be the key - that morning, within a few minutes of waking up, I had two t-shirts on, a polo shirt, a fleece, a hoodie and a coat.

Most of the other teams, probably numbering in the teens by this time, began to wake up. Common courtesy meant nearly all teams were anxious to fire their fine vehicles into life and get the heaters on, no doubt from the very early hours of the morning, although everyone waited until another had taken the liberty to be the first. Which was nice, really. Some people would have been sleeping and perhaps woken by the roars of 1 litre engines starting around them. By 7.30am, an ambulance team decided that this was a great time to kick off the day's proceedings, and they started their engine. Within minutes, a chorus of other engines took heed that they weren't the first to create some noise and kicked into action.

Breakfast consisted of cereal bars, a poor excuse for a breakfast we know, but far too cold to cook anything outside. We'd stocked up on Russian cereal bars on the way through, presuming the Mongolian equivalents to be yak testicle or fermented mares milk flavour. With hindsight, we'd probably give the latter ones a try, as the Russian ones sucked. Grape flavour was just wrong, and all the others were coated with hard yoghurt that tasted terrible. But ah well, they filled you up despite not tasting overly pleasant. As we liked to say - it's all part of the rally!

By the time we'd repacked our sleeping backs, shared our amused frustration with our friends, it was nearly 9am and time to hit up the border control building for some paperwork. We'd arrived too late in the day to do anything before we were impounded, so fingers crossed we'd be processed nice and quickly (only a few teams had arrived before us the day earlier, so we were quietly confident that we'd be out by lunch time).

The border building was larger than the Russian equivalent, and much emptier - staffed by a couple of lone Mongolians, one to process the passports and another to process import paperwork.

Obviously completely unprepared when then presented with a small army of passport wielding rallyers! We all filled the building, queuing up nicely stretching back to the main doors. With hindsight, this was a very small number of rallyers - perhaps 15 cars or so. I'd hate to have seen the Mongolian's when confronted with fifty-something cars the next day.

We eventually got through, getting a quick glance to ensure we looked remotely like our passport photos, and then progressed to the import area of the building. Due to us donating our car in Ulaan Baatar and not removing it from the country, a whole load of paperwork had to be filled in. The Adventurists, organisers of the rally, also had to pay a considerable sum in import tax. Still, we had a lot of forms and paperwork to do.

I say 'we", I mean Will. As he was the registered owner of the car, it was down to Will to queue and complete forms - myself and Mackey had gotten away with a considerable amount of work throughout the entire trip!

Paperwork done, it was then just a case of waiting to see when they'd get around to do us and give us our precious 'pink slip', which meant we were allowed to drive through the wide open border gates and progress onwards. We left the building at 10am, returned to our waiting convoy and began the waiting game….

With hindsight, the twiddling of our thumbs was easier than we thought. To be stuck somewhere for a day or two, with no facilities, penned in like animals, it does sound rubbish. But in reality we tried to make the most of it - lots of reading, listening to music, and a hell of a lot of chatting. That's certainly one thing we'd learnt whilst on the rally, a skill that we could take away from it and keep forever; the art of waiting. Being stuck at numerous border points for hours at a time, completely restricted to the general vicinity of Pete the Saxo and very little to keep you entertained; or relegated to the back seat of the car (aka the "lounge") and for hours upon hours having nothing to do other than admire the scenery. Without noticing it, we started the Mongolian border waiting game without complaint, and happily played it the entire day, all without declaring ourselves bored.

We had a little game of football inside the pen, and a Mongolian guard even came over for a kick about with us - although he was quite rubbish. At one point, Mackey kicked the ball over the border fence - something which would have most definitely rendered the ball a lost cause, if we were at any other border crossing in the world. As it was Mongolia, and the front doors were always open (literally), all Mackey had to do was wander out the front to retrieve it.

Some local kids also noticed the brightly coloured collection of strange vehicles, and managed to break into the impound lot. Most of these kids were nice and polite, wanting nothing more than a kick around (or some sweets they'd seen in the car - you see, Mongolian's have no concept of privacy whatsoever. They, of any age, were more than happy to peer inside your car and have a look around. The same with their gers, as they were more than happy for you to poke your head inside and view their houses.)

A couple of the kids were little buggers. They'd rifle through the car's rubbish for things they could steal, continually bug and ask for things, and generally lower the tone of the entire place. One in particular was very annoying, the ring leader of the group, who strategically rifled through team's belongings for things to pilfer. Getting rid of him became the sole aim of our car, as well as our comrades. Mackey I think won the battle by throwing peanuts at him. It might sound a little mean, but we really weren't - this kid was the bane of Mongolia!

Lunchtime came around, although the concept of time did seem to disappear when you were waiting for so long. Every now and then you'd check the time on a phone, completely unsurprised if it was three or four hours before or after your estimated time; waiting was a strange game.

The wind was still blowing hard, bringing down frigid air from the snow-topped mountains. As a result cooking on our little stove was quite a difficult task. To help, we moved Pete the Saxo horizontally in front of the Mongol Mongrels and the Two Mongoleers, to form a crude U shape with the cars and a basic windbreak. It did its job! Lighting the stove then became possible, and we made Russian Super Noodles for everyone (they had nothing on our UK equivalents, but they did make up for their lack of flavour with a handy eating tray and a fork).

Mackey the mechanic was called into action shortly after we'd finished, to have a look at the other Citroen Saxo; it was refusing to start, the diagnosis by the owner being somewhat lacking in anything definitive. All he knew was it wouldn't start and he only reached the Russian border by luck (the car had stopped completely as he reached the top of the last hill, allowing him to coast downhill the last mile to the checkpoint!). He'd been towed through No Man's Land, and now was stranded with us at the Mongolian border. Still, he was happy - he'd made Mongolia! Unfortunately though, even Mackey with the assistance of the very handy Haynes manual couldn't quite figure out what was wrong with it…

The afternoon soon came, watching as we all sat around in our cars and read/listened to music, chatting to our convoy mates about everything and anything. I think I went on about Tresco too much, sounding more like a timeshare salesman than just a content resident. Hopefully I've managed to sell a few holidays though! By 4pm, we had some great news; Ed & Emma had been given the "pink slip", the hallowed piece of paper we'd all been waiting for whilst impounded. The slip meant that the car had officially been imported into Mongolia; the taxes had been paid, the paperwork completed - they were free to leave! (Ironically, the pink slip that had been drummed into us since the beginning about not losing as soon as we received it, never to lose the pink slip, cherish and protect the pink slip etc.; whereas in fact it was a white slip. No trace of pink. Small things like this entertained us, hence the mention).

Percy the 206 was the first of our convoy to leave, a lovely sight accompanied by cheers around the compound as it crept towards the open gates, and traversed that country line we'd all been aiming for. One car done, four to go. This was good progress - Ed had only been waiting 31 hours since first arriving at the Russian border before being unleashed into Mongolia. Next up was Laura and Paul from the Two Mongoleers, who too began the simple task of picking up their now completed pink slip and getting a once over on the car. Not exactly searching for contraband, more just checking the vehicles out, as the lone guard strolled around them inspecting funny little things like the light in the boot, and electronic wing mirrors.

Somehow though, the combination of the two cars and two pink slips meant it was now 5pm; the Mongolian border shut at 5pm. Not good when two of our convoy were allowed out (one of which was actually out), and three of us remained.

My complete hats off to Laura though, for she pulled the best bit of bribery we had ever seen. Basically offering to pay their overtime, plus "a bit extra", Laura actually managed to convince the border guards to stay late and process the last three cars! Laura, we salute you. The border guards did as bribed, and typed like mad on their ancient computers to get Pete the Saxo and his two friends entered and finished.

But, as you know, it was rarely as easy as that on the rally; the computers started crashing. A lot. Rather than just a simple problem, perhaps one that even I could have offered to fix, it turned out to be an internet problem. As I'm sure you can imagine, Mongolia (in particular, it's sparsely populated mountain region) didn't offer the fastest of broadband. Well, it didn't actually offer broadband at all, instead relying on good old fashioned dial up. This is where the problem lay - the border control building, a rather impressive new-ish establishment of ample size, apparently only had one phone line going into the building. A single line supplying every phone and the Internet. So old school in fact, that they'd have to disconnect the Internet to make a call.

The border guards tried for two hours before giving up for the night, even offering us back the "overtime" we paid them. Laura refused to take it but made them promise we'd be first out the following day (which would be Wednesday, day three of our imprisonment). The guards agreed and we retired to our prison, defeated and frustrated. Laura hadn't yet moved her car out of the impound lot, which left Ed as the only one who had been released and enjoyed the freedom of Mongolia.

Ed's independence was not to last. Determined to re-join the convoy despite his brief taste of the liberating air, he drove back up to the gate, and enquired with the guard if he could be let back in.

The bemused guard agreed, more out of amusement than anything else, and Ed willingly re-joined his team mates.

The convoy was whole again, unfortunately though in exactly the same predicament as it was 24 hours prior.

We felt like frontier veterans - we knew how to get through the gates, we knew how to get to the village, we knew where to buy food. Rally teams, having only entered the yard that day, were coming up to us for advice. We were the old lags, been in the longest, had the most knowledge. As such, we greeted complaints of a six hour wait from fellow teams with a nonchalant shrug.

I'll admit it began to get a little frustrating. It was another night in the concrete yard. The temperature was plummeting as once again the day began to slide into night. The lack of hot food was a serious concern and so the five of us decided to go for some more mutton dumplings. We locked up the cars, wrapped up very warm and headed back through the border gates towards the township.

Our usual buuz-shack was shut, something which panicked us a little. We relied on their fantastic dumplings of mutton for warmth and sustenance, without which we'd be forced to try and cook outdoors in the bitter wind and temperatures already touching zero. Luckily though, our noses provided the answer as we caught the waft of buuz as we began to stroll back towards our waiting cars, and found another small cafe. This one was open, although only just. Most definitely open for food, as the lady enquired how many we wanted (and we answered with finger counting), but only just; it was dark. Very dark, both inside and out. I spotted a light bulb a short distance above our heads, but no sign of electricity. The entire place, holding three tables and enough seating space for 18, was illuminated by a single candle struggling to emit enough light to fill a single place let alone the room.

All was fixed with the presenting of the dumplings though - steaming hot, incredibly tasty, and an instant morale booster. Yeah, we were still stuck at the border. Yeah, we'd have been there fifty something hours. Yeah, it probably meant we'd miss the four week party. Yeah, we were cold and tonight would be rubbish. Yeah we hadn't had a shower for three days. Yeah, toilet facilities involved a single hole in the frozen ground shared by many...

But we were filling ourselves with a hot meal, we were in some of the best company we'd ever known, and we were still chatting and laughing despite all those things thrown against us. We were all in the same boat, exhausted and cold, and all laughed at the trials we'd gone through to get this far. Strange I know, but that meal felt like one of the high points of the rally, a huge sense of accomplishment and a weird understanding of the rally began to emerge.

As we finished our meals, the lady serving us did the universal hand signal for sleep - she was asking if we needed somewhere to sleep. Usually, this meant them giving up their own beds to make a few quick Togrogs - about £2's worth per person, a very small price to pay for the luxury of stretching out your legs through the night. A quick team chat, and a few very much wanted that luxury. We also agreed it was necessary for the cars to be watched, especially with the little Mongolian chavs lingering around. Ed & I volunteered for car watch duty, happily reminding ourselves that a terrible night sleep in minus-six degrees temperature whilst in a small family car in a concrete impound yard was, like many other things - all part of the rally.

Mackey, Will & Emma (along with Laura) took them up on the offer of beds, and Ed & I retired to our individual cars to begin the hurried task of constructing a bed setup. I had the back seats once more, providing a little space to lie down with the exception of completely bent knees throughout the night. Ed went for a more vertical position (as their back seats were full of equipment), sleeping in the driver's seat for the whole night.

Darkness had fallen - we'd temporarily split the convoy, the cold Mongolian air that had filled the cars was slowly being warmed by body heat alone, and I drifted off for the second night in the yard....

The border pen, our home for a few days

Waking up in sub-zero temperatures

Our U shaped car formation provided precious little protection

Day 26 – Freedom!

Waking up in a car is never an overly pleasant situation. Don't get me wrong; Pete the Saxo was a god amongst cars. After all, the little French car that attracted so many laughs and doubts had proved so many people wrong, as we sat within 20 feet of Mongolia. But cars were designed for sitting, and not lying.

With the majority of the convoy visiting the local town's hotel (i.e. a local villager's bedroom, very willing to give it up to bring in £8), I had Pete the Saxo and Ed had Percy the Peugeot. Choosing the backseat rather than the front, the sleeping arrangement offered a full 4-foot of length, and two foot of width. Not really a problem, apart from the legroom. Or lack of it. Or the non-existence of it.

It was another cold night, falling to minus six (our coldest of the rally so far). The temperature wasn't really an issue, thanks to our 4 season sleeping bags – the minimal insulation provided by the windows and roof helping, but these bad boy bags probably would have kept us warm enough outside. The leg space though... That was the killer, having my legs at a constant 90 degree angle meant that waking up every 10 minutes to try and move them was an unavoidable definite.

The sunlight poured through the windows at day break for the second morning in a row. The pathetic attempt at curtains made by odd items of clothing in the windows did very little to stop the determined sun's rays, and it was another early start. 7am and the car had filled with the harsh reality that we were still impounded, we were still without comfortable sleeping arrangements, and I was still in the car. Although I (and Ed in Percy) woke up at 7, looking out at the day through the frost covered windscreen gave us reason enough to spend as long as possible in the relative comfort of our sleeping bags, and I happily lay there (scrunched up against a door and a fuel can) delaying the inevitable rush of cold air when I got up.

The rest of the party strolled back into our confine at 8.30am, Will & Emma much happier after a night with leg room. Mackey almost indifferent as he had yet to experience the joy of a car's night sleep. With the motley crew strolling back, I knew it was time to arise and bit the bullet as the back doors of Pete the Saxo were opened, and the frigid air came to greet me.

Getting dressed wasn't a problem, as none of the "hard core convoyers" (aka those that had roughed it in their Mongol Rally vehicles) had bothered to get undressed to sleep, a combination of the temperature and impossibility of undressing in such close quarters. I muttered something about breakfast after re-welcoming everyone back to our prison, contemplating a culinary luxury such as a Russian breakfast bar, the "all natural" snack brighter than the luminous wrapper. The hotel crew had actually been offered morning sustenance, all part of the bargain £2 a night bed & breakfast deal.

According to Will (and keep in mind, the boy will eat anything), they had to resort to subtly putting the various breakfast components into their coat pockets before they left; they didn't want to seem ungrateful when presented with a fine feast, but it seemed Mongolians have a bit of a sweet tooth, and presented them with a range of hard, sugar based candy, each packed full of sweetness and threatening to put anyone who tried them into a diabetic coma.

My lone sleeping bag packed away, it was minutes before we'd settled back into impound life; various seats in various cars occupied by various team members, talking about any subject under the sun. Music was playing quietly around the pen, stories were swapped and water was being boiled for teas and coffees, everyone anxiously awaiting a hot drink to keep the bitter cold out a little longer.

The landscape surrounding the compound still held a certain wow factor, every morning we were greeted by rolling hills and mountains in every direction, all with a light dusting of snow from the cold night before, the tallest peaks never shedding their whiteness in days. The Mongolian border was a strange place, no doubt made even stranger by the now 50 Mongol Rally cars that filled the fenced-off yard in a mish-mash of European engineering, eccentric colours and countless sponsor's stickers. But, we weren't overly stressed with it; we weren't getting angry at the fact we were basically prisoners, we weren't disgusted with the fact we had no facilities whatsoever (other than the 15ft hole they called the toilet), we weren't disgruntled that we'd come so far and now all just sat around… doing nothing… I think we actually started to become adjusted to impound life.

It did give us a chance though to talk, with each other and our team mates, and talk a lot we did. Everything that we'd ever done, ever thought of, ever aspired to be, ever achieved, ever failed at, we talked about it all. I was chatting to Emma about the rally, and how people thrown together from all walks of life (but with similar enthusiasm to do zany challenges) seemed to end up such good friends after a comparably tiny amount of time. Emma's response was of agreement;

"Other than you three boys, I don't think there's anyone else I'd let see me after a week without showering or hair washing in the whole world".

9.30am soon came around, and with it the handful of border guards arriving for work as they strolled through the front gate along the only road, separated from us by a small chain link fence. There was only four or five of them, the most armed wielding a biro or clipboard (I'm sure I wasn't the only one weighing up the risks of making a break for it at some point on our 50+ hour border crossing) and no doubt smug with the attention and smiling faces they received as they passed 130 weary and desperate rallyers. I take that back actually – although many thought that, they were genuinely nice people, just unable to do their jobs with the 1970s style equipment provided for them. We were happy to see them, and for a good reason; for the previous night, we'd attempted to bribe them to get us out with the rest of the convoy…

The guards had just stepped inside the office building, and the doors barely had time to close behind them before the convoy car owners (including Will) had darted in as well. Mackey and I both agreed, it was a great thing Will ended up being the registered car owner on the V5 – any tedious paperwork, and problems at borders and the car owner would often be the one called to sort it out. Poor Will, but I think he began to enjoy it in the end!

Despite the fact that our three remaining impounded cars were the first to go, the car owners were gone for a few hours before any sign of action (another testament to the ancient Mongolian technology they have to use. I almost considered giving them my Macbook if it meant securing our freedom a day or two earlier).

The action did arrive though, in a spectacularly anticlimactic fashion – our wait of 50+ hours, being locked inside a concrete yard and fenced off, anxious to see the stunning country that lay so close (and yet so far), the metal gates and fences keeping us as political prisoners, was all over and done within seconds.

A scrupulously clean-shaven border guard emerged from the control building, the first we'd seen that wore a suit and armed with a clip board. He wandered through the compound towards our car. Attracting the eyes of over a hundred fellow rallyers, all he did was glance at the chassis number, laugh at our face stickers on the rear bumper and gave us the hallowed pink piece of paper. The pink piece of paper (that was actually white) that gave us our freedom, the pink/white piece of paper we'd waited days for, casually handed over after a 10 second inspection.

Not to worry though – we were free!

Although we were re-packed and in the car, mentally revving and ready to go, we had the issue of the other two teams in our convoy to wait for; The Desert Beagles and This Is Our Everest. Luckily though, the comedy mountain of inspections and checks meant the rest of our convoy were done within the hour. Each with our slip of paper in hand, we began to leave the compound and headed towards the (already) open gates towards Mongolia. Sending ourselves off with a torrent of horn tooting and even some cheers from those poor, poor prisoners still locked up, we pushed onwards and the cars tasted Mongolian roads for the very first time.

Whatever happened from here on it, it didn't really matter. Technically, we'd done what we set out to do (in a technically, almost sort of way). Driving from the UK to Mongolia – we had officially driven thousands of miles, in pathetic (sorry Pete the Saxo) cars, across unbelievable terrain and through incredible countries. If we broke down a couple of miles down the road, for me anyway, it wouldn't have been the end of the world.

The Mongol Mongrels lead the way, leaving the compound (as they'd actually been allowed to leave the previous day) and headed a few hundred meters up the road, towards the border village. It was here Ed was flagged down by a man in a little hut – if you've seen Chitty Chitty Bang Bang, it was a "grandpa's hut" sort of hut. In our experience, we found these huts to be occupied by two sorts of people

1. Official police/border soldiers
2. Chancers looking to make a quick buck

Ed duly pulled over, not risking smashing onwards in the case of the occupier being a number 1. The man, although dressed like a number 2, claimed to be an official insurance salesman. His goods for sale? The official Mongolian insurance that we needed to buy, most definitely required to buy, despite looking like something he'd just typed out on notepad and printed on a cheap printer. Ed and his sensibly cynical mind decided that this guy wasn't the real deal, and obviously spotted us Westerners with untold riches, and wanted some for himself. What followed was a hilarious example of the language barrier accelerating an already brewing argument...

Ed tried to gauge how essential this essential insurance really was, and asked basic questions. What with the salesman's inability to speak English, he assumed he was questioning his legitimate nature (which he sort of was), and began threatening Ed with the police if he didn't buy the insurance then and there. Ed, realising that causing trouble for $20 wasn't the best thing to do, agreed to purchase it but told him to wait five minutes – Ed would get his friends (aka us), and we'd all buy in a big group. Lots of insurance sales for the man!

Of course, trying to act out this little plan didn't go to well, and involved the Mongolian salesman and his wife chasing after Ed and his car, whilst taking a photo of his number plate and shouting "SEND NUMBER TO POLICE". Usually that would be cause for worry, but we were soon to find out that it would have taken the nearest police officer about a day to get here. Not really worth it over an argument!

Once the last few convoy cars had caught up with Ed, we re-approached the insurance salesman, his crazy wife and little tiny shed, and started smiling, nodding and waving dollar notes around. Funnily enough, the Mongolian soon changed his tune and happily provided us with the very legitimate insurance documents (although no doubt chuckling away to himself, how he'd just made more Mongolian Togrogs in one day than he did the previous month).

Now fully within the law (although we all think we were firmly legal from the second we entered the country), we finally left sight of the border and our home for the past three days, and pushed onwards. We were in Mongolia! And within 30 minutes, we realised that Mongolia was as epic and mysterious as we'd all imagined (and hoped) it to be. The scenery was incredible, rolling mountain ranges all around us, the entire landscape swathed in a monotonous colour of greeny grey. The roads were… well, there were no roads. We thought we had it bad going through the Ukraine or Kazakhstan – but in Mongolia, there was absolutely no sign of tarmac! Instead, we followed well-worn paths through the plains stretching out as far as the eye could see, yet still managing a maximum of 30mph dodging the natural obstacles that littered our way – boulders and rocks, pot holes and crevices, each with the potential to cause some serious damage to convoy.

We had no idea where we were going – road signs would no doubt be erected as the Mongolian's discovered tarmac, and instead used the age old method of following the sun. The convoy of five cars headed in the best direction we could, following the paths and passed a single vehicle in a few hours of driving (a rather bemused local in an ancient truck), before reaching another small village nestled amongst the hills.

We thought it might be a good idea to check we were headed in the right direction, and stopped at the settlement. As it turned out, we stopped directly in the centre – we think in the village square, on the common green, even though the village had no roads. Just gaps amongst the gers we drove through, before finding a Mongolian man on a motorcycle.

Out came the map (luckily we had a map in Cyrillic, kindly donated by Tim Holyomes – a previous entrant into the rally. If you ever find yourself travelling across Russia, the 'Stans, Mongolia or surrounding area – don't buy a map with the place names in English, no matter how tempting it is) and pointed at our destination. Within two minutes, half the village had come out to greet us, all excited about a random car let alone five of such strange origins. Children ran from their gardens with smiles and waves, locals watched us intently (although seemed to keep a few meters away, as if we were an unknown evil) – such attention, such friendliness, was incredibly endearing. We'd officially been in Mongolia a few hours, but we'd already fallen in love with the country.

The motorbike rider offered to take us past some deceiving paths, paths that we'd no doubt take the wrong one, and point us in the direction we wanted; if we'd be so kind to pay him $2. Bargain! And so we followed a speeding Mongolian on his dirt bike as we waved goodbye to the hamlet and continued towards the first city of Olgii.

The convoy pushed forwards, each car deciding which route to take in the local area – countless paths cut through valleys, all ending up meeting a few miles down the road but each providing their own set of obstacles. Some looked like soft sand, willing to swallow the car up to the axles; others looked more like the lunar landscape with countless boulders. Water became an all-too frequent feature, as our five cars made every effort to avoid the boggy routes. At one point, all five of us had taken different routes; separated from the next car by only 50 meters or so, convoying in a horizontal formation. If we only had a film crew in a helicopter, it would have looked incredible.

Despite our best driving, the cars took a hammering, with 35mph being a convoy top speed for the entire morning. We moaned so much about the Romanian and Ukrainian roads – in their own right, they were terrible. Compare that though to the complete non-existent road surfaces we now travelled on, and we realised we'd acted like spoilt children all that way back.

 The scenery continued to amaze us, driving for hours in wonder as we climbed up and down hills, snaked through valleys and crossed wide steppe. Half way to Olgii, the Beagles at the tip of the convoy came to a stop. As with the camaraderie of the rally, and even more so in the brotherhood of a convoy, we all came to a stop. First thoughts were of a puncture, although no doubt every member of the convoy sharing that deep down fear it was a more serious car issue. As it turned out though, the car was fine. The team was fine.

The reason they stopped however, was a large sign in the middle of the road – a notice, five foot high, declaring 'explosive mines in the area'.

Do we continue? This was the only way we could head, the only path (or group of paths) we'd seen going in this direction for a few hours. Mackey decided to test the water by throwing some rocks ahead into the road, and alongside, perhaps hoping to detonate the waiting ordnance and clearing the way. No explosions though, probably a good thing but I know us males of the group were hoping for some dramatic excitement. Still, we remained parked up with trepidation. Luckily though, a few minutes later, we saw the tell-tale dust cloud of an approaching vehicle, a Mongolian truck older than us all, charging down the road towards us without sharing our worries. That was good enough for us! As soon as he passed, the huge wheels kicking up a dust storm which too rushed passed us, we again set off.

By lunch time, I noticed that Pete the Saxo was struggling a little – third gear just didn't provide power any more, and I relied on second to continue along the road. Before too long however, even second gear (the usual workhorse of any small engine) began to stumble, and first gear had its chance to shine.

Looking at our team mates, it didn't seem to be a problem limited to Pete the Saxo – all cars had slowed to a crawl, and began to get slower. Looking at the car behind us gave us the answer. Without really noticing, we'd ascended half way up a mountain, the sprawling valley below giving us an idea of how far we'd actually gone. As far as the eye could see, sweeping contours of the mountain range carpeted the area in hues of browns and greens. Very little foliage grew in these conditions, arid grasses solitary in their struggle for survival.

There was still a mountain to climb ahead of us however, and it was no longer a regular drive. Each car was shed of its excess passengers, and we drivers had the sole responsibility to drive up the gravel-topped path. The Desert Beagles, Jason and Matt, took first attempt. The 997cc of the Suzuki Swift rallied up the path, kicking up dirt as the tiny engine dragged them to the top. Next were the Two Mongoleers, their Marco (1 litre Volkswagen) Polo driven by Laura. Not being an overly aggressive driver, and probably worried for the potential damage to the car, she decided to take a run up. Laura reversed 50 meters back down the path to a slightly flatter stretch, in order to give herself some forward momentum before the push onwards and upwards.

In her enthusiasm Laura reversed a little too much and straight off the path into a natural ditch. The loose rubble that sat, undisturbed for countless years, happily collected the car as it slid down. Our collective hearts skipped a beat, as we helplessly watched the event unfold. Within a few seconds, the passengers of our faithful convoy had rushed to Laura's aid, pushing the car back onto the path. Back on terra firma, Laura accelerated in a cloud of burning clutch, and the Polo reached the summit.

Ed, avoiding the ditch, took heed of Percy the 106 and followed her without problems. I took control of Pete the Saxo, and with some exciting wheel spinning before traction was finally found, I too began skidding and sliding up the steep trail towards the top. As each of the cars successfully reached the top, cheers and applause echoed around the expanse from jubilant team members. The Terios boys were the last to saunter up, followed by the pedestrian passengers.

At the top, Ed and I checked on our GPS units to find out what sort of altitude we'd reached. Fear not though, as I imagine we have a few readers that would be appalled to read that acronym on a Mongol Rally blog – this GPS unit provided nothing other than longitude, latitude and altitude!

2,535 meters above sea level (roughly 8,300 feet). No wonder the cars were lacking in their usual aggressive power, and we too felt some effects of the thinning air. Will, someone who spends his working day outdoors and rowed competitively, was completely out of breath after the 250 meter walk to the top. Mackey followed quite a long way behind, but eventually made it, struggling for breath and took a well-deserved seat to regain his composure. In true Mackey style, he accompanied this breathless sit down with a Marlboro.

Once at the top though, apparently the tallest peak we'd be facing and signalling the end of the Bayan-Olgii Aimag mountain range, we continued our drive and reached Olgii a couple of hours later.

Olgii was as expected of a Mongolian city, a cluster of buildings of varying styles, condition and age, the local inhabitants still looking slightly unsure about their own city. Mongolia is generations behind even the most underdeveloped nations that I'd ever experienced; but certainly not in a bad way. Olgii, and Mongolia in general, had already struck me as being one of those untouched places on earth where development and progression hadn't started, but because it hadn't been needed. This had been going on for millennia, and only began to creep its way in now.

We stopped for a spot of lunch, or rather a convenience store to pick up some lunch worthy items. This sort of stop was a game in itself, the plethora of random goods with Cyrillic wrappers, where we hoped they showed at least an artist's illustration of the goods inside so we could make an educated guess of what to eat. We managed some strange cheese, some peculiar meat and some very regular bread, along with some biscuits to keep us company on the hundreds of miles still to go.

We received word that another team was on its way to Olgii, and the Beagles really wanted to wait for them. Without knowing how long we might be waiting for (it could have been a matter of minutes, or could have been a day), we were anxious to push on. Ourselves and Ed & Emma had the weakest cars (I'm sorry Pete the Saxo for saying that), and we decided to continue to the journey towards Khovd. We knew that our slower speed would mean the convoy would catch us up before too long. All was agreed and the much-reduced convoy of two set off once again.

10 minutes after leaving the city limits (by city, it was a quarter of the size of Penzance, if not smaller), we'd again been thrown into the Mongolian outback. The steppe now stretched ahead of us as far as we could see, distant hill ranges on either side providing a landmark to ensure we were going the right way. The road and the tarmac we so loved had still failed to form, our driving surface just a worn route through the grassy steppe.

We passed herd after herd of camel and dozens of gers as we drove onwards. Gers are incredible structures – providing ample warmth and space for a traditional Mongolian family, yet able to be constructed within a few hours by a knowledgeable few. There is no owned land in Mongolia, the thousands and thousands of square miles of emptiness simply shared between the people. A family and their herd of livestock, usually goat/camel/horses, would simply pack up their ger once the animals had temporarily stripped the nearby grassland of food, and move somewhere else. Such a simple, sustaining way of life; no materialistic desires to make them unhappy, as they all seemed completely content with their lives and at one with the earth.

Before we knew it, the sun began to set as we approached a grouping of hills and meant our driving for the day was over. We were surprised that the other half of the convoy hadn't yet caught us up but presumed they'd waited longer than anticipated or perhaps found somewhere comfortable to sleep for the night. Driving without the sun to light the way had been a dangerous game for the last few thousand miles, and no more so than Mongolia – the paths we had to follow, that would hopefully take us to the next city on our journey, were hard enough to spot at noon – let alone in the dark.

With 15 minutes or so of dusk remaining, we drove a short way towards the foot of a hill and set up camp. Being just the two teams now, and such veteran campers, we had our sleeping arrangements organized and erected within minutes. Being such close friends, and the fact the temperature was dropping alarmingly fast, we decided to do without a tent each. I shared with Mackey in one of our new, luxury tents (bog standard two man tents, although comparative luxury when imagining the coffins) and Ed & Emma invited Will along to share their palace – their tent was so big, it had rooms. Actual rooms! Their foyer was twice the size of a coffin. Oh, how they lived.

The cooks got about creating a culinary feast, Emma as head chef and myself as Sous/KP, and before long we were sat under the stars between the cars, eating army rations and marvelling how we'd managed to actually get to Mongolia. This was proper camping in the wilderness – other than us, there was no sign man existed. No artificial lights, no roads, no pylons or cables, absolutely nothing for miles around us.

It wasn't long before we all headed to sleep, another day of constant driving taking it's physical and mental toll on us all, and we quickly drifted off anxious to see what the next day would bring....

The convoy is free!

The convoy is lost!

Curious local Mongolian children from a small village

An alarming sign to come across when following the only road in sight

Giving Laura (Two Mongoleers) a 'helping hand' out of the ditch

Climbing the Altai Mountains

Day 27 - We should have brought a boat

We drifted off to sleep the night before quite easily, as every night, as our bodies became impressively adjusted to Mongol Rally life. Despite our beds being nothing more than 1cm of foam to protect against the jagged, rock strewn floor on which we slept, the night soon brought sleep to us all. Until now Ed & Emma had lived in comparative luxury. They had the foresight to bring a double airbed, offering ample comfort against any terrain the world would throw at them. Unfortunately after nearly a month of sleeping in the great outdoors, their precious airbed had developed a puncture.

Any storms aside, we'd normally sleep through until daylight penetrated our tents and stirred us from our rest. Not tonight though, as we were rudely awakened at 2am by some headlights fast approaching our makeshift settlement. It woke me up with a start, not being able to see anything from within the tent other than two glaring lights getting closer and closer...

A very unsettling thing, seeing fast approaching lights through the translucent tent walls accompanied by the sound of a struggling family car as it climbed towards our camp. We had our tents in front of our vehicles, and the approaching car would have nothing to stop it ploughing into us before reaching the mechanical obstacles that were Pete and Percy. As we lay there, our imagination suggesting the car was much closer than it actually was, I tried not to think of the carnage that would be caused if this approaching vehicle didn't stop in time and ploughed straight into our waiting heads.

Perhaps it was the fact we'd just been awoken with a start, but I think I did panic at one point, before relief was granted as the car pulled to a stop close enough to Camp Scilly Mongrels. We were too tired to venture out and see which car had joined our camp, and couldn't stay awake to listen to their tent erecting, and once again drifted off...

The weather picked up whilst we slept, a hard wind and rain buffeting our camp sight but not bothering us too much. After all, it had been nearly a month of roughing it in the great outdoors (with the odd questionable hotel here and there) - I'd pretty much forgotten the luxury of having four walls and a roof, and accepted the bad weather like a seasoned traveller.

The sun slowly rose over the Mongolian steppe as early as ever, and Ed was once again up before anyone else. Our two teams had become one incredibly smoothly over the past week, unwritten rules becoming part of our daily lives. The first up would wake the others, and especially this far into the journey, we were aiming to set off as early as possible each day. It was about 6.30am as we began to rise - first hearing Ed & Emma chatting not too far away, as I stretched (as was possible in the two man tents and not the coffins) and sat up, ready for the day.

Not the most welcome start to the day however, was the sight of Mackey smoking. In his sleeping bag. Inside the tent. The shared tent that housed the both of us. A foot away from me. The boy had issues! Shouting at him to get outside, physically kicking him out much to the amusement of the others was certainly a good way to get out of the warm comfort of my sleeping bag!

We emerged into the cold, fresh morning to inspect any damage the strong winds might have inflicted upon our little village. Straight away we realised the car that had joined us in the middle of the night had attempted to set up camp in the midst of the storm. One of their tents had been erected but then abandoned in preference for the safety of their car. Probably a good thing somehow, as no pegs or ropes held their tent down, instead finding safety by resting up against ours! Without our cars, their bivouac would no doubt be half way to the finish line by now.

No signs of movement from the guest car, the team name of which escapes me, as we went about the regular dismantling and packing of our campsite. We jumped in the cars and began our second day of driving through the Mongolian wilderness. The fresh sun was rising above the distant hills, casting their slow moving shadows across the plains as we continued our journey along worn paths carved into the grassland.

Mongolia was quite a cold place, or certainly at 7am. Hoodies and jackets were a must, as the cars slowly warmed enough to use the heaters to thaw us out a little. Within half an hour of driving though, the morning serenity punctuated by our morning chatter across the CV radios, we came across our first obstacle of the day - a river.

Our first river crossing of the entire trip! We had originally planned to travel the northern route through Mongolia, but had been sensibly warned away from the idea by some kind locals in the first village due to huge amounts of flooding across roads. Rivers would form from no-where, fed from melting snow and ice in the mountains, and cut through the already primitive road system. Despite taking the comparatively safer Southern route, it seemed those darned mountains refused to keep their fluid run offs to just one area of the enormous country.

Luckily for us, it wasn't overly deep - perhaps eight foot wide, but only a foot or so deep. Bowing down to Mackey's immensely more impressive resume of driving experience, Will & I stepped out of the car to let him drive. This gave us a chance to take some photos and video our "first time" at crossing the river, and watched as Mackey did true to his word and successfully traversed the freezing water.

Ed, captaining Percy the 206, followed soon after and managed to get across the torrent of raging water (actually, more babbling brook than a tempest of disaster). We continued along through the wilderness, hoping we were going in the right direction with nothing to follow other than a dirt path and compass heading. Before long however, we came to another river. This time though, it was bigger - twice as wide, deeper, and without the gentle incline of the earth to let us down. Instead, we had a two foot drop from a bank into the water...

Our two cars realised this would be harder than the last, and we parked up on the bank and began to inspect our options. The river looked shallowest where we were, but that large drop from the bank would no doubt plough our front ends into the water, and leave us a little bit stuck. A couple of minutes' walk down each side of our location gave way to no other alternatives - either the river was deeper, much deeper, or the steep bank that slowed our progress only got bigger. We had one option - to enter where we had arrived.

A previous vehicle, be it a rally car or local, had used a 2x4 plank of wood, the wood still remaining embedded into the bank and the other end in the river. A crude ramp, four inches wide, and probably doable. The right hand wheel would have this gentle wooden decline into the water. The left hand wheel though would still have to negotiate the steep drop into the river. With no other choices however, this was to be our way across.

Once again, veteran Mackey volunteered to make the crossing. We all jumped over to the opposite bank (thankfully using some discarded tires in the river - it was 8am, the river was fed from frigid mountain melt water, and none of us particularly wanted to get hypothermia this far away from civilization!) and took our places. Will would guide Mackey to ensure one half of the car remained on the singular plank of wood, Emma took some dramatic photos and I filmed the action. Slowly but surely, Mackey inched his way towards the wood and began his descent into the water...

With lots of shouts of "left", "right", "straight", Pete the Saxo descended well - one half remaining on the plank as the other dipped rather worryingly. As the front bumper entered the water, realising that the car was partially down, Mackey took the decision to hit the accelerator hard - the 1.1 litres of pure grunt roared into action, and with an almighty splash, Pete the Saxo threw itself into the water and powered through, stopping for no man and successfully climbing out the other side.

This was tense. This was worrying. This was all part of the rally!

Ed followed suit, keeping an eye on Mackey's path and planning to follow it to the safety of the opposite side. Percy the 206 was lined up, again one half using the risky plank of wood to descend, with Will directing which way to turn. Inch by inch, Ed set off as the front wheel touched the plank of wood, the rest of our collective team watched with anticipation...

Downwards the car went, the tire wider than the plank by several inches but hanging on as Ed made the half way mark, the silence hanging in the air only broken by the roar of the 206 (what with its broken exhaust) and the bubbling of the fast flowing water. Slowly but surely, the tire continued down its straight path as the front bumper too hit the water.

And then, it all went wrong. The wood, having been soaked by the river and incredibly slippy, had decided to lose its hold of the tire and pushed Percy off. Rather than just have the car slide down into the water however, Percy jumped forward and came to rest on top of the plank - wheels spinning in the air, completely stuck on the wood. This wasn't good.

A silent collection of profanities was shared - the front of the car dipped into the water, and the radiator fan churned up the river and dispensed it through the front grill. Percy had its own water fall, looking much more critical than we hoped it actually was. Straight away, Mackey & Will jumped into action - off came shoes and socks, and they waded into the frigid water to assist Ed. Of course, someone had to film the drama, so unfortunately I remained dry and comparatively warm on the opposite bank.

No amount of pushing or pulling the car provided any movement - Percy was stuck. Out came a spade, a staple tool in the rally (for the spade allowed us to dig holes for fires and the calls of nature) and we began the arduous yet essential task of trying to dig the embedded wood from the bank. Luckily though, the ground was soft (as apparent from the deep channel the water had carved in a short amount of time), and Ed made quick work of digging around the plank of wood.

As the wood began to loosen up, Mackey pulled off a superhero-esque move and grabbed Percy by his wheel arch, lifting with all his might. In truly spectacular fashion, this lifted enough pressure from the wood for Ed to kick it away, and once again leave the 206 free from obstruction. There was the fact that the car was currently at a 45 degree angle with the front bumper implanted in the river, but a few seconds of screeching revs and Peugeot power pushed the rest of the car through the river, and out the other side. Percy was out!

Well, almost. Despite all the previous excitement, eventually getting in the water and traversing the river, Ed didn't quite have enough power to climb up the opposite bank to freedom - the wheels spinning without hope on the wet muddy bank. In such an emergency, who you gonna call? Why, Pete the Saxo of course!

Having already made it to the opposite side, we unravelled our tow rope for the first time (not bad considering we were already in our destination country!). As Mackey and Will were experiencing a little touch of hypothermia after their little paddling session in the freezing river, and had lost all use of their limbs, it was up to me to tow our comrade car out of the river and up to safety.

Which, I'm sure, would be no problem for a veteran driver. Actually, I'd go as far to class us all as veteran drivers after the thousands of miles we'd already driven through some extreme conditions. But towing a car? Something I'd never done. Ah well, in for a penny…

We connected the two cars. I inched Pete the Saxo forward with trepidation. The thought of burning out the clutch whilst thousands of miles away from a replacement weighed heavily over me. We won't go into detail with how many times I stalled, however we eventually did get Percy the 206 out of the river, up the bank and to safer ground.

And so began some truly authentic Rally driving. It was still early in the day, the sun gaining strength and so still requiring more than one layer of clothing. Our first river crossing was an eventual success. Within 10 minutes however, still jubilant that we'd crossed such an enormous raging torrent of water and disaster (that's how we'd tell it to everyone), we came across the second river crossing of the day. Luckily though, this one had kind and gentle inclines going into the relatively shallow water, and we pushed on through like professionals.

As we continued along the Mongolian steppe, the landscape changing every few hours from utter wilderness to rocky mountain paths, we continually bumped into a couple of teams (including some Nissan Micras - these things were unstoppable, the Compact Pussycat girls and the lone rallyer in the Polo). This other convoy had a habit of driving a lot faster than us (a LOT faster than us), but had to stop on a regular basis to fix their wheels and cars. The result was a yo-yo effect we'd have with them - one hour they'd fly past us, a profusion of car horns as they left us in a cloud of desert dust, and the following hour we'd see them all along the side of the road, car jack in hand and usually a hammer, still waving as we overtook and passed them. A true example of The Tortoise and the Hare!

We pushed onwards, not a clue where we were but a destination in mind, the only help we had was from a small key ring compass and by following the ever changing paths carved into the desert. The plan was just, in theory.

You'd never come across a simple path linking A to B. Well, I'm sure there must have been at one point, but as a path became too worn, exposing rocks or just delving too deep into the desert, a new one would be started. As this one became a little bit too well used also, another new one would be born. And so on, and so on. A few decades of this, and what you were left with was a definitive maze of paths that snaked around each other - turning the wilderness of the steppe into the craziest 10 lane motorway you've ever seen. (Not that 10 lanes were needed; you'd probably see one vehicle an hour as you drove along them).

It became an art to navigate these paths, trying to work out which was the "freshest", the one that would cause least damage to the car. The oldest would have churned up jagged rocks or deep trenches, just dying to wreak carnage on the underside of the car (although as we'd proven over and over again, Nick Shiles does make the best sump guards known to man).

As we pushed forwards, we spotted a beautiful sight – a few hundred metres of tarmac entering the city of Khovd, a red carpet for us to drive down, giving us the chance to stock up on supplies and hopefully find the fabled "Mongol Rally Camp". This camp had been advertised at the start line at Goodwood, so many weeks ago, and had promised us such luxuries as hot food and showers. Of course, back then, as we sat on the start line surrounded by UK facilities, we never imagined we'd get so excited about the thought of food and water. As we approached Khovd, we saw the billowing flags alongside a collection of gers. We knew we'd reached the camp.

Although not consisting of much else other than some gers, a few toilets, a makeshift shower and some picnic benches, it was fantastic. Every other rally team would drive through Khovd, thanks to the Northern route through Mongolia now pretty much underwater, and every team stopped to recharge for a few hours.

The hosts were fantastic, and spoke better English than us. They offered us hot food, a tasty noodle dish, and we spent a few hours sat in a homely ger surrounded by fellow rallyers. Not sitting in the cars, not on the move, not being beaten constantly by the rough Mongolian landscape – just chatting, eating and relaxing. It was heaven.

The shower facilities however left a little to be desired. When they worked, they were pretty impressive. A corrugated metal shower cubicle in a field, a power shower (!) fed by an electric petrol generator and a bowser full of water. When the generator worked, and there was water to be used, they did live up to their promise. But... there was only one, and a congregation of 30 rallyers had formed by lunch time! The first few who took advantage of these showers did receive the experience as promised. The rest of us however, had to make do with a literal trickle of cold water. When the bowser ran out of liquid, they did well by improvising – collecting water from a recently dug well, a couple of meters deep, and filtered using a pair of ladies tights.

Still, we all managed to wash, ridding ourselves of the desert dust. We put on some fresh clothes, even if we only stayed that clean for seconds once we got back on the road. It felt amazing.

It also gave us the chance for the biggest car sort out we'd had to date – absolutely everything came out of the cars, each covered in a thick layer of dust, and we filled bin bags of rubbish and junk we'd not be using again. Mackey got called on for some makeshift repairs on Percy the 206, the exhaust again experiencing another bodge job in keeping it attached to the car.

We spent a good couple of hours here, and it was just the refreshing pick up we needed. The cars were more organized, we were much cleaner, well fed and ready to push on. We waited around for the other half of our convoy that we managed to lose the day before, and it wasn't until we pulled out of the rally camp and onto the main road through the city when we spotted them approaching along that short piece of tarmac.

It was very good to see them – the Two Mongoleers, The Desert Beagles and This Is Our Everest, and we chatted about the last few days. Whilst talking however, they were eyeing up the showers and hot food just behind us, obviously desperate to experience the same highs as we just did. Unfortunately though, we'd made the decision to push onwards, and leave the others for a night of camping here.

We all agreed we'd like nothing more than to reform the most excellent convoy that pushed through Kazakhstan, Siberia and the beginnings of Mongolia, and shared the trials of that impound; but, we were approaching our time limit and couldn't afford to waste any more time. Having been stuck in the Ukraine for three days, and the Mongolian border wasting another three days, meant we were very behind on our schedule.

We said our goodbyes, and pushed forward, knowing we probably wouldn't bump into our friends until the finish line. We drove the couple of minutes through the "city" (or in UK scale, the "village") and the precious flat surface was soon replaced by the desert path once more.

The afternoon was filled with the "washboard effect" – the worn desert paths giving way to a washboard surface, which shook the car to pieces. Literally, things started falling off. Crossing them at 20mph just exaggerated the bumps and the car would soon have to be stopped. Eventually though, we found the only way to cross this weird terrain was to travel at MORE than 20mph – 30mph seemed ideal, the fastest we'd travelled in a week, and kept the tyres bouncing over the top of the ridges rather than finding time to implant themselves into the mini troughs.

This was how we spent the entire afternoon – pushing forward in roughly the right direction, absolutely no way to tell our position other than the key ring compass and a lot of silent praying. The two cars swapped their occupants, us all taking turns between Percy and Pete. Believe it or not, but the daily swap was an exciting part of our trip, breaking up the usual monotony of identical companionship as we drove on.

Before we knew it, the sun once again began to set behind the rolling mountains adjoining our flat steppe, the afternoon having disappeared to time. It's a funny thing, driving. A short few hours' drive could seem like a lifetime back in the UK (where a two hour drive qualified as a distant voyage), but on the rally, time had no meaning. Well, it had a meaning, but it had no reference point – we had no appointments we had to remember, we had no start time to our day, we had no finish time. We just... drove. Even boredom had lost its place in the car, its trivial nature of no use when you were an entire world away from normality.

As Mongolia was a little too risky to drive in the dark, what with the spontaneous river systems that sprouted up every now and then, we began to look for a camp. Whereas a week ago, where we'd all spend up to a few hours looking for an ideal camp site (away from the main road, behind the cover of some useful trees, ideally away from popular roads etc.), our requirements were somewhat simplified in the magnificent country that was Mongolia. For as long as we were out of the way of the beaten path (the literal path), then that would be our home for the night.

There were no trees to sleep behind, there were no built up areas to avoid – as far as the eye could see, that was our option. We took a turn off the long, straight path and headed a quarter mile towards some rolling hills nearby. The ground was hard, flat but covered in rocks absolutely everywhere. No matter where we chose to sleep, or even how we slept, we wouldn't be having a comfortable night (our half inch roll mats unfortunately hadn't grown magically whilst in the boot of the car, and Ed & Emma still had a puncture in their luxurious air bed).

Still, we were adventurers, and we pulled up together and began the regular activity of setting up camp. Step one, turn off the car and get out. And, step one was as far as we got. The second we pulled up and the doors were opened, swarmed the most unnatural cloud of mosquitoes the world has ever seen. The moon like landscape, barren and arid, seemed to be the perfect place for mosquitoes to hang out. Words cannot describe the little bastards. Every mosquito, usually enjoying the summer in the UK and Europe, obviously decided to do without their annual vacation this year and all stay at home on the Mongolian lunar-esque surface. And, by the looks of it all, we were their only dinner option in many miles.

We were all out of the car for about 10 seconds before we realised what was happening. In the chaos that followed, I think Mackey actually began to drive away whilst leaving his team behind. Two small European cars ploughed down a slope at dusk, chased by desperate team mates, followed shortly by a cloud of blood hungry bugs following the lights and the smell. It was as if God sent a biblical plague for evil sins we'd carried out. (Probably Mackey).

After that little lesson, we perhaps learnt that the land wasn't ours to inhabit, albeit for just one night. Maybe we'd have to look a little more in depth to find our promised land, and that we did. The sun had set, and the sky was already passing from pastels to deep blues and purples. Light was fading fast, along with any hope we had of finding the perfect camp site. Actually, scrap that, any sort of camp site that wouldn't eat us.

We pushed on for 15 minutes, as day turned into night, and soon it was time to stop. As it turned out, pushing on for that quarter of an hour was the best decision we could of made. Instead of a slope of a mountain, the surface covered with stones and rocks and home to 90% of the world's mosquitoes, we found an indubitable Eden.

The floor was soft sand, no trouble for the cars and heaven for our weary backs; low sand dunes and grasses provided us with our own little private room amongst the thousands of square miles that surrounded us. Best of all, of course, were the very sparse population of local, blood sucking insects. A few, of course, but nothing like the pestilence that bothered us earlier.

With our new home sorted, our entire team happy (Pete & Percy included), we set about our usual chain of affairs – team Supermarket Sweep would get about making dinner for the five valiant rallyers and Ed, Mackey & Will would set up camp, and before long we had a superb armed forces ration pack for dinner. Once again, a huge thanks to our anonymous donor for these – they kept us alive!

Whilst setting up the stove, I thought I heard a noise. An animal noise. But then again, we were in the middle of a pitch black desert and no doubt the scarce plant life would hold a number of insects and small animals. But, being such a veteran camper, I thought nothing more of it, and carried on setting up.

Looking up from the camp stove however, I came face to face with a horse.

It made me jump, the little ninja horse inching its way closer to me without anyone else noticing. Only when I regained my composure, and reeled in my expletives, I realised the horse was not alone. Sat on its back was a small Mongol boy, no older than nine or ten, but in awe at the strange cars that sat near his camp. Luckily he had no idea what I was saying during my little outburst.

Before long, the boy was joined by two others – brothers, friends, who knows. But the three of them were very friendly, watching in amazement at the stove, and our boil in the bag meals. We tried to communicate the best we could, sharing absolutely no words between us, but mutual understanding based on nods and laughs. They got very excited when we offered them a bit of Russian brand cola, each taking a sip and offering it back. We let them keep it, much to their enjoyment (both for the drink contents, and the plastic bottle they'd keep. What a very different world.)

They were very polite, very inquisitive, but I had no idea how we looked to them. These boys lived in nearby gers, fantastically efficient mobile homes/tents without water or electricity. They rode horses from an early age, lived completely off the land, learnt from their elders; to see our cars turn up, with our iPods and our laptops, our boil in the bag food and pop up tents, and Mackey. All very bewildering no doubt, but awe inspiring for the both of us as well.

Once we'd eaten, it took a good five minutes of the universal "sleep" sign before the lads finally got the hint and trotted off on their horses. Well-fed after the meal, comfortable with the sand underneath our sleeping bags, and still over the moon we were somewhere in Mongolia, it wasn't too long before we all drifted off, yet again unaware of what the next day would bring.

Pete the Saxo crossing our first river

The car slips from the plank of wood and Ed is stuck

Mongolian Gers nestling into the mountains behind

Day 28: The comforting expanse

Compared to some of the places we'd woken up (the swamp springs to mind, or the hard ploughed fields), this was heaven. Soft sand to bed down on, small dunes with towering reeds surrounding us, affording a small amount of privacy from the outside world. Yeah, there were a few mosquitoes here and there, but nothing like the swarm of blood suckers we'd considered bunking with an hour before we found our home for a night.

We all got up, bright and early, as was custom on the rally. Ed was yet again the first one up, almost relishing in his first task of the day to wake the rest of us up. Not an overly hard job however, as Will once again bedded down with Ed & Emma inside their palace of a tent, and I shared with Mackey.

There we no signs of our visitors from last night, and the soft sand suggested we had no further guests as we slept. A subconscious effort was all that was needed to pack our camp, and it was time to push onwards.

We managed three meters until we noticed one of the front tyres was completely flat. Not bad going, only a couple flats so far, and we were nearly eight thousand miles into our trip. Will set about changing the tyre, Mackey assisted, and I went about improving Pete the Saxo with things I could find around the local area. The result of which, was a real camel toe, taped to the bonnet. Well, it was more than just the toe - more, a real camel's lower leg. Perfectly preserved in the arid Mongolian sun, it added yet more sense of adventure to the already heroic car.

The wheel was quickly changed, mental notes were made to have it fixed at the first sign of civilisation, and onwards we went. Today our target was Altai - a large city (well, for Mongolia) and the capital of the Govi-Altai province. We'd heard that there was an airport here, and so looked forward to the hustle and bustle of a metropolis after the last week of wilderness.

First though, we had desert and mountains to cross. Without road signs to follow, and certainly no GPS to answer to, we did what we did best - headed East, and followed any track we could. This sounds easy, of course. Just follow the road, or the closest thing to a road. We found tracks, the same worn paths through the desert made over a hundred years, but they never stayed in one direction.

The path we followed swooped North, then swooped South; other paths seemed to merge into our own, before shattering into half a dozen paths a couple of miles further, the correct one merely an educated guess. The conditions remained shockingly bad; almost comical, we looked back as we complained incessantly about the Eastern European roads. To be fair to our original moans, they were terribly bad - but at least they were straight, at least they were tarmac'd (mostly)!

Pete the Saxo and Percy the Peugeot continued on none the less through our final country, performing their job admirably. They took a constant beating on these rough paths, their shock absorbers and suspension getting absolutely pounded by the corrugated surface on which they happily bounced over. Imagine some car testing video you might have seen on TV - some specialist machine causing the wheels to bounce to their maximum safe levels, just to test their ability. It was like this - but constantly, for 12 hours a day.

As we drove through the wilderness, half of the landscape dominated by the Altai mountain range to our north, and the Gobi Desert to our East, we came across another group of rally teams - the two Micras, and the Compact Pussycats in their Hi-Jet. These guys made a regular appearance as we travelled through Mongolia - they absolutely tore across the desert, the poor Micras merely skimming the top of the rough surface as they easily doubled our speed. But, they reaped the problems from this aggressive tactic!

Before we knew it, it was lunch time - and we happened to stop by a truck stop café. Well, I think it was more suited for anything and everything that passed, a lone group of whitewashed outbuildings in the middle of no-where, offering much needed sustenance to anyone who passed - us included. We parked up, careful not to run over the owner's dog napping in the midday sun, and stepped inside. A long banquet style table, complete with the benches you'd find at school. We were the only guests, so we sat at one end and began to chat amongst ourselves.

As we sat and talked about the day so far, Will seemed unhappy with the woollen blanket that lay behind him on a raised flat surface, and so pushed it further away. Possibly more than a push -

a shove would probably be more accurate, but the weight underneath it seemed to surprise him. It was only at the third shove, did the blanket move; along with the snores and grunts of the Mongolian local asleep underneath! Little did we know, we weren't alone at all - instead sharing the room with a sleeping trucker, which Will had seen fit to push out of the way. Of course, the rest of us found this hilarious, as we giggled under hushed tones as you would do at the back of a classroom.

The cafe owner stepped into the room, and asked us what we wanted. Luckily, we asked for tea - it seemed to be the only drink on the menu, and before long our host reappeared along with two floral flasks and cups. Emma did the honours and poured our cups - tea, whether it was beautiful PG tips or Mongolian Chai, was a fantastic thing. Very stereotypically British, we all looked forward to it.

As the liquid was poured, we looked a little disappointed at the colour - very weak, far too milky. Perhaps only a singular tea bag struggled to diffuse an entire flask of water? Either way, it was welcome fluid after a morning of dusty driving. We all took the bowl-like cup in two hands, and took a deep mouthful.

Salty tea.

Who in their right minds would think salty tea would be a good idea?! After Ed, Emma, Mackey, Will and I struggled to swallow the first mouthful, we all burst into laughter. Here we were, in the middle of the Mongolian wilderness, in a strange roadside cafe, sitting in front of sleeping trucker Will had just abused, drinking hot salted tea. A slight dawn of realisation perhaps, but any frustration we had with the day soon got swallowed by the tears of laughter we all shared.

It was a good feeling - there'd been good times in the last few days, but a lot of tough times as well, the relentless grit at bashing through our expedition. We'd pushed on and on, so close to the end, but seemingly so far. To end up drinking the vilest drink in the world, in a situation that probably no one else would find funny, was a welcome distraction from everything else.

Before too long, as we ordered lunch (with absolutely no idea what was to come out - just nodding when the Mongolian owner motioned for food), we were joined by the Micra lot (Hass and company). The school-esque style bench and lunch table was now full, 10 on each side, anxiously awaiting the mysterious lunch. What came out wasn't the worst thing we'd ever eaten; a bowl of watery noodles, strange vegetables and questionable meat (which we couldn't quite work out which animal it had come from), a traditional Mongolian lunch. Some of us on the table appreciated it more than others, but it was nice to sit around as a big collective and take an hour from the relentless and punishing driving.

We settled the bill, comparative pennies, and all bundled back into our cars to restart the journey to Altai. We waited for Ed to reverse the 206 back onto the path, and what seemed like slow motion, helplessly watched as Ed (despite the countless thousands of empty square miles surrounding our small group of cars) reversed straight into a parked Micra! Lots of laughter, a few choked back tears, but luckily not much damage - a smashed front headlight on the Micra, and Percy the Peugeot remained unscathed.

Of course, we were all rally brethren. Accidents happened! The Micra boys laughed it off, much to the embarrassment of Ed, and the second attempt to get back on the road went much smoother - Ed managed NOT to crash into one of the only cars in a hundred square miles, and onwards we went.

The rest of the day was relatively uneventful, still at the mercy of the Mongolian landscape. The desert stretched out as far as our eyes could see, the travelling surface still nothing more than worn tracks we were becoming so used to. The only stop we took for the rest of the day was a David Attenborough style look at a herd of wild camels; a dozen or so of them, in the middle of no-where, obviously keen for some attention. Will, our roving animal expert, took the video camera and decided to see how close he could get to one…

Despite his ninja like steps, the camel didn't hang around too long. I provided some comedy commentary over the CB Radio for our small group to hear, probably the causing factor which resulted in the camel bolting (although, strangely, Will found a camel with a Swastika on its face).

After our little break, an opportunity to take in a minuscule part of this amazing country, we started up our chariots and continued on towards Altai. We'd read in Em's Lonely Planet that there was a hotel that boasted such luxuries as hot water and hot food. That was our target, and to get there meant a long afternoon's drive with minimal stops (which at that moment seemed dependant on whether Percy the Peugeot wanted another flat tire).

The afternoon drive seemed never ending - the landscape never changed, desert expanse for thousands of miles fringed by some distant mountains, completely unable to gauge any sort of scale - for all we knew, they could have been 10 or 100 miles away. For hours upon hours, we drove along the desert paths - one minute along the corrugated hard surface that continually shook our poor cars (and selves) to bits, the next along a freshly worn path that seemed forgiving after the first.

Eventually though, we did approach those mountains that framed our point of view for days. Our location on our maps was nothing more than an educated guess. Perhaps even less than that - we knew we were no longer in Olgii, and not yet at Altai. Somewhere in-between. Too far north, too far south, was anyone's guess. We were in a stretch of desert hundreds of miles wide and blindly heading in a Westerly direction. The £2 key ring compass I'd bought started to turn into one of the best buys of the entire trip.

It was strange; in the UK, anything more than a one hour car trip inevitably descended into aimlessly flicking through radio stations, blindly gazing out towards the repetitive landscape bordering the motorways and A roads. Mongolia though, it was different. Well, not all of it. The landscape probably couldn't get more repetitive - at least you have other cars and interesting road signs to admire in the UK. But Mongolia, there was nothing - literally, nothing. Although it was so repetitive, it still held a certain awe factor within us all.

Music and chats filled the car as it bumped over the rough surface, the back seat passenger perhaps even trying to steal an hours sleep; but even gazing out towards the horizon, the sheer expanse nothing more than dust and sand, or someone's selection of music the only thing filling the air, you still didn't get bored. Maybe the nothingness that lay in front of us, behind us, all around us, gave way for time to think; the lack of trivial distractions like road signs and anonymous drivers gave us all a chance to appreciate where we were; what we were doing; who we were.

Perhaps that last paragraph sounds a little too "new age" - but it's very hard to put into words! Hopefully this is just another reason why you, whoever you are reading this, really do need to do the rally.

After an endless few hours, those mountains that remained just too far to make out any detail began to burgeon before us. What was an obscure prominence of earth began to transform into tangible mountains. The thought of something other to travel through excited us all (simple things, simple minds), and that following hour or two flew by much faster. Before too long, we reached the foot of them, and followed the path as it moved from the level plane of the desert to an ascending, windy trail through the peaks.

A welcome change from the straight lines of the desert, this new road/trail/path was a lot more interesting as it snaked through the hills and mountains. We ascended and descended, the cars never faltering in their mission, and we all felt as if we were getting closer. Perhaps a skill picked up, what with us being veteran adventurers now, but we all felt it - Altai was close.

The 20th hill/mountain we passed over/around, and there it was - the great city of Altai, one of the top 15 Mongolian cities (by population), the welcome oasis in the desert; except, of course, it wasn't the sprawling metropolis we expected. In fact, it looked more in size like a sprawling village. The number of houses/buildings with more than one floor could be counted on one hand, the majority of the place filled with gers and tents of some sort. We did though embrace the tarmac that weaved through this shanty-city. As soon as we reached the city (!) limit, the dirt and dust gave way to this black carpet of indulgence (well, the tarmac still contained pot holes of alarming proportion, but beggars can't be choosers!) and we rode further into the city like triumphant voyagers.

Following the rudimentary map in our Mongolian guide, we set sail for the hotel, which promised a large number of rooms (touching into double digits) and a restaurant. Perfect, we'd all agreed, just as we wanted. As mentioned a lot in the last paragraph, it wasn't a large place - but the complete lack of road signs or recognisable, navigable signs or marks meant we were driving blind (again).

A couple of trips around the entire city (literally, driving around the entire thing in 10 minutes and ending up back at the start), we began to get a feel of the layout; Ed & Ems then successfully located our hotel for the night. Understandably, what with the country nestling under Russia, the hotel was in the style of the bygone era. A big imposing building, it was our home for the night. We parked up, grateful for the chance to stretch our legs and shake the dust from our hair, and made our way into the waiting reception.

The receptionist seemed surprised to see such a motley crew enter the double doors, but that look passed when she closely examined the state of us and our vehicles. No doubt many a Mongol Rallyer had passed through those doors in their quest for the finish line. We enquired about rooms, and were told three were available; an en-suite, a double and a single. The happy couple took the en-suite, the cousins took the double, and I had the single.

If you'd visited this hotel as a regular holiday-maker (two weeks in the Summer holidays at a nice Mongolian destination) you'd most likely have stormed right back down to the reception without even unpacking, demanding an upgrade. Whereas in fact, you were in the deluxe suite already. For us weary adventurers, this deluxe suite was deluxe enough for us. We had everything we needed; a bed, four walls and a roof.

Anything more than that, advertised or not, was lacking; the "en-suite" rooms consisted of a toilet, and a shower that didn't work. The other rooms shared a bathroom with half the hotel, a dribble of lukewarm water fed by a hosepipe was the promised shower. Still, it had Western style toilets – no more digging our own hole in the desert!

After a quick shower and freshen up, the five of us headed down to the in-hotel restaurant. Not overly big, probably six tables, a couple of which already in use. We sat down, ordered some cold beers and shared an unspoken satisfaction with the world. The beer tasted surprisingly good, we were comparatively clean, we had a roof above our heads for the night, and were about to eat something that hadn't come out of a foil packet.

It wasn't a huge menu, a single sheet of paper listed with Mongolian dishes;

puntuuztzee khuurga, narnee maksan khuurga, chochgnegei bansh, tomcnee khuchmal, ondogtsee bnooteic, uzzngei budaa.

No, that isn't me haphazardly smashing my hands on the keyboard, that's some real Mongolian cuisine there. Luckily however, the menu did offer a translation – of sorts. They'd made the effort to translate into English, although the translations didn't always make sense:

* puntuuztzee khuurga
   Great string of noodle the beefy

Still, it was hot, it was fresh, and we didn't have to cook it on a stove the size of a tea cup. The menu looked great.

The waitress came over, somewhat amused by us, and asked us what we wanted. Instead of reading, and no doubt failing miserably at the near impossible pronunciation, we resorted to the point and nod. It's a universal constant – everyone knows what the point and nod meant.

We started off with the nice things – "great string of noodle the beef" sounded great, as did "breast chicken cheese nice cheese". But as we went through the motions and chose our meals, the waitress uttered "no have" all too many times. In fact, out of 15 items, they only had three dishes available! It would have been much, much quicker for her to have just pointed to the ones we wanted first, rather than let us go through everything else. Maybe that was her evening entertainment!

To give credit where credit was due, what came out was lovely, as was that evening – the five of us, sat around the table, still ecstatic with our progress so far, very happy with a good day's driving, and inching closer and closer to Ulaan Baatar and the finish line that awaited us. We didn't have a late night; contrary to popular belief, sitting down for 12 hours a day was very tiring. With a few beers and a good (yet unknown) meal inside us, a couple hours of chatting about the day (and journey) so far amongst company you couldn't tire of, we all retired for the evening, ready for the final push to UB.

Salty tea

Will realising he's been pushing a sleeping Mongolian trucker

Attempting a career in animal documentary

Day 29 - Loving/Hating the Desert

I was going to start this day with "Waking up in the hotel…", but it sounds far too much like a nice vacation somewhere; a European city break perhaps. The word "hotel" usually conjures up feelings of luxuries, of thoughts of extravagant living, ideas of relaxation and the concept of tranquillity. True, we were technically in a hotel, but I wanted to dispel that myth straight away for any doubters reading this blog. To give it credit it was warm, dry and hospitable. Quite clean as well, with only a few stains on the bed sheets and curtains. But this wasn't the "hotel" break you might have subconsciously evoked in your mind - this was just a fleeting chance we had to sleep in a real building (with walls! and ceilings!) in a real bed (albeit a little firm and basic) with real facilities (running water).

We had a bit of a lie in for once, the brick walls offering somewhat more of a barrier against the morning sun than our tents, and it was at least 8.30am before we all began to stir. I think I speak for the five of us when I say, that short lie in was inspiring - a brief chance to recharge our batteries that had so worn out over the last week of sleeping and eating rough. Breakfast wasn't an option within the hotel, so we were in no real rush to get up, instead enjoying the chance to properly gauge the amount of (or in reality, how alarmingly little) clean clothes we had and the chance of another shower before we re-joined the dusty Mongolian wilderness.

What with Ed & Emma's "en-suite room" being slightly faulty (a more accurate description would have just been "room"), we all made do with the communal showers. They weren't too bad - wet room style, a hose pipe attached to some taps with a shower head screwed to the wall. I went first, and straight away made the rookie mistake of mixing up the taps - it seemed the hot water came out of the cold tap, and vice versa. A close, nippy call. But crisis averted, and once again the shower washed away the remnants of the Mongolian dust hiding in my hair, and replenished my energy like a withered plant.

Will though, didn't quite get over that first hurdle - having felt the cold water coming out of the red-topped tap, he gave up; instead just manning up and showering in the cold stream out of necessity rather than indulgence. Poor Will. With our bags packed up once more, we headed out of the hotel (considering the very limited selection in the restaurant, we correctly surmised that breakfast wasn't on offer) to sort out the cars. Despite not camping last night, and so the cars didn't need the enormous daily repack as usual, they still needed a good sort out every day.

We had a few tasks to complete whilst in the relative civilisation of Altai - several punctured wheels needed repairing (especially if the last few days were anything to go by), we needed to restock with food and water, and the small issue of flights home was beckoning - we were theoretically only a couple of days away from the finish line, but had no idea how the three of us were going to get home! Ed & Emma were their usual delightfully organised selves, already had their UB > Beijing > UK trip all booked.

Mackey and Ed took our faithful chariots off into the maze that was Altai in the search for a mechanic. We all agreed that these mechanics would no doubt be making an absolute fortune; not only from fleecing weary rallyers such as ourselves (after all - who know how much a wheel repair really cost in the middle of Mongolia?) but from the locals who unquestionably suffered from punctures several orders of magnitude more than us UK folk, spoiled with abundant smooth tarmac. Will, Ems and I were given the restocking mission; enough food and water to keep us going to the finish line, and hopefully some internet (but we weren't holding our breaths for the latter - we were in the middle of the most geographically inhospitable place we'd ever been!)

Off went the cars, and so the three of us strolled away from the hotel and into "town", which we identified as being a couple of well paved roads and shops flanking either side. Trying to work out the difference between the laundry and the grocery store was merely trial and error, but on the third attempt we found a shop that stocked an interesting variety of edible goods.

One thing I've noticed about shops the further away from home, was how little they had stocked. Of course, you could theorise that this was due to the lower footfall and customer numbers; but their shelves often just had a single product; if someone bought it, there wasn't a big stack behind to choose from, and you were out of luck. Another observation; many of the products were shelved behind the main counter - if you wanted something, you asked the assistant to get it for you. Who knows why, the areas we were in didn't seem to be as crime ridden as this particular shop setup would suggest, but the complete language barrier we all faced when asking for things made our shopping experience very testing at times!

This particular shop however, managed by two local Mongolian women, was very good to us; they were extremely happy to see three smiling European customers, and allowed us behind the counter to select our own goods! They were rather good saleswomen as well, persuading us to buy a whole range of things we really didn't need or want (including some interesting Mongolian fortified wine) and a range of biscuits and snacks that would see us through to the end. With snacks purchased, water stocked up, we departed the shop and continued down the "main" street, past the other two shops, and reached the main city square.

With no idea how Ed & Mackey were faring with the tyre task in hand, we continued with our own mission - this time, to find internet. And as if Тенгери (the Mongolian God of the sky, but you knew that) was looking down at us, what was the only visible commercial building on the central square? Why, a fully stocked modern internet cafe of course! Certainly surprising, giving our current location a thousand miles away from modern civilisation! But, it had exactly what we needed; multiple computers that worked, relatively fast broadband, a chance for us to update the photos and blogs. Oh, and air conditioned as well! I must remember to pray to Тенгери sometime…

A short while later Ed & Mackey walked in - not quite sure how they found us in this sprawling metropolis, but they returned triumphant - all tyres had been patched up at the official Mongol Rally garage (well, probably not overly official, but they were called "the Mongol Rally Garage"!). Whilst we had the luxury of internet, we decided it might be a good idea to buy our flights home, what with us being so close to the finish line.

I hit up the usual flight comparison sites, worrying at some of the prices that were coming up - £1,500 for a single, one way ticket back to the UK? It was probably cheaper to stay in Mongolia and start a new life! Eventually though, I hit the jackpot. £400, one way, straight back to sunny old England. Three Adults... check.... Mongolia to London... check... Add to basket.... check.

Luckily though, eagle eyed Mackey noticed my subconscious desire for the adventure to last a bit longer, and spotted the flight date was the end of October. If I had gone through with the checkout process, we'd all find ourselves in Mongolia for another couple of months (and most likely without jobs to return to). The correct dates were put in, Aeroflot (as predicted) were the cheapest, and probably nothing to do with the fact they have the worst airline safety record IN THE WORLD. The price rose from £400 to £750 each, but still the most economical way of getting home. We'd be flying via Moscow, yet another chance to re-enter Russia, the third time this trip. Well, if you count the big problems we had at the Kazakh / Russian border with our paperwork, and having to go backwards and forwards through both sides, it was more like the 10th time we'd visited the mega-state.

With the blog updated, family contacted, photos uploaded and flights booked, it was once again time to set off into the great unknown.

With the "city" still so very clear in our rear view mirror, the desert wasted no time in replacing the nice tarmac roads with the carved paths once again. I'd like to say we missed it, the roughness of the journey, the adventure on a dirt track - but truth was, it was a punishing drive again - both for us, and the cars. Still, adventurers we were, and we ploughed on regardless.

The drive was filled with an expanse of nothingness. The hills we'd climbed the night before, to find Altai, soon evaporated. Yet again we were surrounding by thousands of square miles of emptiness, void of anything other than sand and dust, and the rough path we followed.

What made things even more difficult though, was when this path split - just, for no reason other than a whimsical fancy, it bisected into a pair of paths, each not quite following the same direction and so separated by an ever growing wedge of desert the further along we drove. After driving for a couple of hours away from Altai, this regular split happened, but both paths strangely headed in roughly similar directions. Which one do we take?! Having realised that the decision would be nothing more than an educated guess and a glance at the compass, we picked one - one that seemed to be headed more Easterly than the other, which we noticed was bending off towards the North. Path number two it was - our two teams agreeing over the CB Radio, and onwards we went.

It wasn't for 45 minutes of following path #2, that we realised that our direction on the £2 compass was slowly moving.... East.... South East East... South South East.... South. Damn. Although I'd have liked to have crossed the Gobi Desert and visited China, this wasn't the right time to do so. We'd picked the wrong path, and we'd travelled a good few miles down this windy, incorrect path. We were in the middle of the desert, no idea where the correct path was - it could have been 1, or 80 miles away.

Ah well - this was what the adventure was all about! Well, not all about getting lost, but you know what I mean - getting into trouble, and finding our way out of it. The land around the road/path was surprisingly good - in fact, it was a better driving surface that the path! Very flat desert, a few withered shrubs regularly dotted the expanse, but minimal obstacles - no big rocks as far as we could see.

The trouble however, was to leave the relative safety of the worn path and to venture into the literal great unknown. Was this just setting us up for disaster? At least the path we were on was occasionally used by vehicles (even if they were annual Mongol Rally teams). Should we really gamble on attempting to re-join the correct path using a blind guess of direction? Or should we double back, waste hours, and play it safe?

We were quite lost really. Not just on the wrong path, but on the map. We knew we'd passed Altai, and spent a day driving. In which direction? Not overly sure. Just somewhere to the right of Altai. "Right" – not even a geographical heading! After a little team meeting, the five of us deciding what to do, our prayers were answered. In the distance, in a general North direction, we saw the tale-tale cloud of dust being thrown up in the air by a large vehicle - a truck perhaps. Mackey, who continued to fancy himself as Colin McRae reincarnated, decided we should try and catch it up - and so we did.

The three Scilly boys jumped into Pete the Saxo, and began to tear across the barren land, leaving the path behind (and the Peugeot to catch up at a less suicidal pace.) Mackey loved the challenge – to catch the bus that was hurtling in the wrong direction, separated by a mile or two across completely unknown ground. I'd have to agree, it was probably the most excitement we'd had in a long time. No doubt the bus/truck saw us, a tiny blue European car hurtling towards them at breakneck speeds (well, about 40mph), but onwards they went regardless. Only one thing to do Mackey - floor it. And so he did…

Five minutes of wild driving, avoiding a couple of rocks and mounds, we had got close enough to the bus (as it turned out) to wave it down, and stop it did. I jumped out the car, smiling to show the perplexed Mongolian driver we weren't crazy, although I'm sure it did no good. Map in hand, we walked up to the bus door as it swung open. We were greeted by a forty-something, vest wearing, cigarette smoking driver along with his collection of passengers, which we suspected were his family.

This weathered driver, bald and with a friendly puzzled look on his face, didn't seem to be hassled by our interception. He tried a few words of Mongolian language, but soon realised we were a long way from home and without the common tongue. His passengers/family also shared the mutual curiosity – a small group spanning several generations arose from their seats, smiling and waving at us.

We had a map - probably the best quality map these guys had ever seen - but trying to ask the question

"Where are we? At the moment, where are we right now?"

in mutually understandable sign language was near on impossible. A group of five Mongolian men, who looked to be the most able of the group, joined us on the desert floor. There was a nice feeling in the air. No suspicious behaviour or sceptical attitudes, just a general ambience of genuine willingness and support.

I tried to ask a simple question - "Where are we?". I was pointing at the ground, I was drawing crosses on the ground, jumping around like a mad man... but to no use. The five simply looked at me, perplexed, amused.

Still, they were nice Mongolians - they laughed at us, the smiled, and the Mongolian driver was so nice as to offer me some of his drink…

Yes, it was that drink we'd all heard about, but managed to avoid up to now. "Kumis" - basically alcoholic horse's milk. Not just that, but warm. Very warm. And this particular driver was kind enough to offer it to me from his own drinking bottle - something that resembled an old Robinson's squash bottle, but looked older than me. Just looking at the bottle gave my stomach a little turn - we'd heard rumours that the taste was similar to Gorgonzola, with a texture not too far away from month old milk.

Ems, of course, found this delightfully hilarious - so much so, she quite loudly stated "It would be very rude not to, Drucey!". Damn that girl. Still, if it didn't kill me, it would make me stronger. (But would probably kill me). With a grateful smile, I took the bottle and took a swig; not too small as to insult the driver, but not too big either.

Result? Yeah, tasted as bad as we'd been told. Quite sweet, but with a definite hint of blue cottage cheese. Lovely. Karma would see the world right though. Having laughed through the entire thing, the driver was kind enough to offer Ems some. Of course, I did the only thing I could, and told her how rude it would be not to...

After ten minutes of chatting/mumbling with the bus-load of Mongolians (the taste of that nasty drink still very much weighing heavily on our stomachs), they decided to continue their cross-desert journey and we bid farewell. With a better understanding on our current location in the world, we felt confident we were heading in the right direction to the next town and waved them off as the bus roared to life.

Before we had a chance to follow suit and continue, we noticed a cloud of dust approaching us - too small to be a bus or car, but completely alone amongst the hundreds of square kilometres that surrounded us.

The cloud of dust was soon seen to surround a motorbike rider, and as it got closer, we realised it wasn't a local - instead, it was a rather nice BMW. The rider pulled up next to our cars, probably as curious to see us as we were him, and took off his helmet. A Belgian man who was touring Asia with some friends, a Belgian man who was really hoping we'd seen his friends.

After a share of pleasantries, we discovered he'd lost them (somehow) in the desert. With little idea of where he was, and absolutely no idea of his fellow rider's locations, he'd stopped to ask us if we'd seen them. Unfortunately we hadn't, and I felt terrible telling him that - mobile phone signal was unheard of in these parts (actually, mobile phones were probably unheard of), and he was desperately trying to find his friends.

We shared what little information we did have - we knew a rough location of where we stood and talked, and a general direction of our next stop, the town of Bayankhongor. The Belgian rider decided that he'd probably find hope in that town, common sense hopefully bringing his party back together, and with thanks, he once again set off.

The little things like this really did put the world into a strange perspective. Here we were, without accurate knowledge of our location, adrift in thousands of square miles of empty land. One second we shared laughs (and kumis) with a travelling Mongolian family going one way, and the next helped a Belgian motorcyclist who'd lost his friends travelling the other. The world is an enormous place, but man makes it so much smaller.

With the desert convoy back to just our two cars, we also set off for the distant town. It was late afternoon by now - any hopes of a hotel or shower were fading fast, as we continued along the desert paths. We did pass through a couple of small settlements, lone beacons of humanity amongst the wilderness, which we hoped was proof we were going in the right direction. As the sun began to set on the horizon, the sky becoming an intense battle between the blue of day and purple of dusk, we came across a little obstacle that needed to be overcome…

The path we had been driving on, along with all nearby paths, ended abruptly at the bank of a very wide river. No doubt this was a young tributary, for no bridges, fjords or ferries were apparent - but still 150ft foot of water intersected our way. Bugger.

A few gers found their home on one side, with a pack of Mongolian children excitedly running out to meet us. We pulled up next to the water, all got out and looked with astonishment and worry at the size of the river in front of us. Much, much larger than anything we'd attempted to cross before. This didn't look good. The kids though, obviously well versed with the techniques needed to cross it, were very happy to offer their assistance. They swarmed around our cars, trying to point us in the right direction to cross - the sort of knowledge that only the locals would know, a sweeping curve across one particular part that seemed to be the shallowest.

One of the kids began to wade into the relatively fast flowing water, showing the level to rise to thigh level. Not too scary when the legs belonged to a five year old, but if anything went wrong with this crossing, we were doomed - hundreds of kilometres away from a mechanic, supplies or help. The kids though, they were confident enough for us all, that we'd make it through. (Which was nice, so nice in fact, that Ed punched one. He claimed it was an accident whilst opening a car door, punching a defenceless four year old Mongolian boy, but tears did flow. We managed to stop them with bribes of Russian sweets..)

The sun was setting very fast now - darkness had won the battle, and we had to turn our headlights on to survey and plan. As I got out of the car, having locked the doors just in case the inquisitive Mongolian children decided they liked the shiny laptop, I heard Will & Mackey in hysterical laughter. I grabbed the video camera, walked over and realised what they were laughing at - a Mongolian bloke on his ancient Soviet motorbike was attempting to cross the torrent of water, aided by some idiot pushing him.

Only after zooming in, however, did I realise that idiot was none other than our very own Ed! Somehow, he'd been roped in to help - and not only the guy on the motorbike, but also the goat tied to the back seat. You read that correctly - there was a live goat, feet bound by rope, tied to the back seat - no doubt wondering what the hell was going on, being pushed through a river by a very well-spoken Notting Hill resident up to his knees in water. Despite the motorbike stalling half way across, and the rest of our two teams crying with laughter on the shore, Ed managed to get them safely to the other side. What a hero.

Mackey prepared as much as he could – he sacrificed his socks to cover the air intake on our two cars, to try and limit any water creeping in and wrecking the remaining journey. To be fair though, I doubt those socks had been washed since the UK. A bit of water would probably have been a good thing.

With the help of the kids, and Ed's motorbike buddy, we worked out the best way to cross. Still 2ft deep in places, enough to cover the headlights of the car with the bow wave, it was time to go. What little light remained in the vast Mongolian sky was fleeting - it was now or never.

Will & I removed our shoes and socks, and began to wade through. Ems jumped in with Mackey, as he took the lead and inched closer to the river. In typical Mackey greatness, the car revved and jumped into the water. The Mongolian kids had made a human barrier in the river, marking out where we shouldn't be driving (as the river seemed to get much deeper off this sweeping curve - Saxos and 6ft of water don't play nice.

With Pete the Saxo charging through the water, the headlights illuminating more underwater than over, our hearts stopped - half way across, we heard a silence as the engine stalled. Pete the Saxo had stopped, half way across an enormous river, the bow wave beginning to fade and water approaching the engine. Whether we had a Mongolian god looking over us (and probably laughing his ass off) or not, Mackey quickly restarted the car, and it roared back into life. Foot on the accelerator, the car pushed the water forward, and actually landed on the other side.

An epic feeling spread around the river banks, as a couple of other teams had somehow made their way to the river, despite it being pretty much night now. With Ed, Will and I still on the first bank, we shared what information we had - listen to the kids, don't punch the kids, drive fast. With Percy the Peugeot also prepared (socks on air filter), Ed stood up to the challenge, jumped in the car and inched closer to the bank...

Mackey and Ems were safely on the other side. Will and I were knee deep in the river, just on the submerged ledge before it got much deeper. The bank was full of Mongolian kids and other Mongol Rally teams, each sharing in the collecting holding of breath, and we all watched as Ed plunged into the water. The Peugeot displaced a ton of water as it created a bow wave, revs screaming, and followed in the wake caused by Pete the Saxo.

Much to my relief, and the relief of the few dozen multinational spectators, Ed was triumphant. The 206 didn't do the party trick of stalling half way through, and powered through to the other side.

Will and I jumped up a bit in excitement, but not too much - it was dark, the water was cold and the riverbed was slippery!

After we regrouped on the far bank, all but the last sliver of dusk light bidding us farewell, we decided we needed somewhere to sleep. We weren't too keen on just pitching our tents at the river side - who knows what could have happened in the night; the river deciding on a new course and wiping our tents away? The local Mongolian families desperately in need of a good meal? Either way, we wanted to find our own corner of the desert to call home.

The two cars, both happy to be back on dry land and headlights blazing, waved goodbye to the river and local kids (who'd been surprisingly helpful, even if Ed did punch one of them), and drove off into the darkness. We could just make out the path, illuminated by four headlights, but realised the dangers of going too far. All we needed was one stray rock to jump out in front of us, and we'd probably be worse off than stuck in the river.

15 minutes of slow, careful driving away from the water, we took a custom made path off the track. Well, we just turned right and drove into the desert. Only for five minutes or so, but to put enough distance between our cars and any passing bandits. With night now truly in charge of the dark blue sky, and far enough from the bustle of the Gobi Desert highway, we found a particularly lovely patch of dirt we were to call our own for the night.

It'd been a month now - a month of living out of Pete the Saxo, and many (many) nights of sleeping in tents. With just the light from one set of headlights, the five of us had camp set up in no time. The usual sleeping arrangements - five rallyers, two tents. Less than 10 minutes after stopping and turning off the cars, we had our homes all ready to go, and we began to feel the effects of a long day driving.

Before sleep though, we decided to eat, and brought out the petrol stove for one of the last times. We were so close to the finish line - we could feel it. And being so close meant we could afford not to nit-pick on the luxuries we had. You see, we started the rally with 50kg of army rations. We ate when we could, but always seemed to save the best things - namely the deserts – for another time. Tonight though, we'd eat like kings (and queen).

Ems, of course, did one better. A huge thanks to Em's mummy for having the beautiful foresight to stock their car with a few treats - namely, the most amazingly posh boil in the bag meals from Waitrose. Venison something, steak something, it was all there. These might have been foiled wrapped for 9,000 miles - but they were divine. Oh, and "Smash". We each filled our mess tins (our plates and bowls for the last month) with superb food, washed down with Thai green Cup-a-Soups, and polished off the last desserts.

We sat on the desert floor, deliciously full with hot food, laughed and chatted about the day, the rally, life. We were hundreds of miles from a town, dozens of miles from the nearest mound of dirt, expanse lay all around us. We were so far away from the start line, from our friends and family… but as the five of us sat in that wide open desert, on a perfect clear night, a reassuring sense of calm and tranquillity fell over us all, followed by a cold dose of realism - we were getting closer to the finish line, so close, that in a day or two or three, this would all be over….

…. but in the meantime, we all just sat there, gazing up at the stars, almost wishing the night would never end.

The Mongol Rally Auto Service – named for their yearly customers

Our desert campsite

Asking for directions in the middle of the desert

Warm kumis

Sharing our very limited geographical knowledge with the lost Belgian rider

Day 30 - The end is near

So, day 30. A month since we started this challenge, a month where we'd crossed 15 countries, a month where the small Citroen Saxo had been our home. Waking up in the desert, in our respective tents, had not got any more affluent - those roll mats we'd brought 9,000 miles ago had been suitably compressed to more resemble a sheet of paper than foam.

Still, it sounds like I'm moaning - if this were a regular camping weekend in the UK, it would be moaning. But here... waking up a thousand miles away from a border, in one of the least populated places on the planet, completely vulnerable to the elements and surroundings, almost at one with the world... it all makes it very much bearable.

As always, we woke up at a very respectable time in the morning (the sun rising over the plains and flooding our tents with light did help), and repacked our cars. Ed & Emma shared the collective skill us boys had at repacking - well, they had a little more space and fantastic foresight; they brought such Western wonders as plastic boxes and containers - every piece of camping equipment had its own special place in their very tidy car!

Once the campsite had been deconstructed (and all rubbish had been packed up - this was an immaculate piece of our planet, albeit a very dusty one. The last thing we wanted to do was leave plastic rubbish lying around), we set off. The excitement between the two cars was clearly apparent - we chatted wildly on the CB radios about what the day would bring - are we really in reach of Ulaan Baatar, the capital of this magnificent country, and our finish line? Will we see mythical tarmac ever again? Who knew... but right now, we had to push on. We were still in the middle of the desert, nothing to be seen in any direction - our trusty key-ring compass providing the only clue to where our finishing line might be...

Onwards we went, the morning silence of the desert rudely replaced with the vicious growling of two very small cars with very broken exhausts

Ed had a flat tyre before we reached Bayankhongor, but an almost daily occurrence for our convoy, and nothing to worry about. We all travelled through the small town until we reached the far side, and found a lovely shallow river running through the land.

This seemed like a good place to stop for an early lunch. Ed and Will ventured out in Percy to attempt to get the tyre fixed, and Mackey, Ems and I made lunch. Ems and I went paddling, which descended into a water fight (using our pots and pans as water flinging weapons). As it turns out, it was the first bath we'd had in a month. It was fantastic feeling, although bloody cold.

Mackey cooked noodles whilst sat on the shore with a grown-up look of disapproval at the two of us having fun in the water. After five minutes of simmering on the stove, Mackey presented lunch - the Russian equivalent of Super Noodles in a polystyrene package, which tasted nothing like the "roast beef" as advertised. I'm betting the polystyrene had more flavour, in fact. Luckily though, those superb Navy Rations each contained a miniature bottle of Tabasco sauce, which flavoured them well enough. Ems, on the other hand, enjoyed couscous, roasted vegetables and pistachio nuts. Can you really say that's true adventure food?!

Ed & Will returned as we were finishing lunch, and they too tucked into the flavourless noodles. Once we'd eaten, washed up in the river and repacked our lunch camp, it was time to push on. We were already on the far side of the small town, and so joined the only road/path leading out of it. Noticeably though, was the presence of several other vehicles. Compared to the vast solitude of the desert for the past few days, this was a comparable traffic jam.

Before long, the noodles still warm inside us, we came across an old friend - the river crossing. Those few vehicles around us realised what naive foreigners we were, and they swiftly overtook us and ploughed straight into the water. Successfully, I might add. Filled with confidence, and without the need to get out and spend half an hour discussing crossing strategies, Ed and Mackey took the two driving seats and followed suit. Ed went first, the 206 smashing into the shallow water, reaching the other side without so much as a lift off the accelerator. Mackey, whose driving experience had not let us down so far, was close behind and revved high as Pete the Saxo pushed through the water to the far bank.

Having paid close attention to our own vehicles, I didn't realise until making my way across (by strolling through the knee high water) that the other bank of the river was filled with quite an impressive crowd of locals. Those vehicles that preceded us were obviously taking bets whether our little European cars would make it, and half a dozen small vans had disembarked their passengers. As both cars made it, a slow ripple of applause went through the crowd (obviously those that had bet on our success).

The hills that seemed to surround every Mongolian town once again gave way to the flat expanse of the desert. We were still on our path, with very little chance of going in the wrong direction (mainly as there were no other options to follow), and we drove blindly in a very rough North-Eastern direction.

Before long, Percy the Peugeot experienced yet another flat tyre. Since we met with Ed & Emma in Kazakhstan, they'd had six or seven flats – and none before teaming up with us. Perhaps Scilly Mission were bad luck...

As the tyre was replaced, we reflected on the status of our car - the gearbox was screwed, very stiff and would only really stay in 1st or 4th gears. Trying to get through a particularly difficult bit of terrain needed low gears for slow moving followed by higher for fast moving (and lots of changing in between). This was getting very difficult. Front shock absorbers had also broken, no doubt the pounding they'd received over the last week across the rough desert. Possibly worst of all though, was the dust – so much dust - a thick layer of desert dust coated everything, including us. That river washing we had a few hours ago? Nothing but a dream now.

With the tyre replaced, Percy's bad luck continued - an hour of driving with four inflated tyres, a new problem presented itself. Clearly visible from us in Pete following shortly behind, was Percy's heat shield - the large sheet of metal underneath the engine block - but this time, the leading edge was dragging along the desert floor. Not so good! Another quick stop, and some of Mackey's mechanics, and we were set to go. Again. For how long this time, no one knew!

Our next target was a small town called Arvayheer, which we knew from previous experience to expect nothing big or fancy. One of the largest "cities" of the region, Altai, had turned out to be nothing more than a large collection of gers and a fuel station. Arvayheer, according the map, was an order of magnitude smaller. As we approached, we noticed those tell-tale hills filling the horizon, and the land seemed a little more alive - sporadic patches of grasses that provided sustenance to large herds of wild horses, who all looked up in bewilderment as our loud, pokey cars tore by.

As we travelled along the desert path, most of it resembling a WRC course, a little accident occurred. You see, despite good visibility as we drove forward, it could sometimes be very difficult to judge some of the obstacles immediately in front of you. A pot hole, from 100 meters away, might seem to be a small dip in the sand, whereas in fact would happily swallow your car. As Ed took the lead, and made the judgement on a little indentation that was getting ever closer, Percy's front wheels fell sharply and the front of the car took the full force of the impact. Straight away, the occupants of both cars knew this could be particularly bad.

As we all got out, we were relieved to see Ed & Emma were OK. Not an overly bad incident from a passenger point of view, but looked very nasty when thinking of Percy. First impressions were good though - the front bumper didn't look too bad, both front wheels looked remarkably spherical, and no obvious damage could be seen (apart from the usual flat tyre, so very common on Percy!)

To was one thing - to hear was another. As we all examined the front of the car, a very loud hissing sound could be heard. This wasn't good.

All eyes went to Mackey (and his mechanics) - could it be a fuel line? Radiator? From the looks of it, the front wheels had jumped up so badly, it had pushed the alternator up and caught a pipe in the spinning belt. It had pierced said pipe, which was hissing ferociously, throwing out its unknown contents onto the desert floor.

It didn't smell like fuel (which was a good thing), and didn't feel too much like oil - so hopefully wasn't brake fluid or similar. Possibly radiator? It wasn't as warm as the Russian heat wave that so punished us, but it wasn't cold either - and the cars had been driving non-stop for hours. Without a working radiator and cooling system, the Peugeot wouldn't have lasted long.

As luck would have it though, and about bloody time, Arvayheer was in sight - literally a mile away, the cluster of single story gers a welcome sight. At this distance, Pete could tow Percy there, and hopefully find a garage (or someone with the tools and mechanical know-how to assist).

This was the second time the tow rope had been used (the first, when we dragged Percy out of the Mongolian river - Pete was proving to be even more of a hero!) and we very slowly headed into the town to seek assistance. Mongolians really were an incredibly friendly race of people, second to none (perhaps maybe Kazakhs) - for as soon as we entered the town/village, the centre obvious from its one petrol station, we were approached by two Mongolian men, asking what the problem was. They had a quick look, but insisted they knew of a mechanic that could fix it quickly. Perfect!

They jumped in their car, and drove 100 meters down the road and pulled in to a closed... well, nothing to describe it really other than a field, with high fences along each side. Perhaps back home, that might be something of a cause for concern - entering a secure, private area with (now) eight or nine strange men. But in Mongolia, and us as seasoned travellers, we knew they meant well, and we followed them in.

Their workshop wasn't the most equipped in the world - the car ramp, enabling the mechanic to look underneath the vehicle, was nothing more than two logs. The mechanic himself, was nothing more than a sleeping man in a chair (although did the Asian mechanic tradition of removing his shirt whilst working under the car. Europe was the last time we'd seen a car mechanic wearing a top!)

As the Mongolian mechanic and his crew/friends/neighbours began to delve into the bonnet and start to investigate, we couldn't help but worry. What would that leak be? Would it be fixable? Would we be safe to continue on our journey, knowing we were SO close to the end?

Luck again - only the air conditioning system! (Luxury or what?! It served Ed & Emma right!). The leak was nothing more than the air conditioning fluid - something that Percy could most definitely do without (and apparently hadn't been used in ages. We didn't believe them).

We set off again through the village, and by this time it was late afternoon. As we excited, we had a brand new landmark to follow - electricity poles! Each were numbered, something like 1888, 1887, 1886 - huge distances between them, but did this mean we were going in the right direction? Definitely close? The excitement filled the air once again. Looking at the map, we realised tarmac must be nearby. Ulaan Baatar was the capital, and capital cities generally had a tarmac "red carpet" entering them. How close were we from this precious road surface? An hour? Eight hours? Either way, it was now a case of hours - and not days or weeks.

We drove for as long as we could, excited to see further signs of civilisation, but darkness soon took the day from us as the sun began to set over the distant horizon. We wouldn't be making Ulaan Baatar today, but we were close. So very close. We began to look for a suitable place to stop up and camp for the night. Overwhelmed with choice (as we were in the vast expanse), we noticed a headlight behind us, and watched as it got closer and closer.

Being a single headlight, us clever folks surmised it was a motorbike, which had caught us up. Not overly strange we thought, so we slowed down a little to let them pass. What was strange however, was they didn't pass. They just stayed behind us, following our tail. Hmmmm. This was strange.

Our two cars talked on the CB Radio - who was this lone rider who was intent on following us? Was this his patch of the desert we were travelling through? Without much of an idea who they were, or what to do, we carried on... slowly. And, as feared/expected, the rider followed us still. Several times as we tried to make out further detail in the twilight, he came closer to us. It was a lone Mongolian man, looking to be in his 50s, with an angry expression and a rifle in his hands.

Yes, he had a rifle. He was a gun wielding motorbike rider, and he was following us. We tried to work out how far we could go on like this, travelling slowly as to avoid any unseen obstacles, but it would only be a matter of time before we had an accident. After all, if Ed could hit a big dip in the road in broad daylight, we were risking it by driving in these almost night-like conditions.

Mackey, driving his usual twilight shift, made the decision to stop. Yeah, he had a gun. But there were five of us. Potentially armed with spades, jerry cans and packets of Russian noodles. Both cars slowed to a stop, and as expected the motorbike rider came to a stop. He had his rifle slung over one shoulder - which we allowed to fill us with a small sense of relief - much better over the shoulder than in his hands, the iron sights lined up towards our pretty little heads.

He sat there, looking at us. Perhaps not with the look of evil rage that we imagined, maybe pure curiosity. After all, here was a traditional Mongolian herdsman on an ancient Soviet motorbike. Here we were, five European travellers in fancy cars (Only in Mongolia could you consider a Saxo and 206 to be fancy). We opened the doors, and Mackey approached him 20 meters away from the car. I couldn't hear a lot from the safety of the car interior, but we noticed Mackey pulling out a packet of cigarettes, and offering them to him.

Darkness had fallen, so much so we could only watch as the two silhouettes, Mackey and bike man, nodded and pulled out cigarettes. A short minute later, although feeling much longer when holding your breath, the bike man restarted the old contraption on which he rode, and sped off into the darkness.

Mackey had done well - "He only wanted a cigarette!"

It could have gone so much worse, but this was Mongolia - friendliest people around! We guessed that this was just as good as any to rest up for the night, and so unpacked our tents and set up camp. It was strange, thinking that this could be the last time the tents would ever be used by us. OK, so we weren't there quite yet. But we were so very close.

It was a collective feeling, and so we treated ourselves. Potentially the last night camping on our little stove, so out came the last of the luxury rations we'd been saving. Treacle sponge and custard; chocolate cake with chocolate sauce; toffee cake with toffee sauce; all the desserts we wanted. Even the main meal was no longer a random pick (to make it fair between us all), and we delved in to the mess of the roof box and chose our own delights. Ems and I, in our usual role of chef and KP, got to work as the table was set up and tents erected.

We sat around, a hundred miles from anything resembling civilisation, and finally let the excitement get to us. We were so close to the finish line, the culmination of months of planning, the atmosphere was electric. If a car went wrong, we could squeeze all five of the team into one and make it. If both cars went wrong, we'd have the encouragement to run the rest of the way! Here we were, one team of five friends, knowing we'd been through more with each other than others we'd known for decades. Tonight, we'd eat well, we'd even crack open the Kazakh brandy we were bought a few weeks ago, and rest our heads on the desert floor for possibly the last ever time…..

(Mackey and Will did spend a few more hours tucked up in Pete the Saxo finishing the bottle of brandy…)

The Citroen Saxo – still going strong through the desert

Still in very good spirits

Fixing yet another puncture in the desert

Day 31 - The Final Push

I woke. The first thought that came into my head as I lay on the now paper-thin roll mat was - this was it. According to my rough calculations, and a whole lot of hope, this was the last stretch before the finish line. The final push

It seemed I wasn't the only one in this frame of mind - the usual morning quietness between the five of us, eyes barely registering the now rising sun, was instead transformed into a miniature metropolis of excitement. We all felt it - we were close, so close, to the finish line at Ulaan Baatar. We felt amazing.

Well, I say "we" - perhaps falsely indicated all five of us. Will was a little jaded, having stayed up drinking Kazakh brandy until the early hours. But even he looked angelic compared to the... well, utter mess that was Mackey. Every word he spoke preceded a toxic cloud of brandy and whisky - and this was at 8am! Still, I think even Mackey felt the anticipation we all shared.

We weren't counting our chickens quite yet - we figured we had around 350 km to go before the finish line - three hundred and fifty kilometres, still crossing unknown terrain, any meter of which could do untold damage to the cars (or ourselves). Without wood to touch (the desert was a very wood-less place), we knew we still had a challenge ahead. But even with that hint of apprehension - this was going to be the last day.

Breaking the schedule we'd followed since France, it was Mackey who took the morning shift. Perhaps not the best idea considering his hungover state, but the boy was determined. And to see that amount of determination in one man's eyes (even if they looked like the tiny eyes of a shrew); I knew we were in safe hands.

Ems, ever chirpy at 8am, started the repacking of the camp. Such an event was second nature to us now - despite detesting camping when younger, something I'd have paid anything to not do (and instead to have slept in a nice warm bed), we were all elites. Erecting our tents, repacking them into that small bag that usually perplexed every alpha male, sleeping in the wilderness, feeling almost as one with the desert - we'd done it all. I know I wasn't the only one that felt a tinge of sorrow knowing that this would (possibly) be the last time we'd collectively act like such adventurers.

Once packed up we tended to the usual morning procedure, including brushing teeth. That was something I knew I wouldn't really miss, having to brush your teeth using a small amount of water from a bottle; inevitably dribbling some minty fresh foam down your chin or on your flip flops. Give me a tap any day. Even the showering - as dirty as it sounds, we'd had one shower since we left our Siberian hotel over a week ago – it was something we'd all relish once we're home, but still look back so very fondly at our time in Mongolia.

Tents packed, the two car team ready, we set off with Mackey in the driving seat. We had a rough idea where to go, which direction to head in, despite the obvious lack of tracks - but before long, five minutes of driving in a North Eastern direction, we found a trail we'd follow for the rest of the day.

The iPod blasted out the usual selection of tunes, ranging from the dulcet sounds of The Verve to the turbulent chords of Poison, when we experienced the first problem of the morning. Percy the Peugeot, which seemed to constantly complain at the world, showed it's frustration by freeing itself of its exhaust! The long arm separated somewhere near the engine block, and transformed itself into a dragging dirt collector, scooping samples from the desert floor.

We all came to a stop in the desert sand, amused by this set back - that Mongolian god we mentioned a few days ago obviously chuckling away to himself on the summit of some Mongolian mountain. Mackey the Mechanic quickly spotted that both ends of the exhaust had decided to quit on us so close to the finish line, and were un-fixable. Ed however, refused to leave a team member behind (even if it was the exhaust pipe), and lashed it on to the roof of the car.

Of course, this just meant that both cars sounded like absolute tanks, their 1.1 litre engines disturbing every sparse living creature in a two mile radius. Personally, I thought we just sounded awesome.

We carried on, the compass giving us hope we were headed in the right direction, but then we came across something that gave us more hope - a road. An actual, physical, tarmac road. Flat! Yes, it was littered with pot holes the size of washing machines, but this was a road! We had to be going towards the finish line!

With a road surface, we did something we hadn't done in a very long time - we broke the 40mph limit. Desert driving was a punishing affair - not only on us, but the cars. The rough surfaces and corrugated trails absolutely destroyed the suspension of cars designed for leisurely supermarket trips in England. Our average driving speed over the last week would probably work out to be something in the region of 20mph. Reaching 40 felt like we'd broken the sound barrier; us all hanging our heads out of the window, smiling, looking more like a bunch of happy dogs.

Of course, it was never going to be that simple. Before the novelty of such ridiculous speeds had worn off, we were greeted by a rather depressing sight - the abrupt end of our precious tarmac, and the reclamation by the parched desert. Were we really going to UB? Had we double backed? Had the Earth's poles somehow shifted while we slept, and instead headed towards the very closed borders of China? Why would the Mongolians go to so much effort to create that little piece of black heaven, only for it to end near some rolling hills?

As we drove on, a little perplexed at it all, we came across a Mongolian biker. Forget the leather jacket and handlebar moustache, this was a traditional Mongolian biker (was there such a thing?), complete with traditional Mongolian attire. We hadn't learned many Mongolian words - "thank you" was about it. But "Ulaan Baatar", with excited smiles that obviously expressed it in the form of a question, was understood by the biker. He pointed along the path we already headed down, and nodded.

So, we were going the right way, still none the wiser about the patch of tarmac however. Still, it wouldn't be long before we'd find the next sporadic patch!

The landscape slowly began to transform as we continued along the desert; slowly shaking off the barren title as green began to appear around us. What was once just dust and dirt began to transform into something more resembling country side. Grasses and shrubs reclaimed the land gradually, and before we knew it, began to win the battle against the infertile dustbowl.

By mid-morning, both roaring cars still ploughing along, we also noticed an ever growing number of gers (the traditional Mongolian tent/house) - some standing solitary amongst the empty lands, but others in collective villages. This was some of the densest population we'd seen in days. Not only that, but we ran into traffic; actual, other-people-driving-along-here-hurry-up-and-move traffic.

Perhaps not quite the traffic we'd grown up with - this time, an over-burdened truck headed in a similar direction to us, kicking up plumes of trail dust. Overtaking wasn't an overly hard thing, but was somewhat exciting - overtaking in general suggested traffic, which suggested population, which suggested we were getting closer and closer to the capital city.

As we emerged from the dust thrown into the air by the Soviet monster, we caught sight of road again - this time, almost freshly laid and heading in a very straight line. It couldn't have been more than a month old, the immaculate darkness clearly visible as we approached it from a mile away. Half a mile away, I swear we could smell it. Although it wasn't until we were five meters away, and could actually taste it, did we realise we couldn't use it.

For this was indeed a tarmac road, and it was indeed perfect in every way. So perfect in fact, that vehicles were not yet allowed to use it! Still "under construction" it seemed. SO CLOSE! Yet so far. Still, to witness the extension of a road that must have started in the heart of UB, was still as encouraging as ever.

Next to the perfect road, almost mockingly so, was more of our old friend, the desert track/path/trail. Worn into the surface, almost glad of its last few days use by the Mongolian traffic before the road opened, was our ticket to the finish line. We also spotted our first road sign in a very long time - ULAAN BAATAR - 348km. The CB radios crackled with excitement as our two cars both read the sign out in gleeful cheers.

Mackey, still ridiculously hungover but in a very uncharacteristically good mood, relished in this continuing road surface - for every turn and bend around a small corner or detour meant Pete the Saxo slid and bounced like the rally vehicle it never was. As I sat in the front seat, I made the mistake of choosing music which further fuelled Mackey's aggressive (yet rather fun) driving style. The Beastie Boys were played, and Mackey took the driving to a whole other level...

To give him credit, his driving was extremely skilful - we tore along that path (all the while within arm shot of the new road), skipping over pot holes and sliding around rocks. Ed, very plain to see, loved the excuse to keep up with the bat out of hell, and swiftly followed suit.

The time came though, a time which couldn't come too soon, for us to join that tarmac. For us to enter the world of civilised driving, complete with such modern monstrosities as road markings and road signs. For us to enter the driving elite, for us to keep to the right hand side of a dual lane road, for us to abide by the laws of the road. And that moment was welcomed with open arms.

The five of us knew, this time, that the road was here to stay. Perhaps it was counting our chickens before they hatched, but we just knew - all the way to the finish line, we would have our road. I laughed like a child. Mackey followed. Ems (who swapped cars with Will for a few hours) joined in. Even more so when the road signs came frequently at us as Mackey accelerated even more - 60mph this time, the first time we reached such dizzying speeds in this country. Every 10 minutes or so, when the music again changed genre completely and Elton joined us, another sign rose up against the highway side. I gazed out at the now green landscape, almost a built up urban area by last night's standards, as Ems dozed in the back of Pete through all of The Greatest Elton John Ever.

It was lunch time - and Mackey was beginning to flag a little, despite running on minimal sleep and the excitement of us all. It gave us a good reason to stop and eat something. We snacked on what remaining food we had in the cars - some biscuits, old crisps, more of a sustenance stop than anything - a chance to top up our sugar levels so we could remain excited for a couple more hours. Pete was also in need of a top up, and we decided to use the jerry can contents rather than fill up unnecessarily - after all, those jerry cans held precious 95 octane fuel from the depths of Russia!

I took the hot seat, which I knew would be for the last time, as we finished our 10 minute break and pushed on. Mackey retreated to the back seat, no more comfortable than the others but still no barrier between him and a needed nap, Will my faithful navigator.

The next few hours driving were uneventful yet exciting, and we covered a huge amount of ground. Pete the Saxo, a huge testament to both Citroen and our faithful Tresco mechanic Nick Shiles, continued on without a single complaint. OK, so the gearbox was pretty much knackered - a trivial battle to get it into 5th gear, but there it stayed. The engine, having covered most environments on the planet, hadn't skipped a beat. We experienced a total of three flat tyres, meaning one had covered a third of the planet without puncturing!

We realised we had left the flat expanse (albeit greener expanse), and started a very shallow climb into some waiting hills. Gers became a frequent landmark, even making way to fixed buildings. Traffic not only preceded us, but followed us. Cars and trucks rumbled by on the opposite side of the road. Clusters of buildings soon gave way to villages, complete with shops and services. Where were we?? On the map, we had no real settlements listed, certainly not of this size. As we continued to climb, still on a wide open road, we approached the brim of the hill and finally comprehended where we were.

For as we reached the peak of the hill, the gradient flattening before it's inevitable decline, lay a sprawling city - and for once in this country, a city is what it was.

Will was excitingly cheering down the CB radio. Emma gave us a word perfect air hostess style welcome to our destination, reminding us all to keep our hands and feet inside the vehicle at all times. Even Mackey, but an hour before slave to a hangover, perked up with alarming ferocity. I didn't accept it though - I couldn't believe it. Were we really here? Surely not. Will, check the map again. This must be another city. I grabbed the CB radio and asked Ed & Ems if they could verify our location.

But there was no mistaking it, as a big ULAAN BAATAR sign came into view.

We had made it.

Never before had I felt such a strong wave of emotion come over me - sweep over us all in fact, as we continued down the hill into the city limits. What seemed like seconds later, we reached the entry to the city, a formidable ULAAN BAATAR sign covering a dual carriageway, a soldier checkpoint waiting to check all vehicles. For a second, a worst case scenario popped into my head - what if the soldiers didn't let us in? What if something was wrong with the cars? What if...

No. We'd come too far, been through too much, fought on for far too long to be turned back at the last hurdle. Just before we passed into the final city, we all stopped at the side of the road, and sat in front of our triumphant vehicles with the UB sign backdrop (much to the annoyance of local motorists). But did we care? We did not. As it turned out, we didn't have any problems - 200 Togrogs was the entry fee, and never before have we been happier to spend 80 pence.

Our excitement held as we entered the city, a very strange place even considering our sights so far. The capital city was in the midst of being dragged, almost kicking and screaming, into the international modern world. The air sat heavy with pollution, adverts adorned every rough surface, and vehicles fought for supremacy on the chaotic road system. Despite feeling like we'd finished, we still had the small matter of physically reaching the finishing line!

We were given instructions to the finish line a month ago - as we set off from Goodwood, a distant memory by now, we were handed an information pack containing the magic directions. As fate would have it, and certainly not due to any real organisation by us all, we dug out the piece of paper from some corner of the car in seconds – just where we left it so very long ago.

As we made our way to the centre of the city, we let ourselves get taken by the torrent of traffic, like a floating leaf down a turbulent stream. The general direction was ours; I let the knowledgeable locals lead the way as we followed suit for nearly an hour, before we recognised a landmark described to us. One of the tallest buildings in Mongolia, it also shone like a beacon - for the finish line was 30 seconds away.

As you can imagine, two cars full of ecstatic team members, there were a few heated moments with directions. Calls of "turn left" came seconds too late and we missed our chance (a couple of times in fact). But we pushed on, as we'd done continuously for the last month. Eventually, we came to a junction where the finish line was visible. Laying eyes on our goal, the culmination of so much emotion, was nothing short of surreal. This last junction proved to be the last test - we wanted to cut across a dual carriageway, and turn left, then into the car park. According to Mongolian road laws, as demonstrated by signs surrounding us, this junction was a "right turn only".

For once, we were above the Mongolian road laws.

We were above any and all laws!

I waited for a chance, put my foot down and shot across towards our target, Ed following close behind. I like to think that this happened so swiftly and smoothly that the Mongolians didn't even notice. In reality however, I'm betting they didn't even care.

We indicated, and pulled into a car park, already full with victorious rally cars. The huge stage, shouting its proud message "YOU'VE FINISHED THE MONGOL RALLY", lay empty and waiting as Pete and Percy pulled up beside each other, and the engines turned off.

30 Days and 17 hours after setting off from Goodwood, UK; over 9,000 miles covered; 15 countries traversed; friendships formed, some of which will never be broken; thousands of pounds spent, but more importantly many more thousands of pounds raised;

We had successfully completed the Mongol Rally 2010.

I jumped out of the car - Ed & Ems had already done the same. We hugged each other with beaming smiles, our weary selves still not realising that the trial was over. Surreal didn't cover it. After a few minutes of laughing and joking, the five of us unashamedly bursting with pride, we wandered past the other cars and found the Rally bar and outside sitting area, complete with other waiting teams sharing in beers and swapping stories.

As we walked in, we noticed a few faces, but they all looked up and smiled. It sounds cheesy, and probably is - but they'd all been through it; overcome similar problems, been part of similar experiences, conquered the same challenge. They were as weary us as, but just as ecstatic.

We walked past the bar into a hotel, and made our way underground to the finishing station. It was air-conditioned, over the top so - freezing in fact, but such a welcome change. There we met Rob, the main Adventurists man behind the rally, who shook our hands and welcomed us to the finishing line. It was nice to finally meet the Mongol Rally top guy, having bombarded him with questions in the preparation stages of the rally. We signed the finishing forms, and were given our finishing certificates - for me anyway, that'll always be one of the most important A4 pieces of paper I'll ever own!

One last thing to do though, before we sat down as the one team we were and ordered a cold beer, was to stake our place on the finishing board. Our final positions: 76th & 77th. Out of 350 teams that started the rally, we couldn't believe how well we'd done. Noticing that there were a large number of vehicles that had to pull out for various reasons (but were still written up on the board), that put our finishing place in the top 60.

With our team names, and our team mottos added to the board ("You want breakfast NOW?" and "Sounds just like a Golf"), we made our way back up to the bar, ordered five large beers, found an empty table, and slumped into the seats.

That was a strange moment. A wave of happiness flowed over the table, all completely in disbelief that we'd completed the Mongol Rally. We'd survived, relatively unscathed, a challenge that was notoriously difficult - a challenge that had tragically taken the life of one competitor, and hospitalised countless others. The three of us in our team had left Goodwood. Now our team of five sat in Ulaan Baatar, with numerous new friends and experiences of a life time.

On the other hand, a dawn of realisation swept over me - like a cold fog, the bitter reminder that it was all done. We'd finished. We'd shortly be saying goodbye to those we'd spent the best part of a month living as one big team. We'd no longer wake up with an insurmountable task ahead of us. We'd no longer have to worry whether we had enough water to last us the day, or how many times we'd get arrested. We'd no longer be doing something so few had done before, and pushing ourselves to the limit.

But it was over. It was done. We traded stories around the bar like football stickers ("Our car has bullet holes when a soldier shot at us!" or "We got thrown in jail for a day!" or "We stayed in the Royal Palace!"), every team as joyful and gratified as our own. We ate a great meal, from an actual menu - with both English writing, colour pictures AND available dishes. We drank some beer, and then some more. Teams retired for the night, soon replaced by others also pulling into the finishing line for the first time.

Before too long, the day had taken its toll. No, the month had taken its toll. We found the name of a hotel, booked rooms, and bid farewell to the remaining parties. One last thing was to be done though – we had to say goodbye to our fantastic cars that had got us this far.

They looked spectacularly at home amongst the dozens of other cars, each as battered and bruised. Despite the cars being full of our things, we were only taking a rucksack back each. The rest was to be auctioned for charity, along with the cars themselves. I grabbed my bag, filled with dirty clothes, and rifled through the car for other important things to take back.

I wasn't alone in trying to take back ridiculous things – Imodium, for example, was a precious commodity on the rally. As were the tools, and even a treacle sponge desert left over. It wasn't until packing these in my bag (and the same went for the other boys), that we realised we no longer needed them.

Rucksacks on our back, we all said goodbye to the two cars – cars that had transcended materialistic sentiments and would be forever remembered as metallic team mates. Whatever their future, we knew they'd remember us too.

As the five of us strolled along the Mongolian city centre, the hustle and bustle of the twilight city all around us, we slowly moved completely oblivious to the outside world. The traffic, the noise, the people; all faded into the background hum as we drifted towards our final beds. Camaraderie almost fell short of what the five of us had - living, eating, sleeping, breathing, drinking, fighting, arguing, laughing, joking, crying, experiencing everything in such a raw way.

Things about what makes a family – years of love and hate, joy and turmoil, we squeezed so much of it into a few short weeks

We found our final stop before too long, and walked in to the reception area. We looked a mess, we knew it, rucksacks thrown over our shoulders and collectively storing a large proportion of the Mongolian desert dust on our bodies.

Almost on auto-pilot, we all paid for the rooms and walked up the air-conditioned marble staircase. In the corridor dividing our accommodations, we all hugged and shook hands – not much more to do really. For we'd done what we set out to do; knowing that, the five of us, collectively, we'd conquered the Mongol Rally.

Arriving at Ulaan Baatar

We finished the Mongol Rally!

Epilogue

It was a strange emotion, finishing the rally. The highs we shared, the lows we persevered and everything in between had been our driving force for the past five weeks, and it was over. For once we had no target to aim for, to strive to achieve. Well, there was always the small case of re-joining the UK and returning to work – but as soon as you consider those issues, you come to realise you're smack bang in reality.

This was always to be the case of course, our once-in-a-lifetime challenge being just this – a relatively short amount of time where we'd shed our day to day lives and worries, and focus on something brand new. Still, it felt strange. One small part of you glad the hardships were over and eagerly anticipating regular showers/beds/electricity; but another part, a larger part, missed the adventure/rawness/challenge.

We stayed in Ulaan Baatar for two days after finishing, the five of us relishing the feeling of success. Finish day was lost to elation and exhaustion, celebrating with our fellow teams whilst battling the overwhelming desire to sleep. Pete the Saxo slept soundly at the Finish Line car park amongst dozens of his fellow vehicles, each looking battle scarred yet triumphant.

We had one free day before flights would take us separate ways (Scilly Mission boys had an Aeroflot journey via Moscow, and the Mongol Mongrels travelled in B.A. style via Beijing). Ems wanted to experience Ulaan Baatar's retail offerings – something that wasn't too high on us boys' list. A good alternative, we thought, was an activity we'd read about months back...

As rumour had it, there was a live firing range somewhere in the vicinity of the Mongolian capital, where dollars could be swapped for heavy weaponry. Being four alpha males of course, the thought of shopping vs. shooting was a no brainer – we had to find it! A quick word with Tom, from the Adventurists, and he confirmed the rumours were true; a short 30-minute car journey and we'd get the chance to visit a shooting range.

The afternoon went as well as we'd hoped; I hoped Emma was having a pleasant time among the Mongolian shopping malls, but I highly doubt it provided as much relief as the time we boys had. I believe there is no better way to relieve a month of pent up frustration that firing heavy weaponry at targets, and RPGs at hills.

That night would be the last we'd all have together on this little trip; we went out for a Vietnamese meal, and retired to one of our rooms for the post-adventure chat. Slumped on chairs and over beds, we laughed and chatted as we relived those testing moments... moments that, at the time, were gravely unfunny. Add a touch of hindsight though, and we appreciated them. We appreciated them all!

A couple of days after we'd pulled into Ulaan Baatar, it was time to leave Mongolia and Asia. Ed & Ems headed off to Beijing, us three island boys took our plane to Moscow. It wouldn't be the last time we'd see the Mongol Mongrels; you can't do something like the Mongol Rally with people like them and not have them part of your life!

Returning to the UK was strange; returning to the island even more so. A welcome party waited at Tresco Heliport, and a proper party held at the New Inn. We recounted the above stories countless times to anyone who'd listen, and felt the support of the entire community as we heard how everyone tracked us at every step of the way.

The full blog articles, photos and videos can be found on our website – www.ScillyMission.com

Afterword

The Mongol Rally was everything I expected it to be, and so much more. It was the hardest thing I've ever had to do – physically, mentally and emotionally. Going a week without a shower wasn't pleasant, nor was roughing it on hard ground for night after night. Living in cramped spaces, driving through a 46°c heat wave, waking up surrounded by snow, travelling hundreds of miles across rough terrain without a true sense of location. So many tests, so many hurdles to overcome to get to the finish line.

But these hardships just made the trip all the more challenging! The deepest lows only gave prominence to the incredible highs; travelling alone in the wilderness, reliant on no one but yourself and your team. It became a true test of friendship, to put up with each other's habits and annoyances after being cooped up in such a confined space.

The Scilly Mission raised £14,624 for the Cystic Fibrosis Trust, a fantastic amount for a fantastic charity. This money was raised not only from director sponsors of the rally, but also varying other events we held before the event – a charity art exhibition, live music nights at the New Inn (Tresco's only pub), a "mobile feast" and the first ever Tresco Triathlon.

On behalf of Will, Nick and myself, thank you to all those that made this trip possible, and to have raised such an important amount of money for the Cystic Fibrosis Trust.

I hope you enjoyed our little story – this is my first attempt at a coherent piece of writing of any sort. If, by reading this, it's given you a slight taste of adventure, perhaps even persuaded you to undertake the Mongol Rally, then my job is done.

Acknowledgments

Extra special thanks go to:

Robert & Lucy Dorrien-Smith (Tresco Estate) – Our employer, and main sponsors, without whom we'd be car-less without a hope of competing, let alone completing. Our sincere thanks to you both for your support at every step of the way.

Dean Whillis – The best contact a team can have, who gave us the professional drive and advice to push on. He never let us settle for anything but the best we could do.

Jo Ash – Mother of the rally, and without whom, we'd most likely be sat in some foreign jail due to incorrect paperwork (if we ever left at all)

Nick Shiles – The Scilly Mission mechanic. Without him, the car (or us) would never have made it – without a doubt.

Our Gold sponsors:

- **Nigel Ostler Harris - Technical Concrete Cutting**
- **Tony Jones - British International Helicopters**
- **St Austell Brewery**

Our Silver sponsors:

- **Liam Nankervis** (Delve & Nankervis)
- **Chris Symons** (Symons Construction)

Our Bronze sponsors:

Skinner's Brewery
WPS Insurance

Lea & Sandeman
Churchtown Farm - ScillyFlowers.co.uk
Petty Woods
Llewellyn Harker Architects
BS Embroidery (Team kit)
Isles of Scilly Steamship Company (Car transport)
Sam @ **The Worksmart Group** (GPS Tracker)
Sharman Multicom (CB Radio)
GoSim (Global Sim Cards)
Mont Blanc (Car Roof Box and Roof Rack)
FastFilms.co.uk (Video Camera Mount)
Signprint.co.uk (Car Stickers)

Special mentions to: Steve Ash, Jane Ash, Lisa Roberts, Pete Marshall, Julie Christopher, Carolyn & John Davies, Bryan Wright, Oliver Plante, Tony Reading, Jackie Hughes, Emma Driscoll, Pete Hingston, Fiona Hingston, Ross Christopher, Keri Jones @ Radio Scilly, Harry Getliffe, Robin Lawson, Alex Christopher, Richard & Maralyn Hobbs, Alasdair Moore, Ian Warren, Trevor & Pauline Washington, Tracey Brown, Ellie Tabron, Faye Page, Rebecca Smith, Kathy Todd, Rob Hesketh, David Hesketh, Janet Druce, Steve Druce, the UK Hydrographic Office, Neil Barbary, Selles Medical, World of Camping, Peter Moore, Lord Phillimore, OCUK members, Tim Holyomes, the Tresco Triathletes, Ruslan Savenko, Okko Alitalo, Vincent Tractors, Alice Chuter, Daisy Chuter, Lily Chuter, Becky Beesley, Chris Potterton, Emma Jeffreys, Derek Bradbury, Edit Toth, Imogen Bone, Jess Corbett, Jo Probert, Laura McCabe, Linda Cunningham, Lydia Birch, Magda Malyszko, Maggie O'Brien, Mandy Hamilton, Millie Driscoll, Nancy Sheridan, Nick Botting, Nicola Hancock, Nicola Lawson, Olivia Krimpas, Peter Jenkins, Rachel Young, Richard Pearce, Stewart Kettle, Susannah Gates, Sylvia Chesterman, Adrienn Szalkai, Tamasin Bridge, Tracey Brown, Miklos Varga, Vickie Heaney, Wendy McBride, Philip Hearsey, Dick Bird, Kim Hopkins, Chris Hopkins & the countless others that have assisted us and donated to such a worthwhile cause.

Appendix

i. Scilly Mission facts & stats

Time taken: **30 days 17 hours 14 minutes**

Total amount raised for charity: **£14,624.14**

Our chosen charity: **The Cystic Fibrosis Trust**

Total distance driven: **Approximately 8,500 miles / 13,680 kilometres**

Number of countries visited: **15 (UK, France, Belgium, Germany, Czech Republic, Slovakia, Austria, Hungary, Romania, Moldova, Ukraine, Russia, Kazakhstan, Siberia, Mongolia)**

Finishing position: **76th (out of 350)**

Total number of flat tires: **3**

Number of working gears at the finish line: **2 (1st and 4th)**

Number of intact shock absorbers at the finish line: **0**

Amount raised by auctioning Pete the Saxo in Ulaan Baatar: **$1,500**

My favourite country: **Mongolia**

Will's favourite country: **Mongolia**

Mackey's favourite country: **Kazakhstan**

My favourite moment: **Laughing until we cried in the Mongolian roadside cafe**

Mackey's favourite moment: **Meeting the Mongol Mongrels & Co in Semey, Kz**

Will's favourite moment: **Being completely alone in the middle of Mongolia – nothing else to be seen**

My worst moment: **Hitting the pothole in Ukraine and fearing the worst**

Will's worst moment: **Hangover whilst stranded in the Ukraine**

Mackey's worst moment: **Rostov, Russia – Corrupt police ransoming my driving license**

Total bribes paid: **Approximately $700**

Did we ever feel our lives were in danger? **A couple of worrying moments, but other than that, no**

Favourite food: **Buuz – Mongolian Lamb Dumplings. Simple, tasty & warming**

Least favourite food: **Kumis – warm, smelly fermented mare's milk**

Money spent: Approximately: **£2000 – including food, petrol, supplies, hotels and repairs**

Most useful car preparation: **Custom made sump guard – saved our car on countless occasions**

Most useful piece of equipment: **A single real pillow for in car sleeping / Whisperlite Stove**

Most useless piece of equipment: **Travel hammock – never used**

Most needed piece of equipment: **Proper tents or a folding down table**

Most listened to album: **Elton John's Greatest Hits (!)**

Appendix

ii.   Equipment List

AC/DC Inverter	Knife
Torches	Saw
Satellite	Cable Ties
Oil Filter	Duck Tape
Fuel Filter	First Aid Kit
2-4 Spare Wheels	Fire Extinguisher
Cam belt	Lighter & Matches
Alternator Belt	Flint Tool
Clutch Cable	Rags
Fuel pump	Bungee Cords
Batteries	Compass
Bulbs	Pens/Paper
Spark Plugs	String
Radiator Sealer	Laptop
Hose Repair Kit	Digital Camera
Exhaust Bandage	Video Camera
Tire Pump	Camera mount
Jerry Can4	IPod
Tow Rope	Cards
Jump Cables	Football
Screwdrivers	Frisbee
Hammer	Maps (for all countries)
Chisel	Tents x3
Socket Set	Sleeping Bags x3
Jacks	Pillows x3
Spade	Roll Mats x3

Stove & Fuel

Water Purification Tablets

Pots & Pans, Cutlery & Utensils

Water Containers

Sun Cream

Wet Wipes

CB Radio

Imodium

Plank of wood

Insect Repellent

iii. Route Map

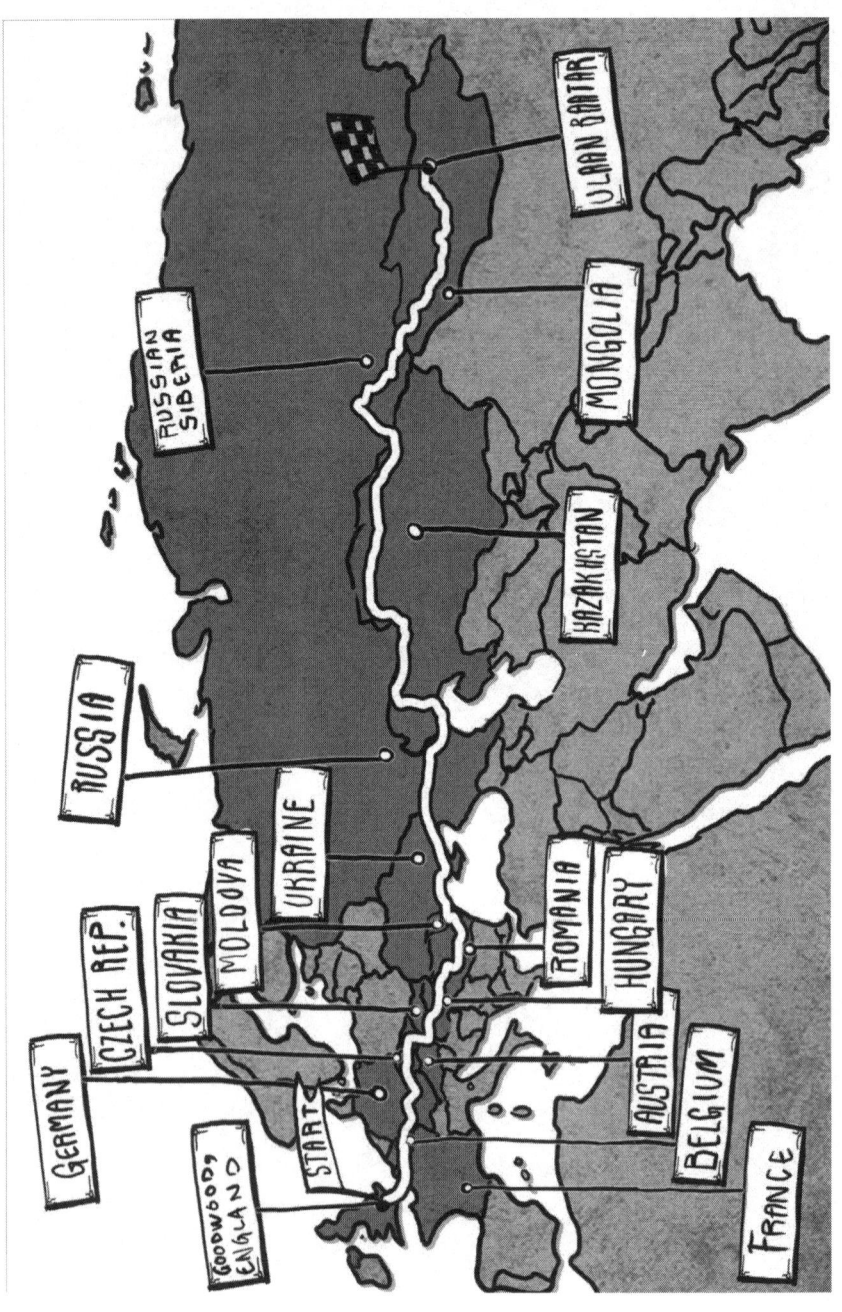

Appendix

iv. Hints and tips for future Mongol Rally competitors

- Expect to be pulled over for "random" checks by Police from the Ukraine onwards.
- Whoever is driving, empty their wallet of large denomination notes – leave a small amount. This will result in very cheap bribes.
- If you do get pulled over by the police, play the dumb tourist! Keep saying "I do not understand" and "We are driving to Mongolia". Eventually they'll get fed up and wave you on your way.
- Take a CB radio – useful for communicating with other teams and car karaoke will pass the long afternoons.
- Take a decent size tent – don't bother with one man coffins.
- Use a decent stove – we took a Whisperlite, which was able to run on petrol. Highly recommended.
- Realise the importance of your fellow rallyers – enjoy other Rally company!
- Set ground rules – song choices, driving patterns, navigation responsibilities etc.
- Remember to buy "Green Card" car insurance at each border from Romania onwards.
- Pack the car efficiently – plastic storage boxes and a place for everything.
- Remember the iPod, and fill it with every album you have
- Air conditioning isn't "cheating" when it's 46°c
- Try to free up as much time as possible – you miss so much when you have such strict deadlines
- Take a laptop or other storage medium – take as many photos and as much video as possible
- US Dollars are accepted worldwide – forget Pounds and Euros
- Install a Sump Guard – it will save your car

v. Team Sponsors

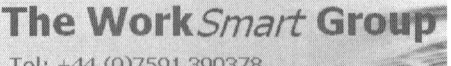

vi. The Car